Penguin Education

Penguin Modern Psychology Readings

The Social Psychology of Teaching

Edited by A. Morrison and D. McIntyre

Advisory Editor
B. M. Foss

The Social Psychology of Teaching

Selected Readings

Edited by A. Morrison and D. McIntyre

Penguin Books

Penguin Books Ltd,
Harmondsworth, Middlesex, England
Penguin Books, 625 Madison Avenue, New York,
New York 10022, U.S.A.
Penguin Books Australia Ltd, Ringwood,
Victoria, Australia
Penguin Books, Canada Ltd, 2801 John Street,
Markham, Ontario, Canada L3R 1B4
Penguin Books (NZ) Ltd, 182–190 Wairau Road,
Auckland 10, New Zealand

First published 1972
Reprinted 1973, 1975, 1977, 1980

Set, printed and bound in Great Britain by
Cox & Wyman Ltd, Reading
Set in Monotype Times

Contents

Introduction

Teaching is both familiar and intriguing; something that most of us engage in during our everyday lives or as professional teachers, but at the same time a difficult set of processes to analyse, hard to describe, and clearly complex and often subtle in its effects upon those we are attempting to teach. This set of Readings presents some of the ways by which we can examine the processes and practices called teaching, and describes findings from studies of teachers on what they do, how they view themselves and their pupils, and how their pupils respond. The articles have been selected against three criteria: that they should present teaching as an applied social psychology; that they should focus upon professional teaching within the settings of school and classroom; and that they should demonstrate empirical procedures and findings of practical interest to practising teachers and a wider audience. The only necessary exceptions to this major emphasis on actual teaching are in those articles which deal with professional training and with teachers' views on their educational roles, and these in themselves may bear closely upon teaching itself.

The decision to represent teaching in largely social psychological terms seems justified on a number of grounds. Historically, some of the most influential ways of looking at teaching have developed from psychological work on leadership styles, group behaviour, attitudes, and role behaviour. More recently there has been the stimulus from social psychology again towards the use of observational techniques and the applications of analytical and experimental procedures in the study of social and professional skills and the processes of interaction in groups. These links represent a common concern for interpersonal behaviour and shared interests in processes of cognitive and affective influence, group relationships, socialization, and the behaviours and perceptions of people in their various social and professional roles. Of course, other ways of looking at teaching – in terms of the curriculum, school organization or subject methodology – are equally legitimate and important; nevertheless, teaching is founded in the characteristics and relationships of individuals and we believe that some of the most important advances in our understanding will come at this level of inquiry.

During its development the social psychology of teaching has undergone some marked changes in its methods and its ways of conceptualizing the characteristics of teachers and their work. From the beginning it has been influenced heavily by the concepts of personality, leadership, role, and attitude. Innumerable studies have been done, seeking to classify and to evaluate teachers in these terms and to examine associations between more or less global characteristics of individuals and the attitudes, achievements and climates of pupils and classes. Many studies, for example, have examined teaching in terms of the authoritarian-democratic styles of individuals in handling their classes, or on similar general personality dimensions such as the abstractness or concreteness of belief systems. They have been particularly useful in revealing fairly systematic differences in class management and in pupils' preferences for some types of control over others. Attitudinal studies have been used frequently in work on professional training where they have provided useful evidence upon certain aspects of socialization into the profession and upon the effects of early teaching experience on the educational outlooks of young teachers. Above all though, it has been role theory which has provided the most popular and one of the most useful tools for studying teachers. Through its elaborate if somewhat loosely connected concepts, such as those of role set and role conflict, it has offered one of the most coherent ways of looking at such matters as the expectations held by different groups about teachers, relations between the settings in which teachers work and their views on their jobs and their pupils, and the conflicts in teachers which may arise because of incompatible demands placed upon them.

Several general comments might be made upon the kinds of approaches which have been mentioned. In the first place, they have often sought to categorize teachers in such general and diffuse ways that they throw little light on what is salient or what is relatively unimportant within a global pattern of behaviours, opinions or expectations, to those who are being controlled or taught. Secondly, since such general characteristics of individuals have usually been assessed through pencil and paper self-reports or the impressionistic ratings of others it may be dangerous to draw inferences from them about the ways in which teachers actually behave. Of course, it is interesting in itself to know what teachers think and feel about their jobs and their pupils; however, it is not only in this respect that such studies have been useful, for through the inconclusiveness of some of this work and through its limited relevance to the events of classrooms it has helped to clear the way for other techniques and for more analytic work on behaviour itself.

The current focus upon the life and work of classrooms has depended upon the development of very different methods of study. In the first place, if we are seeking to describe in detail what is happening in the classroom then there must be means to record the acts of teachers and the patterns of their interactions with pupils. In its most general terms this has meant an increasing reliance upon the use of observers in the classroom; however, this raises questions as to what is observable and in turn what might be important to describe. This is in part a practical matter of recording procedures, but even more, of deciding upon appropriate levels of analysis. In the majority of cases observation has meant recording various verbal acts of teachers such as the frequencies of use of questions, of praise or criticism, of directions to pupils, or of gross amounts of time spent by the teacher in the delivery of his material. More sophisticated categorizing is, however, possible so that observation concentrates upon recording forms of questioning or the logical structures of units of teacher discourse. Systematic observation may also be directed, for example, to providing evidence on the teacher's daily activities, showing the frequency and sequencing of teaching and routine care and preparation activities, or on the ways in which individual teachers distribute their manifest attention to individual pupils in their classes.

The rapid spread of observation and recording has made it possible for the first time to give a more or less objective account of aspects of everyday teaching, removing to a large extent the need to rely upon indirect measures of teaching, separating the process of recording from that of evaluating, and providing an essential step towards the comparison of teachers on different dimensions of behaviour. At this descriptive level alone the findings can be fascinating, but description is an essential tool for two further developments in the study of teaching. Firstly, by providing the means to the comparison of behaviours of teachers and of their pupils it is possible to examine possible associations between teaching and the responses of classes and individual pupils. A great deal of successful work has been done here on relationships between verbal and managerial behaviours and the climates of classrooms and the attitudes of pupils to teachers and schoolwork. And evidence is being accumulated to link specific features of teaching with measurable features of pupils' achievements. On both counts we are achieving a better understanding of what may be significant and what may be relatively non-discriminative in teaching styles. All this work has further implications, this time for the professional training of teachers. The techniques of observation together with analytic accounts of teaching behaviour are the means to systematic inquiry by both student teachers and their supervisors into the teacher's work, and in turn, into the processes and techniques used in training itself. Increasing attention is being given to concepts of skill and to procedures such as micro-teaching in which students can be exposed to models of skilled performance, practise specific skills within small groups, see and criticize recordings of their performance, and get help in translating acquired behaviours to the realistic settings of actual classrooms.

Some indication was given at the beginning of this introduction about the bases of selection of the contents. Inevitably there were further considerations concerning the choice of articles to represent particular topics and about the arrangement of contents. Thus, in some areas of potential interest relatively little empirical work was available; and in others choice was limited by the length of existing articles or by the turgidness of much of the writing. These limitations clearly could not be overcome in an entirely satisfactory way but have been compensated for as far as possible by concentrating upon themes of close practical interest.

In the arrangement of contents we have tried to provide in the two introductory sections general articles, representative of the major theoretical and methodological approaches, which would lead the reader into the more specific school and classroom themes. The third section deals with preparation for the classroom, both as a matter of the socialization of students' attitudes and as one of skills training. The fourth section takes up the theme of the role of the teacher as it is seen through the eyes of teachers themselves and members of their role set such as pupils and headmasters. The remaining three sections are all about teaching in classrooms, but have been broken down into more or less distinctive areas, the first dealing with some general features of personal and managerial styles in teaching, the next with studies of communication with pupils, and the last with some of the more subtle aspects of ongoing informal assessments of pupils such as teachers' expectations, perceptions of the characteristics of pupils, and the interplay of teachers' marks and the expectations of pupils.

Finally some mention is needed about the use of these readings. For the most part we have included articles of potential interest to a wide readership interested in the work of teachers. But beyond this, some of the articles would clearly be most useful if they were studied more intensively under the guidance of workers with specific professional interests and expertise. Whichever the situation, however, it is important to regard these readings as ways in which investigators have looked at matters that have interested them – as means to personal insights to teaching and to criticism. They are not intended to provide some kind of prescriptive view of how teachers should do their job. Empirical studies have a long way to go before we could hope even to provide a part of the breadth and diversity of teaching, and they offer only some of the means towards a wider understanding of the teacher and his pupils.

Part One
Theoretical Approaches

In attempts to provide theoretical frameworks for the study of teachers' classroom behaviour and the effectiveness of teaching, three main approaches may be perceived, concerned respectively with the *role* of the teacher, teacher–pupil interaction *techniques*, and teaching *skills*.

In the first article in this section, Getzels and Thelen suggest a model which is helpful in formulating and clarifying questions about teachers' classroom roles. As yet, however, research based on role theory has focused more on the norms or expectations for teacher behaviour held by different groups than on actual classroom behaviour. It may be that research on such questions as the ways in which pupil expectations influence teacher behaviour or the means whereby teachers resolve various types of role-conflict requires more sophisticated ways of analysing classroom social interaction than are yet available.

Increasing attention has been focused in recent years on more specific aspects of teacher–pupil interaction, and upon the effectiveness of teachers' behaviour in achieving their immediate goals. Argyle's general model of socially skilled behaviour is concerned with ideas which have seemed of central importance to teaching theorists taking this approach; and the parallel Argyle draws between social and motor skills suggests interesting new ways for analysing teacher behaviour.

Gage's article gives the different perspective of an educational researcher; he sees the attempt to identify specific characteristics of teacher behaviour which facilitate the achievement of short term objectives as potentially one of the most fruitful avenues for future research.

1 J. W. Getzels and H. A. Thelen

A Conceptual Framework for the Study of the
Classroom Group as a Social System

From J. W. Getzels and H. A. Thelen, 'The Classroom Group as a
Unique Social System', in Nelson B. Henry (ed.), *The Dynamics of
Instructional Groups*, 59th Yearbook of the National Society for the Study
of Education, Part 2, 1960, pp. 53-82.

The general model

We may begin a description of our model with a consideration of
the most general context of interpersonal or group behavior, i.e.
a given social system.[1] The term 'social system' is, of course,
conceptual rather than descriptive and must not be confused with
society or state, or as somehow applicable only to large aggregates
of human interaction. So, within this framework, for one purpose a
given community may be considered a social system, with the
school a particular organization within the more general social
system. For another purpose, the school itself or a single class
within the school may be considered a social system in its own
right. The model proposed here is applicable regardless of the
level or size of the unit under consideration.

We initially conceive of the social system as involving two
classes of phenomena which are at once conceptually independent
and phenomenally interactive. First, there are the institutions with
certain roles and expectations that will fulfil the goals of the system.
Secondly, there are the individuals with certain personalities and
need-dispositions inhabiting the system, whose observed interactions comprise what we call social or group behavior. We shall
assert that this behavior can be understood as a function of these
major elements: institution, role, and expectation, which together
constitute what we call the *nomothetic* or normative dimension of

1. The same general set of concepts and categories have been applied to
other areas of the school, notably administration, and portions of this
section are paraphrased or taken verbatim from the following: Getzels
(1952, 1957, 1958). Our debt to the work of Talcott Parsons will be self-
evident.

activity in a social system; and individual, personality, and need-disposition, which together constitute the *idiographic* or personal dimension of activity in a social system. In a sense, the one may be thought of as the 'sociological' level of analysis, the other the 'psychological' level of analysis.

To understand the nature of observed behavior and to be able to predict and control it, one must understand the nature of the relationships of these elements. We shall briefly make four points of definition in this connection:

1. All social systems have certain imperative functions that are to be carried out in certain established ways. Such functions as governing, educating, or policing within a state may be said to have become 'institutionalized', and the agencies carrying out these institutionalized functions for the social system may be termed 'institutions'.

2. The most important analytic unit of the institution is the role. Roles are the 'dynamic aspects' of the positions, offices, and statutes within an institution, and they define the behavior of the role incumbents or actors (Linton, 1936).

3. Roles are defined in terms of role-expectations. A role has certain privileges, obligations, responsibilities, and powers. When the role-incumbent puts these obligations and responsibilities into effect, he is said to be performing his role. The expectations define for the actor what he should or should not do so long as he is the incumbent of the particular role.

4. Roles are complementary. They are interdependent in that each role derives its meaning from the other related roles. In a sense, a role is a prescription not only for the given role-incumbent but also for the incumbents of other roles within the institutions and for related roles outside the institutions. Thus, for example, the role of teacher and the role of pupil cannot be defined or implemented except in relation to each other. It is this quality of complementarity which fuses two or more roles into a coherent, interactive unit and which makes it possible for us to conceive of an institution (or group) as having a characteristic structure.

This dimension of the social system may be represented schematically as follows:

social system ➞ institution ➞ roles ➞ expectations ➞ institutional
                    goal
                    behavior

Within this framework then, the class may be conceived as a social system with characteristic institutions, roles, and expectations for behavior. The class as a social system is related to the school as a social system, which in turn is related to the community as a social system, and so on. Ideally, the goal-behaviors of one social system are 'geared in' to the goal-behaviors of the other related social systems. Within the class itself, goal-behavior is achieved through the integration of institutions, the definition of roles, and the setting of expectations for the performer of relevant tasks. In performing the role-behaviors expected of him, the teacher 'teaches'; in performing the role-behaviors expected of *him*, the pupil 'learns'.

So far we have examined the elements constituting the nomothetic or normative aspects of group behavior. At this level of analysis, it was sufficient to conceive of the role incumbents as only 'actors', devoid of personalistic or other individualizing characteristics, as if all incumbents were exactly alike and as if they implemented a given role in exactly the same way. This is not, by any means, to derogate the power of this level of analysis. Indeed, for certain gross understanding and prediction of behavior, this is exactly the right level of abstraction. For example, if we know the roles in a given educational institution, we can make some rather accurate predictions of what the people in these institutions do without ever observing the actual people involved.

But roles are, of course, occupied by real individuals, and no two individuals are alike. Each individual stamps the particular role he occupies with the unique style of his own characteristic pattern of expressive behavior. Even in the case of the relatively inflexible military roles of sergeant and private, no two individual sergeants and no two individual privates fulfil their roles in exactly the same way. To understand the observed behavior of *specific* sergeants and *specific* privates, or of *specific* teachers and *specific* pupils, it is not enough to know only the nature of the roles and expectations – although, to be sure, their behavior cannot be understood apart from these – but we must also know the nature of the individuals inhabiting the roles and reacting to the expectations. That is, in addition to the nomothetic or normative aspects, we must consider the idiographic or individualizing aspects of group behavior. We must, in addition to the sociological level of analysis, include the psychological level of analysis.

Now, just as we were able to analyse the institutional dimension into the component elements of role and expectation, so we may, in a parallel manner, analyse the individual dimension into the component elements of personality and need-disposition. We may briefly make two points of definition in this connection:

1. The concept of personality, like institution or role, has been given a variety of meanings. But for our purposes, personality may be defined as the dynamic organization within the individual of those need-dispositions that govern his *unique* reactions to the environment and, we might add, in the present model, to the expectations in the environment.

2. The central analytic elements of personality are the need-dispositions, which we can define with Parsons and Shils as 'individual tendencies to orient and act with respect to objects in certain manners and to expect certain consequences from these actions' (Parsons and Shils, 1951, p. 114).

This dimension of the social system may be represented schematically as follows:

social system ⟶ individuals ⟶ personalities ⟶ need-dispositions ⟶ individual goal behaviour

Returning to the example of the sergeant and private, we can now make an essential distinction between two sergeants, one of whom has a high need-disposition for 'submission' and the other a high need-disposition for 'ascendance'; and a similar distinction between two privates, one with a high need-disposition for 'submission' and the other for 'ascendance', in the fulfilment of their respective roles, and for the sergeant-private interaction. And we may make similar distinctions in the role-fulfilment and interaction among teachers and pupils of varying personality types.

In short, as we have remarked before, to understand the behavior and interaction of specific role-incumbents in an institution, we must know both the role-expectations and need-dispositions. Indeed, needs and expectations may both be thought of as *motives for behavior*, the one deriving from personalistic sets and propensities, the other from institutional obligations and requirements.

By way of summarizing the argument so far, we may represent the general model pictorially as follows:

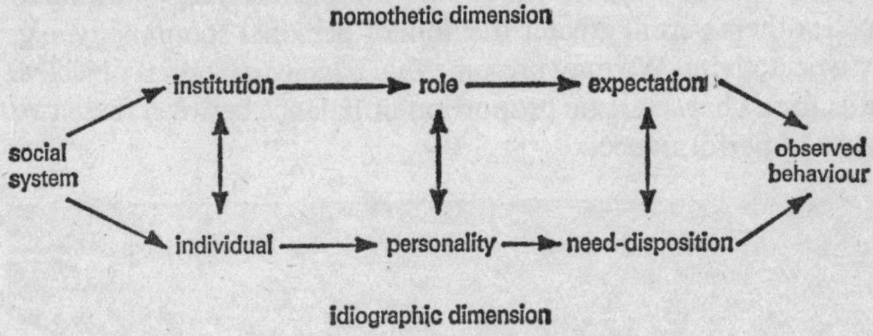

Figure 1

The nomothetic axis is shown at the top of the diagram and consists of institution, role, and expectation, each term being the analytic unit for the term preceding it. Thus, the social system is defined by its institutions, each institution by its constituent roles, each role by the expectations attaching to it. Similarly, the idiographic axis is shown at the lower portion of the diagram and consists of individual, personality, and need-disposition, each term again serving as the analytic unit for the term preceding it.

A given act is conceived as deriving simultaneously from both the nomothetic and idiographic dimensions. That is to say, social behavior results as the individual attempts to cope with an environment composed of patterns of expectations for his behavior in ways consistent with his own independent pattern of needs.

The proportion of role and personality factors determining behavior will, of course, vary with the specific act, the specific role, and the specific personality involved. The nature of the interaction can be understood from another graphic representation as follows:

A given behavioral act may be conceived as occurring at a line cutting through the role and personality possibilities represented by the rectangle. At the left, the proportion of the act dictated by considerations of personality is relatively small. At the right, the proportions are reversed, and considerations of personality become greater than considerations of role-expectations. In these terms, the participants in the classroom situation may define their overt activity along a continuum between two modes of operation from primary emphasis on *role-relevant* performance to primary emphasis on *personality-relevant* performance. Thus, some tasks require maximum adherence to role-expectations, e.g. learning to spell; others permit greater freedom of personal spontaneity, e.g. artistic activity. We may presume that each educational objective calls for a characteristic proportion or balance between these two types of performance.

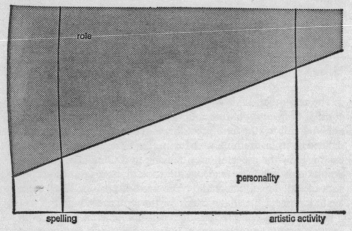

Figure 2

In any case, whether the proportion tends toward one end or the other, behavior in the classroom group remains a function of both role and personality, although in different degree. When role is maximized, behavior still retains some personal aspect because no role is ever so closely defined as to eliminate all individual latitude. When personality is maximized, group behavior still cannot be free of some role prescription. Indeed, the individual who divorces himself from such prescription is said to be autistic, and he ceases to communicate with the group.

The major problem of social or group behavior involves exactly this issue of the dynamics of the interaction between the externally defined role-expectations and the internally defined personality-dispositions. To put the problem concretely, we may ask: How is it, for example, that some complementary role-incumbents understand and agree at once on their mutual privileges and obligations, while others take a long time in reaching such agreement and, quite frequently, do not come to terms either with their roles or with each other?

The essential relevant concept we should like to propose here is *selective interpersonal perception*. In a sense, we may conceive of the publicly described normative relationship of two complementary role-incumbents – the prescribed means and ends of the interaction as set forth, say, in a table or organization or in a curriculum of instruction – as being enacted in two separate private interactions, one embedded in the other. On the one hand, there is the prescribed relationship as perceived idiosyncratically and organized by the one role-incumbent in terms of his own needs, dispositions, and goals; on the other hand, there is the same prescribed relationship as perceived idiosyncratically and organized by the other role-incumbent in terms of his needs, dispositions, and goals. These private situations are related through those aspects of the existential public objects, symbols, values, and expectations, which have to some extent a counterpart in the perceptions of both individuals.

When we say two role-incumbents (such as a teacher and a pupil or a teacher and several pupils in the classroom group) understand each other, we mean that their perceptions and private organization of the prescribed complementary expectations are congruent; when we say they misunderstand each other, we mean that their perceptions and private organization of the prescribed complementary expectations are incongruent.

Like all theoretical formulations, the present framework is an abstraction and, as such, an oversimplification of 'reality' – some factors in the classroom have been brought into the foreground, others put into the background. By focusing on the sociological dimension with the central concept role and on the psychological dimension with the central concept personality, we have omitted other dimensions contributing to classroom behavior. We should like to mention, however briefly, two other relevant dimensions.

There is first the *biological* dimension, for just as we may think of the individual in personalistic terms, we may also think of him in constitutional terms. The individual's personality is embedded, so to speak, in a biological organism with certain constitutional potentialities and abilities. The need-dispositions of the personality are surely related in some way to these constitutional conditions, probably as mediating between constitutional and nomothetic factors. In this sense, we must bear in mind that underlying the psychological dimension is a biological dimension, although the one is not reducible to the other. We may represent this dimension schematically as follows:

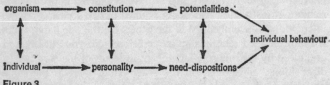

Figure 3

Secondly, there is the *anthropological* dimension. Just as we may think of institutions in sociological terms, we may also think of them in cultural terms, for the institution is embedded in a culture with certain mores and values. The expectations of the roles must in some way be related to the ethos or cultural values. The pupil cannot be expected to learn Latin in a culture where knowledge of Latin has little value, nor can he be expected to identify with teachers in a culture where teachers have little value. In this sense, we must bear in mind that interacting with the sociological dimension there is an anthropological dimension, although again that one is not immediately reducible to the other. We may represent this relationship schematically as follows:

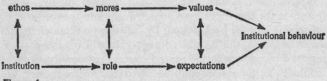

Figure 4

If we may put all the dimensions together into a single, and we are afraid rather unwieldy, pictorial representation, the relationships would look something like this:

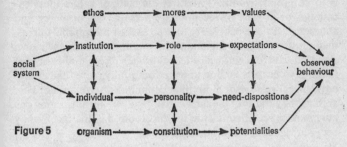

Figure 5

It is our belief that the model can help clarify and systematize important issues relating to classroom behavior. By way of illustration, we should like to apply the model to two of these issues, notably the issues dealing with the *nature and sources of conflict* and with the *nature of teacher choices in changing classroom behavior.*

Application of the model I: classroom conflict

We may identify for present purposes four major types of conflict, although these do not necessarily exhaust the list:

Conflict between the cultural values outside the classroom and the institutional expectations within the classroom. Consider the following instance with respect to the motivation for achievement in the classroom, assuming only the substantive data regarding the state of present values to be as people like Riesman and Wheelis have described it (see Riesman *et al.* (1950); Wheelis (1958)). It is expected by the school that the child will work hard in the classroom in order to achieve to the fullest extent of his potentiality. Accordingly, the child must be motivated to strive and sacrifice present ease for future attainment. But recent studies suggest that our cultural values are coming more and more to prize sociability and hedonistic, present-time orientations, rather than achievement, as goals. In this sense, the criteria of worth in the classroom and in society at large are incongruent, and to this extent the child is subject to conflict with respect to his classroom behavior. Or consider the potential conflict of the so-called gifted or creative child or *teacher* in the classroom. If the potentially creative person is to be productive and inventive, the cultural values must encourage, or at least be receptive to, personal independence and autonomy. If these people are to express their exceptional talents, they must be able to maintain firm commitments to their own standards and to their own beliefs. But again recent studies suggest that our values are coming to prize conformity more than autonomy, moral relativism more than commitment. We are not here arguing the validity of the substantive data – we are illustrating one potential source of conflict in the classroom, i.e. the incongruity between values and expectations.

Conflict between role-expectations and personality-dispositions. Conflicts of this type occur as a function of discrepancies between the pattern of expectations attaching to a given role and the pattern of need-dispositions characteristic of the incumbent of the role. Recall again our example of the individual with high need-dispositions for 'ascendance' placed in the role of an army private. Or more specifically, consider the issues raised by the 'accidental' and compulsory nature of the classroom group. Particular children have not been chosen for particular roles, or particular roles for particular children. There may be mutual interference between the nomothetic or normative expectations for the 'bunch' and the idiographic or differentiated dispositions of each child. In effect, the child is in the classic conflict situation and he must choose whether he will fulfil individual needs or institutional requirements. If he chooses the latter, he is liable to unsatisfactory *personal integration* in the classroom; he is frustrated and dissatisfied. If he chooses the former, he is liable to unsatisfactory *role adjustment* in the classroom; he is ineffective and inefficient as a pupil. In practice, there are usually compromises and accommodations, but the point we want to make here is that the nature of the classroom group activity is quite different when the expectations and the dispositions are incongruent than when they are congruent.

Role conflict. There is a whole range of conflicts that occur when a role incumbent is required to conform simultaneously to a number of expectations which are mutually exclusive, contradictory, or inconsistent so that adjustment to one set of requirements makes adjustment to the other set of requirements impossible or at least difficult.[2] These types of conflict are illustrative of the issues raised by the multiple group and institutional memberships of the participants in the classroom. Role conflicts are evidence of dislocation in the nomothetic dimension of the social system and may arise in several ways.

1. Disagreement within the referent group defining the role. For example, the principal of the school may be expected, by some teachers, to visit them regularly to give constructive help and, by others, to trust them as professional personnel not in need of such supervision. Or, the pupil may be expected by some teachers to emphasize the mechanics of writing, the substance being useful only for the practice of correct form; by other teachers, to emphasize the content and substance, the form being merely an incidental vehicle for the communication. Or perhaps at a more fundamental level, the pupil may be expected by some teachers within the school to conceive of learning as essentially the rote remembrance of information provided by the teacher, and by other teachers as essentially the solution of problems meaningful to the pupil himself.

2. Disagreement among several referent groups, each having a right to define expectations for the same role. To use an example outside our immediate context, the university faculty member may be expected by his department head to emphasize teaching and service to students but by his academic dean to emphasize research and publication. Although these two sets of expectations for the same role do not necessarily conflict, it is clear that the time given to implementing the one set can be seen as taking away time from implementing the other, and to this extent, they *do* conflict.

3. Contradiction in the expectations of two or more roles which an individual is occupying at the same time. It is here that we have all those problems arising from the fact that pupils and teachers are members of numerous different groups in addition to the class-

2. There are numerous empirical studies in the area of role conflict. See, for example, Stouffer (1949, 1951), Getzels and Guba (1954, 1955).

room group. Each group has expectations for its members, and these expectations may be incongruent so that conformity to the expectations of one group may mean nonconformity to the expectations of the other group. Consider here the simple instance of a teacher who is attempting to be, simultaneously, a devoted mother and wife and a successful career woman in her profession. Although the expectations of these roles need not inevitably clash, there is the possibility that attending conferences on teaching may get in the way of keeping up with the progress of her children and husband.

Personality conflict. This type of conflict occurs as a function of opposing needs and dispositions within the personality of the role incumbent as a function of unresolved discrepancies between his needs and his potentialities. The effect of such personal disequilibrium is to keep the individual at odds with the institution either because he cannot maintain a stable relationship with a given role or because he habitually misperceives the expectations placed upon him in terms of his autistic reactions. In any case, just as role conflict is a situational given, personality conflict is an individual given and is independent of any particular institutional setting. No matter what the situation, the role is, in a sense, detached from its institutional context and function and is used to work out personal and private needs and dispositions, however inappropriate these may be to the goals of the social system as a whole.

Application of the model II: classroom leadership in changing behavior

We wish, finally, to apply the terms and categories of our model of the classroom group as a social system to the problem of changing behavior in the teaching–learning situation. In the terms of our model, changing behavior may involve, at one extreme, adaptation of idiographic personality-dispositions to nomothetic role-expectations. We may call this the *socialization of personality*. At the other extreme, changing behavior may involve the adaptation of nomothetic role-expectations to idiographic personality-dispositions. We may call this the *personalization of roles*. In attempting to achieve change, i.e. learning in the classroom, the teacher as the formal group leader always works within these extremes, emphasizing the one, the other, or attempting to reach an appropriate balance between the two. The way the possibilities between socialization of personality and personalization of roles is handled in the classroom determines the kind of group that is achieved and the kind of learning that results.

In this context, we may identify three types of group leadership or, more specifically, three teaching styles:

The nomothetic style. This orientation emphasizes the nomothetic or normative dimension of behavior and, accordingly, places stress on the requirements of the institution, the role, and the expectation rather than on the requirements of the individual, the personality, and the need-disposition. Education is defined as the handing down of what is known to those who do not yet know. It is assumed that, given the institutional purpose, appropriate procedures can be discovered through which the role is taken, despite any personal dispositions of the learner to the contrary, so that he will incorporate the expectations. It then follows that if roles are clearly defined and everyone is held equally responsible for doing what he is supposed to do, the required outcomes will naturally ensue regardless of who the particular role-incumbent might be, provided only that he has the necessary technical competence.

The idiographic style. This orientation emphasizes the idiographic dimension of behavior and accordingly places stress on the requirements of the individual, the personality, and the need-disposition rather than on the requirements of the institution, the role, and the expectation. Education is defined as helping the person know what he wants to know, as it were. This does not mean that the idiographic style is any less goal-oriented than is the nomothetic style; it means that the most expeditious route to the ultimate goal is seen as residing in the people involved rather than in the nature of the institutional structure. The basic assumption is that the greatest accomplishment will occur, not from enforcing adherence to rigorously defined roles, but from making it possible for each person to seek what is most relevant and meaningful to him. This point of view is obviously related to particular individuals who fill the roles at a particular time, and expectations must be kept vague and informal. Normative prescriptions of the sort included in typical role-expectations are seen as unnecessarily restrictive and as a hindrance rather than a guide to productive behavior. The teacher frowns upon *a priori* class 'lesson plans', and is not embarrassed to ask the individual pupil, if we may exaggerate the typical case somewhat, 'Well, what would you like to do today?'

In short, the emphasis is on what we have called the personalization of roles rather than on the socialization of personality. In many ways, neither the nomothetic nor the idiographic definitions of the teaching–learning situation make any demands on the classroom group as a group – the nomothetic mode emphasizes uniform adherence to a given role, the idiographic mode emphasizes the discrete expression of individual personalities. The fact that the roles and personalities exist in the classroom within a group context is more or less irrelevant.

The transactional style. This orientation is intermediate to the other two and is, therefore, less amenable to 'pure' or even clearcut definition. Since the goals of the social system must be carried out, it is obviously necessary to make explicit the roles and expectations required to achieve the goals. And, since the roles and expectations will be implemented by the efforts of people with needs to be met, the personalities and dispositions of these people must be taken into account. But the solution is not so simple as it appears from just saying that one should hew to the middle course between expectations and needs, that is, at some midpoint between the nomothetic and idiographic axes. What we are calling the transactional mode is not just a compromise. Instead, the aim throughout is to acquire a thorough awareness of the limits and resources of both individual and institution within which the teaching–learning process may occur (that is, from the nomothetic and to the idiographic extremes) and to make an intelligent application of the two as a particular problem may demand. Institutional roles are developed independently of the role-incumbents, but they are adapted to the personalities of the actual individual incumbents. Expectations are defined as sharply as they can be but not so sharply that they prohibit appropriate behavior in terms of need-dispositions. Role conflicts, personality conflicts, and role-personality conflicts are recognized and handled. The standard of behavior is both individual integration and institutional adjustment. In short, both the socialization of personality and the personalization of roles is taken into account, and the processes in the classroom may be seen as a dynamic transaction between roles and personalities.

In this mode, the actual balance of emphasis on the performance of role requirements and the expression of personality needs changes as a function of interaction within the classroom group. Account is taken of the common or deviant perceptions of existential objects and roles, and of explicit or implicit agreements on how to deal with conflicts and deviant perceptions. In this sense, the group *qua* group is of crucial significance. It mediates between the institutional requirements and the individual dispositions. On the one hand, it can support the institution by imposing, if necessary, certain normative role-expectations on the group members; on the other hand, it can support the individual in expressing, if necessary, certain idiosyncratic personality-dispositions. In working out this balance between the institution and the individual, the group develops a 'culture' or, perhaps better here, a *climate*, which may be analysed into the constituent *intentions* of the group, and, in effect, the group climate represents another general dimension of the classroom as a social system:

social system ➞ group ➞ climate ➞ intentions ➞ group behaviour

The stability and concomitant flexibility of the group in moving between the nomothetic and idiographic extremes depends on the *belongingness* that the individuals feel within the group. The development of this belongingness is accompanied by increased security for all the members of the group. The greater the belongingness, the greater the ease of significant communication between the teacher and the pupils and among the pupils themselves and the greater the shared pride in the achievement of both institutional *and* individual goals. What was an 'accidental' and compulsory group becomes a planful and voluntary group. The rigidity of the *platoon* or the *instability* of the *crowd* is changed into the resourcefulness and flexibility of the *team*. They 'know' what to expect, what to give, what to take. They find emotional support for their risk-taking, and the consequent increased individual security encourages 'open' transactions between personality and role. The boundaries between the private world and the public world become permeable, and the overlap in the perception of a given situation within the classroom is enlarged. There is, at once, both greater autonomy and heteronomy for the individual. The depth of the person's involvement in the classroom is increased, and, in this sense, learning becomes more meaningful.

Within this framework, this then might be conceived as the ideal-type model of the classroom as a social system: (*a*) each individual *identifies* with the goals of the system so that they become part of his own needs; (*b*) each individual believes that the expectations held for him are *rational* if the goals are to be achieved; (*c*) he feels that he *belongs* to a group with similar emotional identifications and rational beliefs.

By way of summarizing the characteristics of the several dimensions presented, we now offer the final pictorial example selected from the categories of goal behavior.

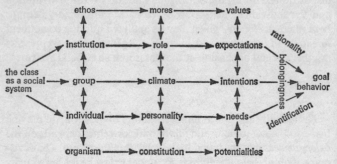

Figure 6

In this final picture we have located the classroom as a social system. From this point of view, the most impressive characteristic of the classroom group, despite its apparent uniqueness, is that it can be studied systematically like *any* other group, be it a board of directors, a neighborhood club, or working team. The fundamental dimensions and concepts remain the same, and in studying any given group within a unified model, we both gain from and contribute to the study of all groups. The dimensions and concepts we have used are derived from the social sciences, and we believe one implication of our effort is that the social sciences have a great deal to contribute to the systematic analysis of education. In so far as there is going to be a 'science' of education, it will be related to concepts, findings, and propositions from the whole range of disciplines called social science. It will be an integrative structure of ideas about the ways in which cultural, institutional, group, individual, and organismic factors interact and, in the process of interacting, change and bring about change.

The appropriate application of science to a particular situation is an art. Educational science is translated into educative outcomes through making choices, and this calls for the exercise of judgment. We see the learning group as an emergent reality developing out of the transactions between role and personality in the classroom. The nature of the group is determined ultimately by the way the teacher responds to the specific behavior of the students. But the judgment of the teacher on how to respond depends not merely on his ability to perceive the behavior to which he is responding as an immediate act but to look behind the act and to comprehend the behavior as a transaction within the social system as a whole. For it is within this sort of comprehension that not only the particular group but the particular individual within the group can be most readily understood. And it is through this understanding that the teacher can wisely judge how to respond.

One fundamental concern of teacher and student alike, then, is surely the nature of the group they are establishing. If they are working at cross-purposes, the likelihood of educational achievement is slim, for the chief preoccupation of the individuals will be the problem of dealing with a situation in which they cannot perceive order and consistency – at least not *their* order and consistency. Yet, if the classroom is to be genuinely challenging – and it must be this to be educative – dislocation in goals, expectations, potentialities, needs, and intentions is bound to arise, for the relationships among the various factors in the social system are continually undergoing change, and are, if we may put it this way, always transacting with one another.

References

GETZELS, J. W. (1952), 'A psycho-sociological framework for the study of educational administration', *Harvard Educ. Rev.*, vol. 22, pp. 235–46.

GETZELS, J. W., and GUBA, E. G. (1954), 'Role, role conflict and effectiveness: an empirical study', *Amer. Sociol. Rev.*, vol. 19, pp. 164–75.

GETZELS, J. W., and GUBA, E. G. (1955), 'The structure of roles and role conflict in the teaching situation', *J. educ. Sociol.*, vol. 29, pp. 30–40.

GETZELS, J. W., and GUBA, E. G. (1957), 'Social behaviour and the administrative process', *Sch. Rev.*, vol. 115, pp. 423–41.

GETZELS, J. W. (1958), 'Administration as a social process', in A. W. Halpin (ed.), *Administration Theory in Education*, Midwestern Administration Course, University of Chicago.

LINTON, R. (1936), *The Study of Man*, Appleton-Century-Crofts.

PARSONS, T., and SHILS, E. A. (1951), *Toward a General Theory of Action*, Harvard University Press.

RIESMAN, D. *et al.* (1950), *The Lonely Crowd*, Yale University Press.

STOUFFER, S. S. (1949), 'An analysis of conflicting social norms', *Amer. Sociol. Rev.*, vol. 14, pp. 707–17.

STOUFFER, S. A., and TOBY, J. (1951), 'Role conflict and personality', *Amer. J. Sociol.*, vol. 111, pp. 395–406.

WHEELIS, A. (1958), *The Quest for Identity*, Norton.

2 M. Argyle

Analysis of the Behaviour of an Interactor

Excerpts from M. Argyle, *Social Interaction*, Methuen, 1969, pp. 179–86.

If it is recognized that an interactor is pursuing certain goals, and that he takes corrective action dependent on the effects of his actions on the other, then we are saying that his behaviour has some of the features of a motor skill. A model of interaction as a kind of motor skill was developed by Argyle and Kendon (1967), and Argyle (1967), from which the following account is taken.

A 'skill' may be defined as an organized, coordinated activity in relation to an object or a situation, which involves a whole chain of sensory, central and motor mechanisms. One of its main characteristics is that the performance, or stream of action, is continuously under the control of the sensory input. This input derives in part from the object or situation at which the performance may be said to be directed, and it controls the performance in the sense that the outcomes of actions are continuously matched against some criterion of achievement or degree of approach to a goal, and the performance is nicely adapted to its occasion (Welford, 1958).

Here we suggest that an individual engaged in interaction is engaged in a performance that is more or less skilled. His behaviour here, as when he is driving a car, is directed, adaptive, and far from automatic, though it may be seen to be built up of elements that are automatized. And here, too, we have an individual carrying out a series of actions which are related to consequences that he has in mind to bring about: in order to do this he has to match his output with the input available to him and to correct his output in the light of this matching process. Thus he may be discussing current affairs with an acquaintance, and be concerned perhaps merely to sustain a pleasant flow of talk. He must be on the watch then for signs of emotional disturbance in his acquaintance, which might signal that he had said something which might provoke an argument. At another level, he must be on the lookout for signals that his acquaintance is ready for him to talk, or for him to listen. He must make sure his tone of voice and choice of words, his gestures, and the level of involvement in what he is saying, are appropriate for the kind of occasion of the encounter.

In the treatment of human performance as developed by such workers as Welford (1958) and Crossman (1964), a distinction is drawn between the perceptual input, the central translation processes, and the motor output, or performance. We will discuss the various elements of the model in more detail.

The goals of skilled performance

The motor skill operator has quite definite immediate goals – to screw a nut on to a bolt, to guide a car along the road by turning the steering wheel, and so on. He also has further goals, under which the immediate ones are subsumed: to make a bridge, or to drive to Aberdeen. He knows when each goal is attained by the appearance of certain physical stimuli. These goals in turn are linked to basic motivations; for example, he may be paid for each

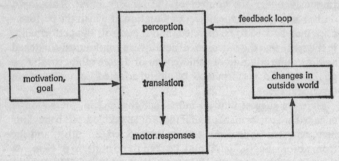

Figure 1 Motor skill model
(Source, Argyle, 1967)

unit of work completed. In much the same way, a 'social skill' operator may have quite definite goals, for example:

conveying knowledge, information or understanding (teaching)
obtaining information (interviewing)

changing attitudes, behaviour or beliefs (salesmanship, canvassing, disciplinary action)

changing the emotional state of another (telling jokes, dealing with hostile person)

changing another's personality (psychotherapy, child-rearing)

working at a cooperative task (most industrial work)

supervising the activities of another (nursing)

supervision and coordination of a group (chairmanship, foremanship, arbitration)

These aims are linked in turn to more basic motivations in the performer, connected with his work. [. . .] Each person wants the other person to respond in an affiliative, submissive or dominant manner, according to his own motivational structure. In professional situations the social skill operator will, in fact, be motivated by a combination of professional and social motivations – he may for example want the client both to learn and to be impressed by his knowledge. Like the motor skill performer, he will also pursue a series of sub-goals in turn. The interviewer first establishes rapport, collects personal data, obtains the answers to a series of questions, and then closes the interview.

Selective perception of cues

The selective perception of cues is an essential element in serial motor skills. The performer learns which cues to attend to and becomes highly sensitive to them. Vision is the most important channel. The performer makes a rapid series of fixations, each lasting perhaps $0 \cdot 25$–$0 \cdot 35$ of a second as, for instance, in reading. The pattern of fixation is itself part of the skill; ideally, information should be collected just before it is needed. The performer also learns where to look at each point, in order to obtain the necessary information: perception is highly selective. The incoming data are actively organized into larger units which are recognized as objects, signals or cues. These in turn are interpreted, i.e. used to predict future events, as with dial-readings or road signs. A number of other perceptual channels are used by the motor skill performer – hearing, touch, and signals from the muscles (kinaesthesis) about the position of the limbs and body. It is common for more use to be made of touch and kinaesthesis when the skill is well learnt: vision is reserved for the cues which cannot be dealt with by the other senses, and for cues at a distance. It is found that as learning proceeds less use is made of external cues. An experienced motorist concentrates his attention on certain stimuli: outside the car he attends to the movement of other traffic and the position of the edge of the road, rather than the architecture of the houses; while inside he is aware of the speedometer rather than the upholstery of the seats. He knows where to look for the cues, and what they mean; he can interpret road signs and can anticipate what is going to happen next. Part of the training for some industrial skills consists in teaching performers to make finer discriminations, to learn the significance of cues, concentrating on particular cues and suppressing irrelevant ones.

During the course of social interaction each participant receives a stream of visual and auditory information about the other. [. . .] The motor skill performer gets quite a lot of information from perceiving his own movements, either by sound, vision or by kinaesthetic sensations. Do social interactors receive any direct feedback in a similar way? People are very interested in the image they are projecting: one of the goals of interaction is to present oneself in a certain light to others. The main source of direct feedback is the sound of one's own voice. Some people are said to be very fond of this sound, but the sound they hear is quite different from what other people hear, since they hear the sound as transmitted through bones. Many people fail to recognize tape-recordings of their voices, and are very startled the first time they hear one. People are often quite unaware of the emotive paralinguistic aspects of their speech. They may also be unaware of the timing aspects of their speech – such as how often they interrupt. Posture, gestures and facial expression cannot be perceived visually by the actor: it is very difficult to see ourselves as others see us. The only way to do this is to have a lot of mirrors, or to study films of oneself. There are however kinaesthetic, muscular cues to bodily movements. People have a fairly definite body image, and do have some idea of their posture.

Central 'translation' processes

Information gathered by the receptor systems is transferred to more central regions of the brain and is converted into an appropriate plan of action. If someone is steering a boat he must learn which way to turn the rudder to go in the desired direction. There has to be some central store of 'translation' processes in the brain, which prescribe what to do about any particular perceptual information. This may be in the form of verbalized information, e.g. 'pull the rope on the side you want to turn towards', in the case of the rudder. Often the translation processes are completely unverbalized and lead to automatic sequences of behaviour with little conscious awareness – as in riding a bicycle. Or they may start as conscious rules and deliberate decisions but become automatic later, as with changing gear in a car. A curious feature of the central system is that it can only handle one piece of information at a time – it has limited capacity. The output from it consists of a plan, i.e. the decision to make a particular series of motor responses, which has been selected from a range of possible alternatives. This involves some prediction about how external events are likely to develop while the response is being organized – as when a tennis or squash player, while he is shaping his shot, anticipates exactly where the ball will be.

We can see how the skill model is able to take account of the differing levels of organization involved in behaviour, from the most automatic to the most reflective. It also takes account of the fact that the same pattern of behaviour can be more or less automatic at different points in time. Social interaction also depends on the existence of a learnt store of central translation processes. In the course of socialization people learn which social techniques will elicit affiliative or other responses from those they encounter. Research has shown how these can be improved upon in many cases. For example, to get another person to talk more the best techniques are (a) to talk less, (b) to ask open-ended questions, (c) to talk about things he is interested in, and (d) to reward anything he does say. The effects of limited channel capacity are seen in social interaction as in motor skill performance: during periods of hesitating and unfluent speech speakers do not scan the faces of the others present – presumably to avoid overloading the system.

Motor responses

Commands go from the central translation system to the muscles, producing a pattern of movements. In fact, there is a hierarchy of goals, consisting of progressively smaller groups of muscular responses. There is also a series of sub-goals: when one sub-goal has been reached the sequence leading to the next sub-goal begins, until the main goal is attained. Driving a car from A to B involves the sub-goals of getting the engine started, getting the car moving in top gear, and getting to the intermediate points X, Y and Z. One of the interesting findings about motor skill is that the series of responses leading to sub-goals become more or less automatic, and can be regarded as larger response units; for example, words rather than letters become the units for morse or typing (cf. Miller, Galanter and Pribram, 1966).

While the essence of the central processes is to *plan*, the essence of the response system is to initiate and control; the desired responses are set in motion and steered with the help of perceptual guidance. As well as learning the perceptual cues and translation processes, it is necessary to learn to perform these patterns of motor response smoothly and accurately. When a motor skill has been perfected, it is faster, movements are eliminated, conscious awareness is much reduced, tension is reduced or sometimes focused at points of difficulty, and there is less need for feedback and some danger of becoming rather mechanical. There are broader aspects of response such as the styles of psychotherapy, foremanship, etc., which have been found to be most effective. These entail rather subtle and complex combinations of social responses, consisting of integrated patterns of social techniques. Establishing rapport, building up a relation of dominance and reducing another's anxiety, are all examples of such higher units of social behaviour, and are probably unitary and automatic sequences of behaviour for many people. Another example is establishing and negotiating relationships and identities in an encounter. These are larger units, composed of smaller units, but interactors are consciously aware of the larger units rather than the smaller ones, and relationships are partly established in terms of the interlocking of these larger units, e.g. relationship between roles.

In considering a performance in this way, we note how it may be said to be made up of a combination of elements, though what we refer to as an 'element' will depend upon the level in the hierarchy we are discussing. It may be noted that 'elements' can be recombined in a fairly flexible way, and it is this that makes a skill so adaptive. On the other hand, once a particular combination of elements achieves, for the performer, an acceptable level of success, and provided the sequence of sensory input is stable upon subsequent occasions when the skill is used, it is found that many sequences of actions in the performance become 'automatized', that is freed from the continuous sensory control. The smaller, lower-level units in the hierarchy are more habitual and automatic than the larger, higher-level units. Feedback operates at each level, so that at the higher levels corrective action involves bringing whole lower-level units into play. More conscious attention is given to the performance of the larger units; their strategy is carefully planned where the lower levels are run off unthinkingly. It seems likely that a similar phenomenon of automatization occurs with social skills. Thus lecturers and interviewers, for instance, who make use of a fairly standard social technique on repeated occasions, may be able to run off long sequences of actions automatically. An experienced interviewer might give considerable thought to the overall strategy of an interview, but much less to particular questions, and none at all to particular words. Museum guides offer a notorious example, where automatization has gone too far. Lecturers have occasionally reported on this process in themselves. Thus Lashley (1951) mentions a colleague who reported to him that 'he had reached a stage where he could arise before an audience, turn his mouth loose, and go to sleep' (p. 184). It is found that speech is accompanied by continuous shifts of head, hands and body, and that these bodily movements are also arranged hierarchically, so that a head position may accompany a sentence, a bodily position a paragraph (Scheflen, 1965). However, these shifts do not appear to be under conscious control at all, except for those who have learnt about these phenomena.

Feedback and corrective action

The motor skill performer uses perceptual cues to take corrective action. He can thus correct a continuous action, like steering a car, when it shows signs of going wrong, or correct later performances in the light of earlier ones, as when firing a rifle at a target. It is in a continuous skill or 'tracking' task that this can be seen most clearly. A beginner motorist tries to steer the car down the road; he sees that he is about to hit the kerb, so he corrects the steering to the right. When he is more competent the same process takes place with greater speed and accuracy. Feedback provides information for corrective action, which makes allowances for variation in the conditions or materials and for error in the initial plan of response. The social skill performer corrects in a similar way. A teacher who sees that her pupils have not understood the point will repeat it slowly in another way; a person who realizes that he is annoying someone by his behaviour will usually change his style of behaviour. The experiments on 'operant verbal conditioning' can be looked at as demonstrations of the effect of feedback – working at two different levels of psychological functioning.

The model is of course only a starting point: it provides a language for talking about interaction, and it is suggestive in a number of ways. We shall have to elaborate it in two main ways.

1. to take account of some of the special cognitive processes taking place during interaction, such as 'taking the role of the other', and

2. to take account of the fact that other interactors are playing the same game, and that there must be a meaningful sequence of responses for social interaction to take place.

The model as expounded so far has however been useful in showing the various points at which social skill training may be needed, and in providing a classification of the ways in which social competence may fail, in mental patients and others.

References

ARGYLE, M. (1967), *The Psychology of Interpersonal Behaviour*, Penguin.

ARGYLE, M., and KENDON, A. (1967), 'The experimental analysis of social performance', in L. Berkowitz (ed.), *Advances in Experimental Social Psychology*, vol. 3, Academic Press.

CROSSMAN, E. R. (1964), 'Information processes in human skill', *Brit. Med. Bull.*, vol. 20, pp. 32–7.

LASHLEY, K. W. (1951), 'The problem of serial order in behaviour', in L. A. Jeffress (ed.), *Cerebral Mechanisms in Behavior: The Hixon Symposium*, Chapman and Hall.

MILLER, G. A., GALANTER, E., and PRIBRAM, K. E. (1966), *Plans and the Structure of Behavior*, Holt, Rinehart & Winston.

SCHEFLEN, A. E. (1965), *Stream and Structures of Communicational Behavior*, Eastern Pennsylvania Psychiatric Institute.

WELFORD, A. T. (1958), *Ageing and Human Skill*, Oxford University Press.

3 N. L. Gage

An Analytical Approach to Research on Instructional Methods

From N. L. Gage, 'An Analytical Approach to Research on Instructional Methods', *Journal of Experimental Education*, vol. 37, 1968, pp. 119–25.

Instructional method constitutes one of the most important and promising but also the most frustrating of the areas of educational research and development. Compared with the areas of learning, subject matter, instructional materials, and organization for instruction, instructional method appeals to the classroom teacher as closest to the heart of her problem. It is all right for a teacher to know about learning, to know his subject matter, to have appropriate instructional materials, and to fit into a given organization for instruction. But what a teacher really wants to know is, 'What should I do in the classroom?' If you ask prospective teachers or teachers on the job, 'Where do you really want help?', I think the reply will deal with some aspect of instructional methods.

Unfortunately, the urgency of this demand has not been accompanied by corresponding success in meeting the demand. Research on teaching has yielded relatively few solid and usable results. The stature of theory and research in other areas puts them well ahead of the study of teaching in the struggle for scientific maturity.

Implicit in what I am saying is a basic distinction between research on learning and research on teaching. The former deals with all the conditions under which learning, or a change in behavior due to experience, takes place. And as I have already indicated, the study of learning is relatively mature, well established, with many volumes of substantial literature to its credit. Research on teaching, on the other hand, deals with a subset of the conditions under which learning occurs in one person, namely, the conditions established by the behaviors of another person, called the teacher. As our schools have developed during the past two or three millennia, we have always attempted to promote and improve the learning process through the intermediation of such another person. Until very recently, the assumption that teachers were helpful or even necessary for many important kinds of learning that society wanted to promote went unchallenged. Even today, the challenge of independent study or computer-assisted instruction and other devices is a mere whisper against the thunder of the assumption that teachers are necessary, that teachers are here to stay. My discussion of instructional methods is going to be based on that assumption. It is the relatively neglected, undernourished, and underachieving subset of research on learning which I call research on teaching that I shall deal with here.

Research on teaching

The Stanford Center for Research and Development in Teaching is devoted to this problem area. In its conceptual framework, teaching, or the behaviors and characteristics of teachers, stands at the center. This domain contains variables that serve as both independent and dependent variables in the Center's program. When the teachers' behaviors and characteristics serve as independent variables, and the pupils' learning and behaviors serve as the dependent variables, then we have research on teacher effectiveness, or, more neutrally, research on teacher effects. On the other hand, when teachers' behaviors and characteristics serve as the dependent variables, and teacher education programs and procedures serve as the independent variables, then we have research on teacher education. Taking both research on teacher education and research on teacher effects as our domain, we have research on teaching, as it is understood in the Stanford Center. My subject is the Center's program of research and development on instructional methods, and my procedure will be to work from the past to the present, from the general to the specific, and then to try for a look at where we are going. When I get down to specifics, I shall be dealing primarily with research in which I am involved, rather than all of the research underway in our Center.

Past research

But first, let us look at where research on teaching has been. As the behavioral sciences go, it has a respectably long history but a regrettably inglorious one. Research on teaching has been going on almost as long as research on learning. Some studies were made in the 1910s and 1920s, and quite a few were made during the 1930s. By the early 1950s, substantial reviews and bibliographies of research on teaching began to appear. And during the last decade, the flow of research on teaching has indeed become significant. But the early years did not pay off in solid, replicable, meaningful results that had considerable theoretical or practical value. Positive and significant results were seldom forthcoming, and they survived replication even less often. The research yielded many findings that did not make sense, that did not hang together in any meaningful way.

Under these conditions, as Kuhn (1962) has pointed out, research workers are impelled to re-examine their first principles, the paradigms by which they guide their efforts. The model problems and solutions of the community of researchers on teaching were accordingly subjected to more and more reappraisal. Licking the wounds inflicted by their negative results, researchers on teaching built up a modest literature of new conceptual frameworks, approaches, and paradigms for research on teaching.

To illustrate, let me refer to one of the dominant paradigms that even today leads many discussions and research projects into the wilderness. This is the paradigm that says that what we need above all, before we can select and train better teachers, is *the* criterion of teacher effectiveness. Here is one example of that kind of approach:

The lack of an adequate, concrete, objective, universal criterion for teaching ability is thus the primary source of trouble for all who would measure teaching. One typical method of attack used in rating scales is to compile a list of broad general traits supposedly desirable for teachers, with respect to which the rater passes judgement on each teacher. This amounts to an arbitrary definition of good teaching, which is subjective and usually vague, but it does not necessarily lead to an identification of it. Only if the traits themselves can be reliably identified can their possessor be identified as a 'good teacher' according to the definition laid down in the scale. Even when the scale is made quite specific, relating not to general traits but to concrete procedure, the fundamental difficulty remains, that there is no external and generally accepted criterion against which the scale can be validated to establish the significance of its items (Walker, 1935, pp. x–xi).

This kind of writing implies that there is some magic variable that applies to all of teaching, for all pupils, at all grade levels, in all subject matters, and in all objectives. The phrase 'the criterion of teacher effectiveness' betokens a degree of generality that has seldom been found in any branch of the behavioral sciences. It also reflects the mistaken notion that such a criterion, largely a matter of values, can be established on the basis of scientific method alone.

Recent research

The so-called criterion problem misled a whole generation of researchers on teaching, embroiled them in endless and fruitless controversy, and lured them into hopelessly ambitious attempts to predict teacher effectiveness over vast arrays and spans of outcomes, teacher behaviors, time intervals, and pupil characteristics, all on the basis of predictive variables that had only the most tenuous theoretical justification in the first place. It is little wonder that, when Berelson and Steiner (1964) dealt with the subject of teachers' behaviors and characteristics in their inventory of scientific findings in the behavioral sciences, they dismissed the 'large number of studies' with the single dismal sentence that 'there are no clear conclusions' (p. 441).

If the global criterion approach had proved to be sterile, what was the alternative? The answer was to take the same path that more mature sciences had already followed: If variables at one level of phenomena do not exhibit lawfulness, break them down. Chemistry, physics, and biology had, in a sense, made progress through making finer and finer analyses of the phenomena and events they dealt with. Perhaps research on teaching would reach firm ground if it followed the same route.

Apparently, a number of students of the problem had this general idea at about the same time. In 1962, writing my chapter on paradigms for the *Handbook of Research on Teaching*, I coined the term, 'micro-criteria' of effectiveness. As I said in that chapter:

One solution within the 'criterion-of-effectiveness' approach may be the development of the notion of 'micro-effectiveness'. Rather than seek criteria for the overall effectiveness of teachers in the many, varied facets of their roles, we may have better success with criteria of effectiveness in small, specifically defined aspects of the role ... a sufficient number of laws applying to relatively pure aspects of the teacher's role, if such laws could be developed, might eventually be combined, ... to account for the actual behavior and effectiveness of teachers with pupils under genuine classroom conditions (Gage, 1963, p. 120).

A group of workers at Stanford University, to which I was to move a few months later, took a similar view. In the Stanford program for training secondary-school teachers, Robert Bush, Dwight Allen, and their co-workers adopted what is now known as the technical skills approach. Technical skills are specific instructional techniques and procedures that a teacher may use in the classroom. They represent an analysis of the teaching process into relatively discrete components that can be used in different combinations in the continuous flow of the teacher's performance. The specific set of technical skills adopted in the teacher-education program at Stanford may be quite arguable. Indeed, the list of skills has been revised a number of times over the past few years. What is important is the approach – the attempt to analyse teaching into limited, well-defined, components that can be taught, practiced, evaluated, predicted, controlled, and understood in a way that has proven to be altogether impossible for teaching viewed in the larger chunks that occur over a period of an hour, a day, a week, or a year.

When analysed-teaching, in the form of technical skills, is made the focus of our concern, we find it possible to do fairly satisfying research both on teacher education and on teacher effects. The satisfaction comes from being able to measure or manipulate relevant independent variables, perform true experiments, or make careful analyses and measure relevant dependent variables.

The idea of technical skills may be illustrated by the terms used in a recent list of such skills. One was called 'establishing set', or the establishment of cognitive rapport between pupils and teacher to obtain immediate involvement in the lesson; one technique for inducing a positive set is the use of relevant analogies. A second technical skill is that called 'establishing appropriate frames of reference', or points of view. A third technical skill is that of 'achieving closure', or pulling together major points, linking old and new knowledge, at appropriate points within a teaching episode as well as at the end. A fourth technical skill is that of 'using questions' in such a way as to elicit the kinds of thought-processes and behaviors desired such as simple recall, or concept formation, or evaluation. Other technical skills are those in 'recognizing and obtaining attending behavior', 'control of participation', 'providing feedback', 'employing rewards and punishments', and 'setting a model'.

Micro-teaching

These technical skills into which important aspects of the teaching job have been analysed are not merely the subjects of lectures and discussions in the teacher education program. Rather, they form the basis for the intern's practice teaching prior to his entrance into actual classrooms. This procedure, well known by now as 'micro-teaching', consists in getting the trainee to teach a scaled-down teaching exercise. It is scaled down in terms of time because it lasts only 5 to 10 minutes. It is scaled down in terms of class size, because he teaches a group of not more than five pupils, who are brought in and paid to serve as pupils in the micro-teaching clinic. It is scaled down in terms of the task, since the trainee attempts to perform only one of the technical skills in any single micro-teaching session. The sessions are recorded on video tape, and the trainee gets to see and hear himself immediately after the session. While he looks at and listens to himself, he receives criticisms and suggestions from supervisors trained to be both perceptive and tactful. Then he 're-teaches' the same lesson to a new small group of pupils in an attempt to improve on his first performance of the specific technical skill that is his concern in that session.

Obviously, the general idea is subject to many variations. The size of the class can be manipulated; the number of trainees teaching a given group of children can be increased; the duration of the lessons can be lengthened; and the nature of the teaching task can be made more complex so as to embrace a group of technical skills in their real-life combinations. But the idea of analysing teaching into technical skills remains the heart of the method and provides its power as a paradigm for research.

The research on micro-teaching and technical skills in the Stanford teacher education program has taken the form of experiments in which various procedures for feedback to the trainee are manipulated. Professors Dwight Allen and Frederick McDonald have organized a program of research on variables hypothesized to influence the learning of the technical skills of teaching. Their independent variables fall into three categories: practice variables, feedback variables, and demonstration variables. A practice variable may consist in micro-teaching versus teaching in an actual classroom. A feedback variable may be the positive or negative character of the feedback, or the mediation of the feedback by another person rather than the trainee himself. Finally, a demonstration variable may take the form of symbolic demonstration, consisting of written or spoken words, or perceptual demonstration, consisting in either live or video-taped portrayals of the desired behavior; and each of these can consist either of self-modeling or modeling by others. Other independent variables have been identified, such as the timing of a reinforcement, the amount of practice, and the amount of feedback.

This condensed description of the Allen–McDonald research program can suffice to illustrate the use of the analytic approach to research on teacher education. Their research takes the form of true experiments in which subjects are randomly assigned to different values of the independent variable.

Technical skills approach – explaining ability

I should like to turn now to an example of the way in which the technical skills approach can be applied to the study of teacher effects. This research has dealt with a technical skill that I call 'explaining', or the skill of engendering comprehension – usually orally, verbally, and extemporaneously – of some process, concept, or generalization. Explaining occurs in all grade levels and subject matters, whether it is a fifth-grade teacher explaining why the time in New York differs from that in San Francisco or a geologist explaining how the ice age may have been caused by volcanic eruptions. Everyday observation tells us that some people explain aptly, getting to the heart of the matter with just the right terminology, examples, and organization of ideas. Other explainers, on the contrary, get us and themselves all mixed up, use terms beyond our level of comprehension, draw inept analogies, and even employ concepts and principles that cannot be understood without an understanding of the very thing that is being explained. To some of us, it has seemed that explaining comes very close to being the inner essence of instruction, so that when a teacher is attempting to explain proportionality to his geometry class or irony to his English class, he is behaving more purely as a teacher than when he is attempting, say, to motivate, promote discussion, or maintain discipline. At any rate, we have made some studies of explaining ability in the attempt to determine some of the characteristics of effective explanations.

Explaining ability study in micro-teaching clinic

The first study was made in the micro-teaching clinic at Stanford during the summer of 1965 by Fortune, Gage, and Shutes (1966). We attempted to determine the generality of explaining ability, that is, the degree to which the ability to explain one topic was correlated with the ability to explain another topic, and the degree to which the ability to explain a topic to one group of pupils on one occasion was correlated with the ability to explain the same topic to another group of pupils on another occasion. We also were able to design the study so as to determine the degree to which there was generality over both pupils and topics, or the degree to which the ability to explain one topic to one group of pupils on one day correlated with the ability to explain another topic to another group of pupils on another day. Because there were only sixty pupils to be shared in groups of five among approximately forty interns in the micro-teaching clinic, the design became quite complex in order to avoid having any intern teach the same topic to the same group of pupils more than once and to avoid having the same group of pupils receive an explanation of the same topic more than once. Accordingly, the forty social studies interns – and we chose to work with the social studies interns only because there were more of them than any other kind of intern – were divided into five clusters of eight interns each. The lectures dealt with twenty different topics, each consisting of an 'Atlantic Report' from the *Atlantic Monthly*. The correlations that we obtained were thus medians of five correlations, each based on four, six, six, six, and eight interns, respectively.

The index of lecture effectiveness, or what I would like to call the micro-criterion of teacher explaining ability, was the pupils' mean score on a ten-item test of their comprehension of the main ideas of the lecture, which was presented by each intern in fifteen minutes under somewhat standardized conditions. This mean score was adjusted for the mean ability of the pupils in the given group as measured by their scores on all of the other topics. Similarly, any given mean score was adjusted for the difficulty of the topic as measured by the mean score of all groups of pupils on that topic. Thus, the variance of the adjusted mean post-test comprehension scores was attributable not to the ability of the pupils or the difficulty of the topic but rather to the differences among the teachers. We then investigated the question of the various kinds of generality by determining the median inter-correlations among the various means. The upshot of this part of this study was that generality over topics was non-existent, and generality over groups was about 0·4. In other words, the interns were moderately consistent in their ability to explain the same topic to different groups on different occasions, but they were not consistent in their ability to explain different topics.

The study dealt with the correlations between explaining effectiveness and the pupils' rating of various aspects of the explanations. The pupils rated the interns' performance with respect to twelve items, such as clarity of aims, organization of the lesson, selection of material, and clarity of presentation. To us it seemed that some of these dimensions should correlate more highly with explaining ability than others. In particular, we hoped that such discriminant validity would be manifest in the form of a higher correlation between the mean rating of the lecture for 'clarity of presentation' than for any of the other items of the Stanford Teacher Competence Appraisal Guide. Our hope was borne out; the correlation of the adjusted mean post-test comprehension scores with pupils' ratings of 'clarity of presentation' was 0·56, higher than that with any of the other rating scale items. This result seems to us to support the validity of both the index of lecture effectiveness and the mean ratings by the pupils.

Explaining ability study in public schools

During the school year 1965–6, I was able, in collaboration with Barak Rosenshine, to undertake a replication and extension of this study in the public schools (Rosenshine, 1968). Because there was no lack of students in the high-school classes, taught by their own teachers, we did not become involved in the complexities of design necessary in the micro-teaching clinic. To put it very briefly, we got forty eleventh-grade social studies teachers each to deliver a fifteen-minute lecture on an 'Atlantic Report' on Yugoslavia taken from the *Atlantic Monthly*. The teachers had been given the article several days in advance, and had been told to prepare a lecture that would enable their pupils to answer a ten-item multiple-choice test of comprehension of the article's main ideas. To guide them in preparing their lecture, they were given five of the multiple-choice questions that would be asked, while the other five questions were withheld. After the fifteen-minute lecture, in which the teachers were permitted to use the blackboard but no other aids, their students took the ten-item test. They also rated the teacher's lecture on items similar to those I have already described. The next day, the same teachers and classes did the same things, except that the subject matter was an 'Atlantic Report' on Thailand; again the teachers had been given five of the ten items as a guide to the kind of lecture that they should prepare and had been told to focus on the explanation of the major ideas, concepts, and principles brought out in the article, which constituted the curriculum for this bit of teaching. On the third day, the classes heard a third lecture, one that was the same for all classes, a tape recorded fifteen-minute lecture on Israel, a verbatim reading of an 'Atlantic Report', and then the pupils again took a ten-item test based on that article.

The class mean on the Israel test was used to adjust the class means on Yugoslavia and Thailand for between-class differences in ability. Our reasoning was that the score on such a test of comprehension of a uniform lecture would be more useful in controlling relevant kinds of ability than would the usual scholastic aptitude test. The class means on Yugoslavia and Thailand were also adjusted for teacher differences in the content-relevance of the lecture, as determined by scoring the transcript of the lecture for relevance to the ten items on the comprehension test. We then assumed that the variance that still remained in the adjusted comprehension test means of the classes would reflect differences between the teachers in what we were concerned with, namely, the intellectual style and process of the teacher's lecture. In this study, the teacher's adjusted effectiveness index on Yugoslavia correlated 0·47 with his effectiveness on Thailand; i.e. there was considerable generality of effectiveness over topics, even after student ability and content relevance had been partialed out.

It should be noted that we were using the micro-teaching idea in this investigation. The teaching was restricted to just one aspect of the teacher's role, namely, ability to explain the current, social, political, and economic situation in another country. The curriculum was also scaled down. We also used another major feature of the micro-teaching clinic, the video tape recorders which made it possible for us to study the teacher's behavior, verbal and nonverbal, at leisure.

One major question was that of whether our criterion, or micro-criterion, of teacher effectiveness in explaining, namely, the mean comprehension score of the pupils, adjusted for both mean pupil ability and content-relevance, contained variance that would be manifested in something about the lecture that was visible or audible. In other words, was there some difference between good and poor explanations that was worth trying to analyse? So we picked two lectures on Yugoslavia that were extremely high on our index of effectiveness and two that were extremely low. We had a group of eight judges read the article on Yugoslavia and take the comprehension test, and then watch and listen to all four of these lectures. Then the judges ranked the lectures in terms of perceived effectiveness in engendering comprehension as measured by the ten-item test. It turned out that the judges' post-dictions were quite significantly more accurate than could have been expected on the basis of chance, and we were accordingly reassured that our micro-criterion was indeed reflected in something that could be seen or heard in the lecture.

But the major concern of this investigation was to determine the cognitive and stylistic correlates of the lecture's effectiveness. For this purpose, we used extreme groups to minimize the labor of scoring a host of variables about which we had no great conviction. So the ten most effective explanations on Yugoslavia were identified and also the ten least effective. From these, we chose at random five of the most effective and five of the least effective. Then, groups of judges and content analysts worked over the transcripts of the lectures, scoring and rating them on a host of variables. Some of these were sentence fragments, the average sentence length, the number of prepositional phrases per sentence, and so on. Other variables dealt with the number of self-references by the teacher, or with various aspects of syntax, or instructional set, familiarization, uses of previous knowledge, mobilizing sets, attention focusing procedures, organization, emphasis, amount of repetition and redundancy, the number of words per minute, and so on.

The variables that discriminated between the five best and the five worst lectures on Yugoslavia were then tried out on the other set of five best and five worst lectures on Yugoslavia to see if they still discriminated. Those that survived this first cross-validation were then tried out on the best and worst lectures on Thailand. At the last accounting, two characteristics of the lectures had survived this kind of validation and cross-validation procedure. These variables were what we are calling 'explaining', or the degree to which the teacher describes the how, why, or effect of something, and the 'rule-e.g.-rule' pattern, or the degree to which the teacher states a generalization, gives examples of it, and then summarizes a series of illustrations at a higher level of generality than the illustrations themselves. These two variables not only seem to be valid in our data but also are reliably rated by independent judges. Nonetheless, these must not be considered to be firmly established findings; they are merely examples of the kinds of conclusions to which research of this kind can lead.

Currently, we are in the process of scoring all of the explanations on all of the variables that appear to hold any promise, and we will then undertake studies of the complete correlation matrices involving not only the indices of explanation effectiveness, but also all of the characteristics of the explanations, and the ratings of the lectures by the pupils who heard them. Such a complete correlational study will throw light on the consistency from one lecture to another of the indices of lecture effectiveness, and the stylistic characteristics of the lectures, and also their inter-correlations.

What I have been describing is of course a correlational study. Along with its advantages in permitting the exploration of a wide variety of possible correlates of explaining ability as they occur under fairly normal conditions, it also has the disadvantage of making causal interpretations hazardous. For this reason, studies of this kind ought to proceed fairly rapidly into experiments in which the different ways of explaining will be based, at least in part, on leads obtained from our correlational studies.

Such experimental research may lead toward quite novel methods of teaching that could never be developed on the basis of studies of teaching the way teaching is. Stolurow (1965) has contrasted the approach of 'modeling the master teacher' with that of 'mastering the teaching model'. The first approach is that of studying the most effective teachers we can find in order to find out how they behave and what they are like so that we can attempt to produce more teachers like them. Many research workers see little promise in this approach. They recommend that we undertake instead to develop wholly new models of the teaching process designed for optimal effectiveness regardless of their similarity to the way teaching now goes on in the normal classroom.

Computer-assisted programmed instruction

The teaching model that many advocates of this approach have in mind is that of programmed instruction, particularly computer-assisted programmed instruction. As Suppes and Atkinson and others have described this revolutionary undertaking in research and development on instruction, it holds out great promise indeed. Before too long, the annoying problems in the hardware will have been solved. After a somewhat longer time, we may expect substantial and well-validated programmed curricular materials to have been developed in all the subject matters and grade levels. As one who has seen the highly developed installations at the Brentwood School in East Palo Alto, California, I must share the optimism of Suppes and Atkinson, and other developers of computer-assisted instruction.

Their very success or coming success, raises problems for the kind of instructional methods with which we have been concerned in this paper. On superficial examination, at least, certain major problems of ordinary classroom teaching seem to be clearly surmounted by computer-assisted instruction. For example, the problem of the cognitive complexity in the teacher's task, of how the teacher can say just the right thing at the right time to develop a concept or formulate a theory, is apparently well handled, at least in principle, by computer-assisted instruction. Its programs can be worked out and tried out in meticulous detail, well in advance, at leisure, by the most skilled curriculum experts in the land, and then made available in all their subtlety and complexity to every teacher who uses the program. Another major problem in the ordinary classroom is that of individualizing instruction. No matter how we group our pupils between schools, within schools, or within classrooms, we still have the problem of adjusting the rate and direction of the teaching and learning process to the needs and abilities of the individual pupil; here again, at least in principle, computer-assisted instruction seems at first glance to have the better of the live teacher.

While pondering these problems, I got some help from a restatement of the idea of individualized instruction in a recent paper by Jackson (1966). He states it as follows:

Individualizing instruction, in the educator's sense, means injecting humor into a lesson when a student seems to need it, and quickly becoming serious when he is ready to settle down to work; it means thinking of examples that are uniquely relevant to the student's previous experience and offering them at just the right time; it means feeling concerned over whether or not a student is progressing, and communicating that concern in a way that will be helpful; it means offering appropriate praise, not just because positive reinforcers strengthen response tendencies, but because the student's performance is deserving of human admiration; it means, in short, responding *as* an individual *to* an individual.

Individualization in this sense is much more than allowing for differences in speed of moving through a program or providing different branches or routes through the material.

Jackson's analysis of this kind of limitation in computer-assisted instruction should be placed alongside the indications by Suppes (1966) that tutoring and dialog, which are higher levels of instruction than drill-practice, are still well in the future, as capabilities of computer-based instruction. Hence, any fears about the rapid obsolescence of live teachers, even where narrowly defined cognitive objectives are concerned, are quite unwarranted. That is, there will still be a need for teachers to use the kinds of technical skills, including explaining, with which the analytic approach being developed at Stanford and elsewhere is concerned. We shall have to continue to grapple with the problems of cognitive complexity and individualization through the medium of the live, human, teacher even in the realm of the well-formulated cognitive objectives. And there will always be the indispensable role of teachers in assisting pupils in attaining various kinds of affective and social learnings in the classroom.

Accordingly, group discussions, role playing, teaching for divergent thinking, as well as the technical skills I have already mentioned, are all the subject of various research and development projects now under way in the Stanford Center for Research and Development in Teaching. We are also looking at the way in which the organizational context influences the teacher's choices among ways to teach. And, in one of our projects, entitled 'The Teacher in 1980', we are looking at the way in which new curriculum developments, television and other technical aids, computer technology, and new organizational schemes in the schools will affect the teacher's role in the foreseeable future.

Conclusion: a need for analysis

In conclusion, let me refer again to what I see as one basic new theme in the research and development in teaching that is now under way at Stanford and elsewhere. If it were necessary to sum it up in one word, my word would be *analysis*, breaking down the complexities that have proven to be so unmanageable when dealt with as a whole. We are no longer crippled by the notion that because there is one word called 'teaching', there is one, single, overall criterion of effectiveness in teaching that will take essentially the same form wherever teaching occurs. Even if none of the analyses of teaching that we have now proves to be viable, they will not be replaced by the old global, conceptually impossible, complex variables that I see as the reason for the fruitlessness of so much of research on teaching in the past. Instead, they will be replaced by other analyses of teaching, perhaps even finer analyses, until we get the sets of lawful relationships between variables that will mark the emergence of a scientific basis for the practice of teaching. It may well be that a fifteen-minute explanation of a five-page magazine article is still too large a unit of teaching behavior to yield valid, lawful knowledge. It may well be that the mean score on a ten-item test of comprehension, adjusted for student availability and content relevance of the lecture, is still too large and complex a dependent variable. But, compared with the massive, tangled, and unanalysable units that have typically been studied in the past – in research on the lecture method, the discussion method, and class size, for example – such units seem precise and manageable indeed. And eventually, of course, we shall have to put teaching back together again into syntheses that are better than the teaching that goes on now. I think it would be safe to say that there is now some hope of our being able to develop a scientifically grounded set of answers to every teacher's central question, 'What should I do in the classroom?'

References

BERELSON, B., and STEINER, G. A. (1964), *Human Behavior: An inventory of scientific findings*, Harcourt, Brace & World.

FORTUNE, J. C., GAGE, N. L., and SHUTES, R. E. (1966), 'Generality of the ability to explain', paper presented at the meetings of the American Educational Research Association, Chicago, February.

GAGE, N. L. (1963), 'Paradigms for research on teaching', in N. L. Gage (ed.), *Handbook of Research on Teaching*, Rand McNally, pp. 94–141.

JACKSON, P. W. (1966), 'The teacher and the machine: Observations on the impact of educational technology', unpublished manuscript, University of Chicago.

KUHN, T. S. (1962), *The Structure of Scientific Revolutions*, University of Chicago Press.

ROSENSHINE, B. (1968), 'Behavioral correlates of effectiveness in explaining', unpublished doctoral dissertation, Stanford University.

STOLUROW, L. M. (1965), 'Model the master teacher or master the teaching model', in J. D. Krumboltz (ed.), *Learning and the Educational Process*, Rand McNally, pp. 223–47.

SUPPES, P. (1966), 'The uses of computers in education', *Scientific American*, vol. 215 (3), pp. 207–20.

WALKER, M. (1935), Preface, in W. H. Lancelot, A. S. Barr, T. L. Torgerson, C. E. Johnson, V. E. Lyon, A. C. Walvoord and G. L. Betts, *The Measurement of Teaching Efficiency*, Macmillan, pp. ix–xiv.

Part Two
Methods of Study

Most observations of teachers' behaviour has been concerned
with assessing their effectiveness. Such assessments have most
commonly been made in the form of a single general rating of
'teaching ability', but repeated findings that such ratings tend
to have low reliability and negligible predictive validity have
led to the development of more sophisticated procedures.

Research workers have increasingly made use of observation
schedules whereby classroom behaviour is systematically
recorded in terms of previously determined categories defined
in behavioural terms; one of the most widely used of these is
that devised by Flanders, which is described in the first article
in this section. Flanders' system, like most of the earlier
systematic observation procedures, emphasizes the affective
aspects of teacher–pupil interaction. In some more recent
systems, more attention is given to the content and logic of
classroom communication; outstanding among these is that
described by Bellack and his collaborators.

In teacher training, systematic observation procedures are
not widely used as yet, but a move towards a more analytic
approach has been made in that many institutions have
replaced general ratings by ratings of different aspects of teacher
behaviour. The article by Lantz reports an investigation of how
such ratings were related to the systematically recorded
behaviour of a sample of student teachers.

Many different kinds of question can be asked with regard to teachers' behaviour, and for each kind of question a different procedure for observation is necessary. Duthie was concerned with teachers' use of their time from the perspective of the amount and nature of training required for each of their various activities and his article reports the distinctive system developed for this purpose.

4 N. A. Flanders

Interaction Analysis and Inservice Training

Excerpt from N. A. Flanders, 'Interaction analysis and inservice training', *Journal of Experimental Education*, vol. 37, 1968, pp. 126–32.

What is interaction analysis?

Interaction analysis is a system for observing and coding the verbal interchange between a teacher and his pupils. The assumption is made that teaching behavior and pupil responses are expressed primarily through the spoken word as a series of verbal events which occur one after another. These events are identified, coded so as to preserve sequence, and tabulated systematically in order to represent a sample of the spontaneous teacher influence.

The most important criterion which any coding system must meet before it can be considered satisfactory is that a trained person can decode the data in order to reconstruct those aspects of the original behavior which were encoded, even though he was not present at the observation. A part of this article will describe inferences which can be made from a blind analysis of coded data.

Interaction analysis has been used to study spontaneous teaching behavior and it has also been used in projects which attempt to help teachers modify their behavior. In the first instance there may be a long period of time between observations and the analysis of the data. The data can be punched on IBM cards as they are collected over a period of several months, but a computer program to tabulate and analyse the data may be used only after all the observations have been completed. On the other hand, when interaction analysis data are collected in order to provide a teacher with information about his own behavior as a part of preservice or inservice training, then it may be advantageous to code directly into a desired tabulation form so that interpretations can be made at the earliest moment after the teaching episode is completed. This article will be more concerned with the procedures of interaction analysis which can be used during preservice and inservice training, and less concerned with applications in more basic research projects. [. . .]

Observation procedures and matrix interpretation

Given ten categories, shown in Table 1, all verbal statements are classified at least once every three seconds by a trained observer. The events are coded by using the arabic numbers from one to ten which are written down in such a way as to preserve the original sequence. The data can then be tabulated in a table of ten rows and ten columns which is called a matrix.

Such a series is entered into a matrix two at a time. The first number of each pair indicates the row of the matrix, the second the column. The first pair consists of the first two numbers. The second pair consists of the second and third numbers, and thus overlaps the first pair. All tallies enter the matrix as a series of overlapping pairs.

With one tally approximately every three seconds, there are one hundred tallies for five minutes, 1,200 tallies per hour; therefore, twenty minutes, or about 400 tallies, provide a matrix with sufficient data for a number of inferences about verbal communication.

In a sustained observation of a teacher covering six to eight one-hour visits, it is necessary to tabulate separate matrices for different types of classroom activities. Each matrix should represent either a single episode of class activity or any number of homogeneous episodes that are combined. We use five activity categories for junior high school academic subjects; they are: routine procedures, discussion of new material, discussion to evaluate student performance or products of learning, general discussion, and the supervision of seatwork or group activities. Different activity categories may be useful for a self-contained elementary-school classroom. In any case, the purpose of tabulating the data in several different matrices, instead of in just one total matrix, is determined by the purposes of observation and the range of expected classroom activities. [. . .]

A tabulated matrix divides into special areas for interpretations that are shown in Table 2. Particular questions can be answered by comparing tallies within and between these areas. Here are some examples.

Areas A ($1+2+3+4$), B($5+6+7$), C($8+9$), and D(10) can be used to find the per cent time the teacher talks, the pupils talk, and time spent in pauses, silence, and confusion. Comparisons between Areas A and B provide information about the relative balance between initiating and responding within teacher talk. Initiating teacher talk is more directive, tends to support the use of teacher authority, and restricts pupil participation. Responsive teacher talk is more indirect, tends to share authority, and expands pupil participation.

Area E is a block of nine cells that indicates the continued use of acceptance and praise, constructive reaction to pupil feeling, and clarifying, accepting, and developing pupil ideas, as well as transitions among these three categories while the teacher is talking. In any inservice training program devoted to increasing the teacher's attention to ideas expressed by pupils, before and after comparisons would require an analysis of these nine cells. In fact, an inservice training program which attempted to teach more subtle differences in the teacher's reaction to pupil ideas might require subdividing Category 3 in order to note the presence and absence of various types of Category 3 statements. For example, 3–1 – merely repeats to show that the pupil ideas were heard; 3–2 – reacts to specific pupil ideas, but only in terms of the teacher's perceptions of these ideas; 3–3 – reacts to specific pupil ideas, but reactions incorporate the perceptions of one or more pupils; and 3–4 – stimulates a reaction to a pupil's ideas by asking questions so that other pupils react. In effect, Category 3 is expanded into four categories for a special purpose. This would result in a 13×13 matrix instead of a 10×10 matrix.

Table 1 Categories of interaction analysis

Teacher talk

Response

1.* Accepts feeling: accepts and clarifies the feeling tone of the students in a non-threatening manner. Feelings may be positive or negative. Predicting or recalling feelings are included.

2.* Praises or encourages: praises or encourages student action or behavior. Jokes that release tension, but not at the expense of another individual; nodding head, or saying 'um hm?' or 'go on' are included.

3.* Accepts or uses ideas of students: clarifying, building, or developing ideas suggested by a student. As teacher brings more of his own ideas into play, shift to category five.

4.* Asks questions: asking a question about content or procedure with the intent that a student answer.

Initiation

5.* Lecturing: giving facts or opinions about content or procedures; expressing his own ideas, asking rhetorical questions.

6.* Giving directions: directions, commands, or orders to which a student is expected to comply.

7.* Criticizing or justifying authority: statements intended to change student behavior from non-acceptable to acceptable pattern; bawling someone out; stating why the teacher is doing what he is doing; extreme self-reference.

Student talk

Response

8.* Student talk – response: talk by students in response to teacher. Teacher initiates the contact or solicits student statement.

Initiation

9.* Student talk – initiation: talk by students which they initiate. If 'calling on' student is only to indicate who may talk next, observer must decide whether student wanted to talk. If he did, use this category.

10.* Silence or confusion: pauses, short periods of silence and periods of confusion in which communication cannot be understood by the observer.

* There is no scale implied by these numbers. Each number is classificatory; it designates a particular kind of communication event. To write these numbers down during observation is to enumerate, not to judge a position on a scale.

Area F is a block of four cells that indicates the continued use of directions and criticism and transitions between these two categories. The two transition cells are particularly reliable indicators of discipline problems. Shifting from directions to criticism is tallied in the 6–7 cell, and indicates that expected compliance is judged unsatisfactory by the teacher. Shifting from criticism back to directions, the 7–6 cell, indicates a return to more directions after criticism.

Areas G_1 and G_2 are particularly interesting because they isolate the immediate response of the teacher at the moment students stop talking. One aspect of teacher flexibility can be discovered by comparing the balance of indirect and direct statements shown in G_1 and G_2 with those found in Areas A and B. The difference between superficial, short, perfunctory praise or clarification, and praise or clarification that is more carefully developed is easily seen by comparing the tallies in Area G_1 with those in E, particularly the 2–2 and 3–3 cells.

Area H indicates the types of teacher statements that trigger student participation. Responses to the teacher are found in column 8; statements initiated by the student in column 9. As one might expect, there is usually a heavy loading of tallies in the 4–8 cell. High frequencies in this cell and the 8–4 cell, but not in the 8–8 cell, often indicate rapid drill.

Area I indicates sustained student participation. These may be lengthy statements by a few students, or student-to-student communication.

So-called 'steady state' cells fall on the diagonal from cell 1–1 to 10–10. Tallies here indicate that the speaker persists in a particular communication category for longer than three seconds. All other cells are transition cells moving from one category to another.

Outlined in the center of Table 2 by dash lines is the content cross. The total number of tallies in this area, compared with tallies not in this area, gives a very crude indication of the content or orientation of the class activity.

In addition to making use of the areas just described, the following procedure can be followed to interpret a matrix.

First, locate the single cell within the ten rows and columns which has the highest frequency. The pair of events, represented

Table 2 Areas of matrix analysis

category	classification	category	1	2	3	4	5	6	7	8	9	10	total
accepts feeling		1											
praise	response	2	area E										
student idea		3											
asks questions		4	'content-cross'							area H			
lectures	initiation	5											
gives directions		6						area F					
criticism		7											
student response		8	area G₁					area G₂		area I			
student initiation		9											
silence		10											
		total	area A					area B		area C		area D	
			response			?(S)	initiation			student talk		silence	

by the cell, is the most frequently occurring and can be used as a starting point in reconstructing the interaction.

Second, from this highest frequency cell, you start forward or backward, in terms of sequence, to begin a sequence diagram. The row of any cell indicates the most likely third event, that is, the event which is most likely to follow, given an original pair of events designed by the highest frequency cell. The column, on the other hand, indicates which event most probably preceded the pair of events in question. The flow of events is properly represented when the eye scans the matrix in a clockwise rotation. Should the highest frequency fall into a transition cell, not a steady state cell, the row or column of either number in the pair can be studied to retrace or advance the sequence of events.

An example of matrix interpretation will be shown later in this article. Skill in matrix interpretation, however, is not likely to develop from reading this article, which serves only to propose guidelines. For that matter, skill in observation cannot develop from reading about how it is done. All aspects of interaction analysis require practice in order to develop skill. It is the opposite of a spectator sport. [. . .]

The assessment of spontaneous behavior must be reasonably objective in order to be reliable. Unfortunately, interaction analysis is not free of bias and error, probably about one out of every ten classifications of an experienced observer is incorrect. Interaction analysis data can be and probably are more objective, when dealt with in summary form, compared with most other procedures for making judgments about spontaneous teaching behavior. Judgments about events which occur within time segments of only a few seconds and which must be repeated again and again tend to become more consistent with practice. Furthermore, noting the presence or absence of a short event is not a procedure which lends itself as easily to distortion and bias.

No matter how objective, reliable, and valid an assessment procedure, the results will be distorted if the behavior itself is distorted. Unfortunately, merely anticipating observation might cause non-representative behavior to appear, not to mention the observation experience itself. Below are some policies and suggestions which we have found helpful in reducing the tendency of a teacher to put on an act while being observed.

First, an observer should be in the classroom only when invited by the teacher.

Second, the invitation should be based on a plan of inquiry which was developed by the teacher and observer prior to any classroom visits. Observation should produce information which is relevant to some problem or question which is considered important to both participants. Thus, a teacher participating in an inservice training program which proposes to improve the way pupil ideas are handled during classroom discussion may be curious about this aspect of interaction before and after training. Such a question might involve creating two similar lesson plans in which a teacher would be confronted with opportunities to react to pupil ideas. One lesson would be observed before training and the second lesson after training. The plan could be embellished to provide greater insights by collecting additional data. For example, predictions about pupil perceptions, teacher perceptions, pupil attitudes and similar phenomena could be made, one lesson compared with the other. Then, instead of merely counting the incidence of constructive teacher reactions to ideas expressed by pupils, certain theories about the consequences of such teacher behavior might be investigated.

Third, the status and power difference between the observer and the teacher should be a minimum. Another teacher who is a best friend might make the most appropriate observer, providing skill in observation is present. [. . .]

Fourth, the entire procedure including planning, execution, and analysis usually works more smoothly when the teacher, as well as the observer, has had approximately equal experience in observation. For example, setting up hypotheses, designing two comparable lesson plans, and knowing where to look in a matrix for the proper information are phases of the experience which should be shared by two partners who are equally competent. When the observer is more experienced and competent, the teacher defers and becomes the dependent member of the team. Both members of the team should have had previous experience in both teaching and observation.

Illustrations of practical procedures

For purposes of illustration, let us assume that the goal is to increase the teacher's skill in making use of ideas expressed by pupils. In an article as short as this one, only four aspects of such a training program will be mentioned. First, some initial performance data provide a before-training performance pattern with which subsequent observation data can be compared. Second, skill training procedures can be closely correlated to observation procedures. Third, data in addition to interaction analysis are helpful in deciding whether or not a change in behavior is an improvement. And fourth, more advanced training designs and more complex data collection procedures will be necessary to push progress beyond the initial results. Each of these four topics will be discussed in turn.

Initial performance data

Initial performance data might be in the form of a short observation during a class discussion. Table 3 shows a matrix of a teacher which will now be interpreted to show how the observer and teacher make an initial diagnosis before training. The same data,

Table 3 Observation matrix

cate-gory	1	2	3	4	5	6	7	8	9	10	total
1	—	—	—	—	—	—	—	—	—	—	—
2	—	1	1	1	2	—	—	1	5	—	11
3	—	—	5	1	4	—	—	—	—	—	10
4	—	—	—	23	2	1	—	42	3	5	76
5	—	2	1	22	80	1	2	3	3	3	117
6	—	—	—	1	—	—	1	3	—	—	5
7	—	—	—	—	2	1	1	—	—	—	4
8	—	5	—	22	19	—	—	45	7	—	98
9	—	3	3	3	7	—	—	3	32	—	51
10	—	—	—	3	1	2	—	1	1	—	8
total	—	11	10	76	117	5	4	98	51	8	380
% of total	—	2.9	2.6	20.0	30.8	1.3	1.1	25.8	13.4	2.1	100

% of total	25.5			33.2			39.2		2.1	
	teacher total: 58.7						student total		silence	

$I/D = 0.77$ content cross = 70.8%
steady state = 49%

of course, can serve as a before training standard in order to determine whether change has occurred.

Since the total tallies equals 380, one can estimate that the matrix represents about 19 minutes of interaction (100 tallies = 5 minutes, 20 tallies = 1 minute).

A number of percentages and other ratios, which help to form an initial picture, can be found at the bottom rows of Table 3. For example, the teacher talked 58·7 per cent, the pupils 39·2 per cent, and silence and confusion was 2·1 per cent. The teacher was fairly directive, that is he initiated more than he responded, as shown by an $I/D = 0·77$ (divide all tallies in categories $1+2+3+4$ by $5+6+7$ to obtain this ratio). The highest cell frequencies are found in the steady state diagonal cells, such as the 5–5, the 8–8, and the 9–9 cells. This suggests that the teacher and pupils were able to continue a particular mode of expression once it started. Higher frequencies in these steady state cells indicate that the tempo of exchange was slower, for example, than might occur in a drill period. All silences were three seconds or less (note no tallies in the 10–10 cell) and most pauses followed teacher questions ($N = 5$ in the 4–10 cell) and teacher lecture ($N = 3$ in the 5–10 cell) rather than pupil statements. In six of these eight transitions, it was the teacher who broke the pause by talking (note that $N = 1$ in the 10–8 and 10–9 cells). This analysis of silence supports the interpretation that the teacher tended to initiate and did not permit a pupil more than three seconds to respond.

The matrix is sometimes more easily understood when it is translated into a flow pattern illustrated in Figure 1. In this diagram the most frequently occurring steady state cells are shown as rectangles and the size of the rectangle indicates the relative frequency of the pair. Transitions among these cells are indicated by arrows and the thickness of the arrow is roughly proportional to the frequency of these transitions. Anyone can learn to draw such a pattern flow diagram from a tabulated matrix. Begin with the highest frequency cell, in this case the 5–5 cell with eighty tallies. Proceed across the same row to find out the next most likely occurring events and inspect columns to identify the most likely preceding events. The arrows in Table 3 illustrate the clockwise direction of the flow. Thus in both the matrix and in Figure 1, begin with the 5–5 cell, sustained lecturing. The next most likely event is that the teacher will ask a question. Next, pupils are most likely to respond to this question, see category 8. There are two events of almost equal probability following pupil response talk, one is that the teacher will ask another question and the other is that the teacher will lecture. The four transitions

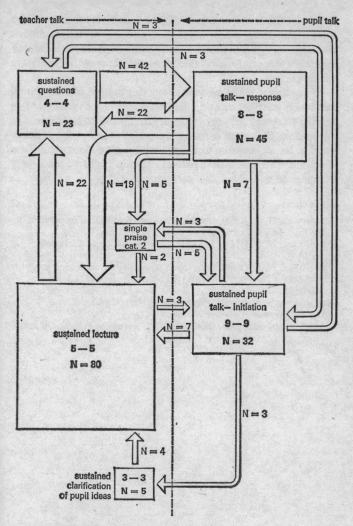

Figure 1 Initial flow pattern before training

shown by the heavy arrows in Figure 1 account for most of the interaction: these are, 5–4, 4–8, 8–4, and 8–5. Other transitions do occur, but the transitions just listed and their associated steady state cells account for 285 tallies or about 75 per cent of the entire observation.

Many things could be said about this pattern of interaction, but by far the most certain inference is that in the event that this teacher increased his use of category 3, it could be clearly seen in the matrix. The use of category 3, especially the 3–3 cell, is below average for a classroom teacher. After training along these lines a second matrix and flow pattern diagram could be made as a comparison with this initial performance. [. . .]

References

FLANDERS, N. A. (1963), 'Intent, action and feedback: a preparation for teaching', *J. Teacher Educ.*, vol. 14, pp. 251–60.

FLANDERS, N. A. (1963), *The Role of the Teacher in the Classroom*, Amidon.

FLANDERS, N. A. (1965), 'Interaction analysis in the classroom: a Manual for observers', (rev. ed.) School of Education, University of Michigan.

FLANDERS, N. A. (1965), '*Teacher influence, pupil attitudes, and achievement*', *Cooperative Research Monograph no. 12*, US Office of Education, OE-25040, US Government Printing Office.

5 D. L. Lantz

The Relationship of University Supervisors' and Supervising Teachers' Ratings to Observed Student Teachers' Behavior

From D. L. Lantz, 'The relationship of university supervisors' and supervising teachers' ratings to observed student teachers' behaviour', *American Education Research Journal*, vol. 4, 1967, pp. 279–88.

Little of the research in teacher education has been concerned with the relations of supervisor ratings of student teachers to independent objective observations of the behaviors reported in the rating responses. The major purpose of this study was to explore certain relationships of independent ratings of teaching behaviors observed in the classrooms of women elementary student teachers to supervisors' perceptions of student teachers' interpersonal behavior.

Supervisor perceptions of student teachers' interpersonal behavior were studied in relationship to both the kind of influence (direct or indirect) exercised in the classroom and classroom emotional climate.

Subjects

The subjects had a common background of professional preparation and were student teaching for two successive quarters. The median age of the student teachers was twenty-one, and the range was from twenty to twenty-three. The student teaching assignments for the thirty-six subjects over two quarters involved thirty-eight classrooms and supervising teachers in thirty different schools. The schools were within four geographic areas in a midwest urban area that were equated for their socio-economic characteristics. Each subject was assigned a lower elementary grade (one through three) during one quarter and an upper elementary grade (four through six) during the other quarter. The subjects were stratified according to their grade level (lower or upper) preference. The subjects on each stratum were then assigned an experience order (lower-upper or upper-lower). The subjects were randomly assigned to classrooms within one of the four geographic blocks (Wilk, 1963).

Student teachers were in their classrooms two weeks prior to the first observation each quarter. This allowed the student teacher to become acquainted with her students and adjusted to the particular classroom.

Thirty-eight supervising teachers and seven university student teaching supervisors participated in this program. Each of these supervisors had experience in the supervision of student teaching. The university supervisors visited their respective student teachers in the classroom three to five times each quarter.

There were five observers who were psychologically trained but who had had no professional experience in the elementary school. The team of five observers spent a month of intensive training in the use of the two observation instruments prior to the actual observation of student teachers. An observation schedule was arranged so that each subject was observed five different times during both the fall and winter quarters. A thirty-minute time sample of each student's behavior during both quarters was recorded by each observer. This resulted in a five-hour sample of behavior which was used as the criterion of teacher behavior.

Instruments

Two instruments were used in measuring and classifying teacher behavior. The first instrument was the Interaction Analysis (Flanders, 1960) which was used for classifying classroom communication. Two types of verbal behavior are classified with this system: namely,

1. indirect influence by the teacher and
2. direct influence by the teacher.

A second instrument used was a modified OScAR (Medley and Mitzel, 1958). The only scale from the OScAR used in the study was classroom emotional climate.

The observer reliability coefficients for pooled ratings of five observers, adjusted by use of the Spearman–Brown prophecy formula, ranged from 0·90 to 0·97 for indirect influence (Wilk and Edson, 1962). The reliability for the classroom emotional climate criterion score was estimated by using analysis of variance (Hoyt and Stunkard, 1952). The reliability coefficient for classroom emotional climate was 0·725.

The independent variables were derived from the supervisor's ratings on the octant scales of the Interpersonal Check List (ICL) (La Forge and Suczek, 1955). Each octant scale of the ICL consists of sixteen adjectives and traits which have varying degrees of social acceptability. Supervisors were asked to indicate how frequently each adjective or trait was characteristic of the student teacher under their supervision. The reciprocal averages technique was selected as the appropriate scaling device to handle the problems of items with varying degrees of social acceptance since the score so derived has the maximum internal consistency.

The analysis of variance technique for unrestricted item scoring (Hoyt and Stunkard, 1952) was the procedure used for estimating the reliability on each scale of the ICL. The scores used in calculating the reliability coefficients were the weighted scores derived from the reciprocal averages scoring procedures. One of the characteristics of the reciprocal averages score is that each item is weighted in such a way that the internal consistency of the total score is maximized. The reliability coefficients for all ICL variables for university supervisors' and supervising teachers' perception of student teachers' interpersonal behavior are presented in summary form in Table 1.

At the end of the first and second quarters of student teaching, the supervisors rated each student teacher under their supervision

Table 1 Analysis of variance reliability estimates for concept of elementary student teacher of ICL variables for university supervisors and supervising teachers

Variable		University Supervisor	Supervising Teacher
AP	Dominant – Advising	0·86	0·87
BC	Proud – Rejecting	0·84	0·93
DE	Punitive – Critical	0·88	0·84
FG	Complaining – Distrustful	0·89	0·91
HI	Modest – Submissive	0·84	0·94
JK	Docile – Dependent	0·87	0·94
LM	Cooperative – Loving	0·90	0·61
NO	Supportive – Generous	0·92	0·95

by means of the ICL. Supervisors were requested to estimate student teachers' interpersonal behavior in the context of the classroom. The ratings from the two supervising teachers were pooled for each student teacher, and likewise, the university supervisors' ratings for each student were combined into a single score. These two different supervisors' ratings (university supervisors and supervising teachers) were considered as assessments of the student teacher as perceived by her supervisors in the classroom.

The intercorrelations for ratings of university supervisors' and supervising teachers' perceptions of student teachers' behaviors are presented in Table 2. Correlations of each of the independent variables with criterion scores and intercorrelation of the separate criterion scores are also presented in Table 2.

A set of multiple regression equations was developed to predict each of the criterion variables of (a) direct influence, (b) indirect influence, and (c) classroom emotional climate from supervisors' perception of student teachers' interpersonal behavior as classified by the ICL. Following the initial development of equations further analyses were completed using variables thought to account for significant portions of criteria variance. The beta weights associated with the initial equation are presented in Table 3.

The resulting betas from each of the analyses were tested for significance in predicting the criteria scores for each of the dependent variables. The multiple Rs and beta weights are summarized in Table 4 for each of the final equations. A correction formula (Guilford, 1956) was applied to each final equation for purposes of adjustment due to small sample sizes.

Discussion

Supervisors' perceptions were not equally useful on all eight interpersonal variables. If the variables were placed on a continuum from hostile, unfriendly behavior to friendly behavior, those variables related to some form of unfriendly or hostile (dominant, rejecting, critical and distrustful) interpersonal behavior were least useful in predicting classroom behavior. It is possible that one of the reasons perceptions of unfriendly behavior may not have been useful in predicting behavior is that student teachers have a

Table 2 Intercorrelations among supervisors'* perceptions of student teachers' interpersonal behavior as classified by interpersonal check list and correlations with criteria

	AP Dominant Proud Advising	BC Dominant Proud Rejecting	DE Punitive Critical	FG Complaining Distrustful	HI Modest Submissive	JK Docile Dependent	LM Cooperative Loving	NO Supportive Generous	DIR Direct Influence	IND Indirect Influence	CEC Classroom Emotional Climate
AP		0·55	−0·18	−0·00	−0·56	−0·50	0·49	0·25	0·09	0·47	0·16
BC	0·48		0·45	0·72	−0·12	−0·28	−0·23	−0·21	0·10	0·19	0·11
DE	0·46	0·90		0·80	0·58	0·45	−0·74	−0·56	0·28	−0·29	−0·43
FG	0·61	0·84	0·83		0·26	0·04	−0·66	−0·48	−0·13	−0·02	−0·20
HI	0·37	0·71	0·60	0·69		0·84	−0·54	−0·41	0·05	−0·51	−0·31
JK	0·31	0·84	0·76	0·76	0·91		−0·33	−0·48	0·28	−0·54	−0·33
LM	0·08	0·77	0·72	0·64	0·74	0·91		0·72	−0·24	0·31	0·34
NO	0·26	0·82	0·74	0·72	0·83	0·93	0·94		−0·49	0·16	0·24
DIR	0·04	−0·13	−0·10	−0·03	−0·08	−0·11	−0·11	−0·02		0·06	−0·29
IND	−0·03	0·02	−0·02	−0·08	−0·26	−0·10	−0·05	−0·14	−0·06		−0·55
CEC	−0·15	−0·05	−0·10	−0·15	−0·26	−0·10	−0·08	−0·10	−0·29	−0·55	

* Note: correlations for university supervisors are represented above the diagonal and for supervising teachers below the diagonal.

Table 3 Summary of the multiple Rs and beta weights for initial equations in predicting student teachers' classroom behaviors from university supervisors' and supervising teachers' ratings of interpersonal behavior

Classroom Behavior	Rating	Mul-tiple R	Beta weights							
			AP Domi-nant Advising	BC Proud Reject-ing	DE Punitive Critical	FG Com-plaining Dis-trustful	HI Modest Sub-missive	JK Docile Depen-dent	LM Coopera-tive Loving	NO Suppor-tive Generous
Direct Influence	Univ. Sup.	0·63	−0·28	−0·12	0·46	−0·34	−0·46	0·26	−0·08	−0·49
	Sup. Tchr.	0·38	0·03	−0·55	0·06	0·23	0·19	−0·22	−0·61	1·18
Indirect Influence	Univ. Sup.	0·67	0·34	−0·43	−0·06	0·40	0·34	−0·83	0·52	−0·48
	Sup. Tchr.	0·51	0·13	0·60	−0·40	−0·12	−1·01	1·09	0·23	−0·67
Classroom Emotional Climate	Univ. Sup.	0·55	0·16	−0·47	0·56	0·66	0·43	−0·51	0·44	−0·29
	Sup. Tchr.	0·54	−0·16	0·37	−0·42	−0·13	−1·48	2·00	−1·10	0·44

Table 4 Summary of the multiple Rs and beta weights for final equations in predicting student teachers' behaviors from university supervisors' and supervising teachers' interpersonal behavior

| Classroom Behavior | Rating | Multiple R | Beta weights | | | | | | | |
			AP Dominant Advising	BC Proud Reject-ing	DE Punitive Critical	FG Com-plaining Dis-trustful	HI Modest Sub-missive	JK Docile Depen-dent	LM Cooper-ative Loving	NO Suppor-tive Generous
Direct Influence	Univ. Sup.	0·48*			0·12		0·23			−0·52*
	Sup. Tchr.	0·07		−0·24					−0·52	0·64
Indirect Influence	Univ. Sup.	0·60†						−0·60†	0·42*	−0·43
	Sup. Tchr.	0·39					−1·02†	1·27†		−0·47
Classroom Emotional Climate	Univ. Sup.	0·46*			−0·74†	0·39		1·54*		
	Sup. Tchr.	0·40					1·24†		−0·57	

* 0·05 level of significance.
† 0·01 level of significance.

particular role expectation which inhibits unfriendly behavior in the presence of supervisors.

University supervisors

Each of the three equations that made use of university supervisors' perceptions of student teachers was capable of predicting the criteria scores beyond chance expectation. The final Rs for direct influence, indirect influence, and classroom emotional climate were 0·48, 0·59, and 0·46, respectively. The F ratios were 3·22, 5·84, and 4·51, respectively. The independent variables based on university supervisors' perceptions that were significantly related to the criteria are discussed below.

Direct influence. The only beta weight that was significant in predicting direct influence was the Supportive–Generous (NO) variable. Psychological observers recorded less direct influence by student teachers who were perceived by university supervisors as being supportive and generous.

Indirect influence. The beta weights for Docile–Dependent (JK) and Cooperative–Loving (LM) variables were significant in predicting indirect influence scores. The Docile–Dependent variable was negatively related to indirect influence scores; thus, student teachers who were perceived as manifesting a higher degree of dependency were observed using little indirect influence in the classroom. The Cooperative–Loving variable was positively related to the criterion scores indicating that student teachers who were perceived as amicable and desirous of establishing harmonious relations were observed utilizing more indirect influence in the classroom than those who were perceived by university supervisors as demonstrating less of this variable.

Classroom emotional climate. The only beta that was significantly related to the prediction of classroom emotional climate scores was the Punitive–Critical (DE) variable. Student teachers who were perceived as high on this variable received low scores for classroom emotional climate.

Supervising teachers

None of the equations utilizing supervising teachers' perceptions was able to predict significantly the three criteria. The final Rs for direct influence, indirect influence and classroom emotional climate were 0·07, 0·39 and 0·40, respectively. The F ratios were 0·05, 1·92, and 2·03, respectively. The independent variables based on supervising teachers' perceptions that were significantly related to the criteria are discussed below.

Direct influence. Perceptions of supervising teachers were not significantly related to criterion scores of direct influence.

Indirect influence and Classroom Emotional Climate. The beta weights for the Modest–Submissive (HI) and Docile–Dependent (JK) variables were significantly related to the criteria of indirect influence and classroom emotional climate score. Student teachers who were rated relatively high on the Modest–Submissive variable received lower scores on the criteria of indirect influence and classroom emotional climate.

Student teachers who were perceived as docile and dependent were observed as having more indirect verbal behavior than those who received lower scores.

Some comparisons

Not only does one note differences in the predictability of the equations based on the two different supervisors, but also differences of perception on the separate variables of interpersonal behavior. Differences in these perceptions raise some interesting questions. For example, why should university supervisors' perceptions of punitive–critical behavior be more highly related to observed student-teacher behavior than supervising teachers' perceptions on this variable?

In the final equation for predicting direct influence scores, the beta weights are reversed for the two different supervisors on the supportive–generous variable. Student teachers who were perceived as supportive and generous by university supervisors were observed as showing less direct influence in the classroom than those student teachers who were perceived as demonstrating less of this type of interpersonal behavior. The reverse was true for supervising teachers' perceptions. The higher student teachers were perceived by supervising teachers on supportive and generous behavior, the higher direct influence scores would be predicted for them.

A similar situation existed with the docile–dependent variable for indirect influence scores. Student teachers who were perceived as rather docile and dependent by university supervisors would be predicted to receive low indirect influence scores. Student teachers who were perceived as highly docile and dependent by supervising teachers would be predicted to receive high criterion scores for indirect influence in the classroom.

In considering the variations in perception of interpersonal behavior on a given variable by the two different supervisors and the usefulness of the beta weights in predicting criterion scores, a logical concern is whether the perceptions are really different or the result of maximizing chance errors in a small sample. This can only be answered by replications of this study with larger samples.

What possible explanations are there for differences in predicting student teacher behavior as made by the two different supervisors' perceptions? It might be expected that, since the supervising teacher spends considerably more time in observing the student teacher than the university supervisor, supervising teachers' perceptions would be more closely related to observed student teacher behavior. Why is it that university supervisors' perceptions are more closely related to observed student teacher behavior than the supervising teachers' perceptions?

Since university supervisors observed and supervised several student teachers during the quarter while the supervising teachers supervised a single student teacher each quarter, could it be that university supervisors observed a wider range of behaviors which enabled them to make comparative judgments? Could it also be that university supervisors were trained to make more discriminating observations? Although somewhat unrelated to the study, it is also possible that one of the weakest links in the teacher education program is the lack of sufficient financial support for supervising teachers which would enable better training programs relative to supervision and remuneration for teachers' supervisory services.

Summary and conclusions

In an effort to study the relationship between supervisors' perceptions of student teachers' interpersonal behavior and independent observation of student teachers' behavior, multiple regression equations were utilized.

The independent variables used were the responses of supervisors relative to their perception of student teachers' interpersonal behavior as classified by the ICL.

Student teacher behavior described as direct and indirect influence was quantitatively estimated in terms of verbal interaction by trained observers using the Interaction Analysis. Classroom emotional climate was assessed by the same observers using the OScAR.

It should be noted that university supervisors and supervising teachers' perceptions on a given variable may be quite different. The best example here is the variable docile–dependent which was positively related in predicting indirect influence and classroom emotional climate when rated by supervising teachers, and negatively related to indirect influence when rated by university supervisors.

Equations that used supervising teachers' interpersonal behavior were unable to predict observed student behavior above chance expectations.

University supervisors' perceptions of student teachers' interpersonal behavior were significantly related to observed teacher behavior. University supervisors' perceptions of student teachers' interpersonal behavior as the independent variables for the prediction of indirect influence and classroom emotional climate was significant at the 0.01 level and at the 0.05 level for the prediction of direct influence.

References

FLANDERS, N. A. (1965), *Interaction Analysis in the Classroom: A Manual for Observers*, (Rev. ed.) University of Minnesota, 35 pp.

GUILFORD, J. P. (1956), *Fundamental Statistics in Psychology and Education*, McGraw Hill.

HOYT, C. J., and STUNKARD, C. L. (1952), 'Estimation of test reliability for unrestricted item scoring methods', *Educational Psychological Measurement*, vol. 12, pp. 756–58.

LAFORGE, R., and SUCZEK, R. F. (1955), 'The interpersonal dimensions of personality: III. An interpersonal check list', *J. of Person.* vol. 24, pp. 94–112.

MEDLEY, D. M., and MITZEL, H. E. (1958), 'A Technique for Measuring Classroom Behavior', *J. educ. Psychol.*, vol. 49, pp. 86–92.

WILK, R. E., and EDSON, W. H. (1962), *A Study of the Relationship Between Observed Classroom Behaviors of Elementary Student Teachers, Predictors of Those Behaviors, and Ratings by Supervisors,* University of Minnesota.

WILK, R. E. (1963), 'The use of a cross-over design in a study of student teachers' classroom behavior', *J. exper. Educ.*, vol. 31, pp. 337–41.

6 J. H. Duthie

A Study of the Teacher's Day

Adapted by the author, J. H. Duthie, from *Primary School Survey*, Scottish Education Department, 1970.

Introduction

Of the enormous output of educational research published each year, very little is specifically directed toward educational innovation in the classroom. A recent exception is 'The Primary School Survey' (Duthie, 1970) commissioned jointly by the Scottish Education Department and the Nuffield Foundation. The Scottish Education Department was concerned that any large-scale employment of auxiliaries in Scottish primary schools should be based on a systematic analysis of teachers' duties. Accordingly, a research team of five was appointed consisting of practising teachers and social scientists. The team, directed by the author, was under the general guidance of a consultative committee representing the Educational Institute of Scotland, the Colleges of Education, The Scottish Education Department, The Nuffield Foundation, The Scottish Council for Research in Education and other bodies.

The remit which we were given by the Scottish Education Department was two-fold.

1. To examine the possibility of employing auxiliaries in primary schools in Scotland;

2. More generally, to make an objective analysis, based on systematic observation, of the educational activities on which primary school teachers spend their time.

At the beginning of the study our hope was to tackle both parts of our remit in one comprehensive investigation of teacher behaviour. We hoped in this way, not only to examine the teacher's task, but in the process of doing this to establish the kinds of duties which might be undertaken by auxiliaries. As a theoretical framework for this endeavour we examined various instructional models including those implicit in such observational systems as Medley and Mitzells OScAR and Flanders' Interaction Analysis Technique. Neither these nor any of the other models which we examined, however, provided the sort of framework which would enable us to distinguish potential auxiliary duties. If our initial intention was to be realized the model of the teaching process which we required would have to meet two general criteria: it would need to reflect those variations in teachers' use of time most likely to influence the nature and effectiveness of pupils' learning; and it would also need to differentiate among teacher activities in any ways which might be relevant either to the nature of auxiliary duties or to the manner in which auxiliary staff might be deployed.

Classification of teacher activities

In the hope of developing such a model for ourselves, we paid the first of many visits to Primary Schools. Not surprisingly, we found ourselves overwhelmed by the complexity of the situation – what to record, how to get it down on paper in time, how to describe what we saw. And when we returned to base there was little agreement among team members as to what we had seen. One thing by which we were struck was that the teachers we observed often seemed to be involved in more than one activity at a time. For example, a teacher might be putting away materials while also carrying on a discussion with some pupils, completing a register while also supervising the class's work, or telling a story to the class while also comforting a child who had hurt himself. Apart from the impossibility of recording all aspects of a teacher's behaviour which might be relevant to one or other of our concerns, a major problem appeared to be that of judging with any confidence what a teacher was aiming to achieve by any particular activity. Not only would such a judgement require a high level of inference on the part of the observer; it would also no doubt be difficult on many occasions for teachers themselves to formulate explicitly their aims in behaving as they had done.

In this respect the model and the system of observation which we required were fundamentally different from most of those we had examined. For many research purposes it is useful simply to *describe* aspects of teacher behaviour with as much objectivity as possible. Because of our remit to consider the possible functions of auxiliaries, however, it was essential that we should look at teaching as a *purposeful* process and categorize teachers' use of time in terms of the different intended functions of their various activities. For this reason, and because observation could only be sufficiently reliable if it were highly selective, we restricted ourselves (in the part of the study described in this paper) to the part of our remit concerned with the possible duties of auxiliaries. It was felt that for this more limited purpose we could, on the basis of what we had seen and of our general experience as teachers, identify the functions of many teacher activities as non-educational. By this we meant that such activities are not in themselves intended to lead to any changes in pupils' behaviour, attitudes or thinking.

A preliminary list of such duties, subsequently named 'Housekeeping Duties', was constructed. It included such duties as bringing children in from the playground, determining milk numbers and giving out travel tickets.[1]

Having constructed the list we then went back into schools and used it as a basis for subsequent observation. On this occasion, the ways in which the duties were performed were noted and on this basis we classified duties as:

A Duties: fixed (in that they must occur at a particular time in the school day).

B Duties: partly fixed (in that they must occur within certain fixed time limits).

C Duties: non-fixed.

D Duties: those duties which are related to the educational work of the teacher and which occur at times which cannot be predicted.

1. It was accepted that in some educational settings these duties might be conceived by some teachers as having an educational function. For example, infants teachers may use the activity of helping children with shoelaces and problems of clothing as an opportunity for relating with their pupils and where this is the case it is clearly inappropriate for an auxiliary to undertake these functions.

E Duties: unpredictable duties which are not related to the work of the teacher.

We presented a list of auxiliary duties, classified into these categories, to the Consultative Committee, and sought their advice as to the appropriateness of our classification. This advice was felt to be necessary since it was not sufficient for our purposes that the classification should be rationally justifiable; it also had to be consistent with the ways in which teachers, and particularly leaders of opinion within the teaching profession, perceive their own activities. The list, modified in the light of the Committee's comments, was then tested by further observation in schools to ensure that it included all activities judged to have no educational function, and to ensure that the various activities on the list were defined with sufficient precision. Examples of the final list of these housekeeping duties are as follows:

Category A: e.g. bringing in children from the playground; cloakroom duty; dinner duty.

Category B: e.g. registration; determining milk numbers; issue of milk.

Category C: e.g. giving out travel tickets; maintenance of audio-visual aids; objective marking.

Category D: e.g. distribution and clearing of materials in classroom; collection and return of pupils' work; record keeping.

Category E: e.g. accidents and first-aid; lavatory supervision.

Several of the duties can be classified in more than one way, e.g. distribution and clearing of materials in the classroom can be classified as a *B* duty (partly-fixed) or as a *D* duty. How we classified the duty on any particular occasion depended upon how it was performed by the teacher whose work we were observing.

It should be clear from the description of our work thus far that we found it impossible to establish even the most basic distinctions among teachers' duties without making *a priori* decisions and following these decisions by observation of teacher activities. Indeed the rationale for the whole of this part of the study is that there must be an interplay of *a priori* criteria, observation and, if there is to be any hope of implementing the results of the investigation in schools, authoritative opinion. Each supports the other. Unguided observation is valueless; and authoritative opinion, without direct observation, is unlikely to be sufficiently well-founded to be of much use as a pointer to educational innovation.

All of these duties occur within class hours. From talking with teachers it became clear that there were some housekeeping duties which were performed out of class hours – at lunch time, at intervals and at home. We produced a check list of such duties, modified it, added to it in discussion with teachers and finally produced a list of 'Housekeeping Duties Out of Class Hours'. Examples from this list are as follows: making expendable materials (work cards etc.); correspondence for obtaining project material; stock and requisition; duplicating; objective marking. Again it can be seen that lists overlap, depending upon how the teacher performed the duty on that particular occasion.

The framework which was established in this way concerned those duties about which there could be little disagreement, i.e. concerned distinctions which were fairly easily made. However, it became clear during observation of housekeeping duties that there were other duties which were less easily distinguished from teaching but which nevertheless do not require the full professional competence of the teacher. In carrying out such 'Supervision' duties, the teacher in general observes the work which pupils are carrying out and helps them with those aspects which have to do with the execution rather than with the understanding of the work in question. To determine which teacher activities fall within this category, *a priori* distinctions again had to be made; but in this case such distinctions were not enough nor indeed were they easy to make. In order to analyse these activities we first of all collected verbal descriptions of them through direct classroom observation. (Although the team agreed that there was an area of potential auxiliary duties to be defined, the lack of a clear rationale at this point made it impossible to construct as before an *a priori* list of duties.) The descriptions which were collected by the team were discussed, some were accepted, others rejected on purely intuitive grounds. We then attempted to formulate the principles upon which our selection had been made since we had to justify both to ourselves and ultimately to the teaching profession the allocation of these duties to auxiliary personnel. The main principle which emerged from these discussions was this: that auxiliary duties must not involve 'structuring'; i.e. they must not involve the definition and description of relationships present in a situation so that pupils may be aware of them; nor may auxiliaries set forth data so that relationships may be seen.

There appear to be two main kinds of teacher activity, other than housekeeping duties, which do not involve structuring and which are therefore potential auxiliary duties;

1. *Activities in mechanical situations.* e.g. Help pupils with minor problems in uses of material; general supervision of class while children are engaged in activities and the teacher is dealing with a small group; check that children are following their work cards in order.

2. *Activities in affective situations.* e.g. Child brings work for admiration; encouragement to children working in groups while teacher works with individuals.

Using these principles, we spent several more days observing in classrooms, searching particularly for duties which might qualify as 'Supervision'. On these occasions, two observers worked independently in the same classroom, and on their return to base, analysed their data independently. Although these principles did in many cases enable observers to produce identical independent decisions as to which activities were to be classified as 'Supervision' and which as 'Teaching', the overall level of agreement was not adequate. Reliable categorization was attained only after we had established a set of specific rules to deal with various circumstances for which the general principle gave insufficient guidance.

Procedures for obervation and analysis
Observation schedules

For the purpose of the study it was important that our observers record the occurrence and nature of auxiliary duties, the time of occurrence of these duties and their duration. The simplest and most effective way of doing this was to provide observers with sheets of paper ruled across in one-minute intervals, ten minutes to a page, and to ask them to keep a longhand record of teacher activities, focusing on those aspects of her behaviour relating to auxiliary functions. It proved quite simple for observers to keep a reliable record in this form, provided they transcribed their data on to a systematic observation schedule at the end of each observation day. These schedules enabled us to record our observations in a standard way so that later analysis was facilitated. The observation schedules (see Figure 1) had time-scales and space for explanatory comments for both Housekeeping and Supervision, together with space for a record of the content and organization of lessons. Possible auxiliary duties were entered (and in the case of Housekeeping, categorized) as continuous periods recorded to the nearest minute and shown by continuous lines, or as untimed 'instances' if the time involved was less than half a minute.

Reliability of observations

A pilot study was then undertaken to try out the procedures which we had developed and to check inter-observer reliability.

Inter-observer reliability was checked with regard to (i) times taken for the performance of each of the six types of duty to be recorded; (ii) corresponding starting times; and (iii) the classification of the duties.

Two pairs of observers each visited different sets of three classes and each pair made independent records for the classes they visited. Agreement on timing was very high. One pair agreed exactly on the time taken for 129 of the 133 activities they recorded and in no case did they differ by more than two minutes; in only three cases did they differ by more than two minutes in their recorded starting times. The second pair agreed exactly on the time taken for 41 of the 50 activities they recorded and differed by more than two minutes in only two cases; they agreed to within two minutes on all the starting times. No significant variation was found in the reliability of observation of different classes or of different duties.

With regard to the classification of duties, the first pair were in agreement in all 133 cases, while the second pair agreed in 47 out of 54 classifications. It was concluded that the observational procedures were sufficiently reliable, and subsequent informal checks showed a similar high level of agreement among all six possible combinations of observers.

school name
number of teachers **4**
total pupils 133

class **P. 1–2**
number on class roll 39
number of pupils present 30

housekeeping			content etc.		supervision	
comments		H		S		comments

register (9.00–12.15)
dinner money (9.00–1200)
T puts out material
T helps P with overall
T helps P get material

T and P put away material

T gives out material

T gives out material

T gives out books

Instructions re milk (9.00–10.40)
collects jotters

P gets straws
milk tops collected

P collects straws

8.50
9.00
9.10 — B2'
— B2'
— D1'
— D
— D
9.20

9.30

9.40 — D4'

9.50 — D2'

10.00 — D

10.10 — D

10.20

10.30 — B
— D1'
— C2'
— C
10.40 — C

groups-activities
class-news
counting-activities
groups and individuals

8.50
9.00
9.10
9.20
9.30
9.40
9.50
10.00
10.10
10.20
10.30
10.40

T helps P with material

T interrupted: P unoccupied
"
P brings work for admiration
interruption: P unoccupied
P waits for attention
"
interruption: P unoccupied
"
P brings work for admiration
Interruption: P unoccupied
P brings work for admiration
interruption: P unoccupied
85'
"
"
P has difficulty with material
interruption: P unoccupied
"
"
"
P brings work for admiration
interruption: P unoccupied
P brings work for admiration
P sits down unattended

P having difficulty with material
queue
interruption: P unoccupied
T tells waiting Ps to sit down
interruption: P unoccupied
"

Figure 1 Observation schedule

The main experiment

Selection of schools

1. *Stratification.* The sample was stratified by size of school and by yearly stage within the schools observed. School sizes were classified as follows: 1 class, 2 classes, 3–4 classes, 5–6 classes, 7–9 classes, 10–13 classes and 14+ classes. Yearly stage was classified in terms of the distinction Infants (Primary 1 and 2), Junior (Primary 3 and 4), Senior (Primary 5, 6 and 7).

2. *Sampling (stage two).* The Scottish Education Department drew up a complete list of schools, stratified according to these variables, and we entered this list, using a table of random numbers. We selected schools until we had enough in each category to be representative of these schools in the whole population. The second stage in the sampling procedure was to select classes within these schools. The sample which we obtained in this way – a one per cent sample of classes in Primary schools in Scotland – included most areas of the country: the Highlands, the Islands, and the Lowlands.

3. *Statistical design.* Our statistical advisers prepared an experimental design to check whether the incidence of duties varied with the size of school and yearly stage of the class. The technique employed was analysis of variance.

4. *Entering schools.* Teachers are understandably reluctant to have observers in their classrooms and for this reason we were particularly careful to go through the proper channels in making our approaches to the schools. We, first of all, with the backing of the Scottish Education Department, approached Directors of Education, informing them of the schools which had been selected in their area and explaining carefully the purposes of the study. In this we were greatly helped by the Association of Directors of Education. The Directors of Education then approached headmasters on our behalf and we followed up this approach by sending information to the headmasters of the schools concerned in the study. We finally obtained permission from the head teachers to approach teachers in their schools. As a consequence of this careful approach we had no refusals and were able to visit each of the classrooms which we had selected at random. In almost every case, teachers were visited by team members on the previous day

to acquaint them with the purpose of the exercise and to enable them to ask questions. On the observation day proper, two members spent one full day in each of the classes selected, arriving before the first children entered the class and leaving after the last of them had gone home.

Results and conclusions

The results of the investigation are summarized in Table 1. One of the remarkable features of these results is their considerable variability. In many cases the standard deviation is greater than the mean. This finding indicates that from one classroom and one school to the next there are very large differences in the amount of non-teaching work undertaken or available. These variations occur within the sub-categories of the stratified sample, and are thus not the result of differences in school size or age level. Any systematic variation in Housekeeping associated with these variables is hidden by the wide variations within categories. The only significant difference found between categories was that, within the larger schools, there was significantly more Supervision for younger than for older pupils.

Although there are wide variations between teachers in the amount and nature of their non-teaching activities, there is always a large amount of auxiliary assistance required; and on the basis of the results obtained, it has been possible to suggest the number of auxiliaries likely to be useful in schools (one for every two teachers if maximum use is to be made of their services), the ways in which their work could most effectively be organized, and the nature of the training they should receive for this work (Duthie, 1970, chs 4–7).

In conclusion, three methodological points became very clear to us from this investigation. First, we were able to obtain reliable evidence relevant to our remit only because we developed an observation system designed to give us answers to explicit questions: classroom teaching is such a complex phenomenon that one is most unlikely to gain any substantial knowledge about it unless one has formulated the particular questions one wants to answer in such a way that a few precisely defined aspects of behaviour can be selected for attention. Second, although the information we required was relatively simple compared with that necessary

Table 1 Means (*M*) and standard deviations (*S.D.*) for various school sizes, levels and duties (*times in minutes*)

	A Duties		B Duties		C Duties by observation		C Duties by interview		Total C duties		D Duties		E Duties		Supervision Duties	
	M	s.d.	M	s.d.	M	s.d.	M	s.d.	M	s.d.	M	s.d.	M	s.d.	M	s.d.
School size: 1 class																
Infants ⎫ Junior ⎬ Senior ⎭	16	21	9	8	11	12	64	45	75	50	14	9	4	4	135	56
School size: 2 classes																
lower level	21	1	9	5	6	6	103	53	108	58	20	22	5	7	54	64
higher level	14	15	11	3	12	16	48	52	59	44	16	4	5	4	75	40
School size: 3–4 classes and above																
Infants	22	14	12	7	6	8	69	50	74	53	20	11	9	6	84	51
Junior	16	16	13	11	11	10	61	43	72	45	24	24	7	5	72	56
Senior	17	11	16	12	9	10	77	92	85	93	15	10	8	12	49	52

for many important questions about teaching, a large number of man-hours had to be expended to develop an adequate system of observation: reliable classroom observation, for whatever purpose, is dependent on a system which has been thoroughly tested and revised in the light of experience, and on extensive training in the use of that system. Finally, we were forced to abandon our original intention of relating teachers' non-teaching activities to their methods of teaching because we could find no adequate conceptual framework for describing teaching activities: the greatest barrier against discovering more about what happens in classrooms is the absence of theoretical models in terms of which teaching behaviour can be examined.

Reference

DUTHIE, J. H. (1970), 'The primary school survey: a study of the teacher's day', HMSO.

7 A. A. Bellack and J. R. Davitz

The Language of the Classroom

Excerpts from A. A. Bellack, J. R. Davitz *et al.*, 'Language of the classroom', US Department of Health, Education and Welfare, Cooperative Research Program, Project nos 1497 and 2023, New York Institute of Psychological Research, Teachers College, Columbia University, 1963 and 1965.

Purpose and procedures

The purpose of this research was to study the teaching process through analysis of the linguistic behavior of teachers and students in the classroom. Observation of what goes on in elementary and secondary schools reveals that classroom activities are carried on in large part in verbal interaction between students and teachers; few classroom activities can be carried on without the use of language. This study, therefore, focused on language as the main instrument of communication in teaching. The major task was to describe the patterned processes of verbal interaction that characterize classrooms in action. A subsidiary aim, viewed primarily as an exploratory phase of our general line of research, was to study linguistic variables of classroom discourse in relation to subsequent pupil learning and attitude change.

The subjects were fifteen teachers and 345 pupils in Problems of Democracy classes studying a unit on international trade. The fifteen classes, located in seven high schools in the metropolitan New York area, ranged in size from fifteen to thirty-five pupils, with a mean of twenty-three pupils. To establish reasonable limits within which the classes could carry on their work and to provide a relatively stable basis both for testing changes in knowledge and for analysing the substantive meanings of the classroom discourse, a unit of instruction was selected for the participating classes. This unit was based on the first four chapters of the pamphlet *International Economic Problems*, written by Dr James Calderwood (1961). Teachers were asked to teach in any manner they believed appropriate; no effort was made to control their methods of instruction. The experimental class sessions consisted of four periods on four successive days during the regular school schedule. Transcriptions of tape recordings of four sessions for each of the fifteen classes served as the basic data for the analysis of the verbal interaction of teachers and pupils.

Theoretical view of classroom behavior

We began with the assumptions that the primary function of language is the communication of meaning and that describing linguistic events in the classroom in terms of the meanings expressed by teachers and students is a potentially fruitful direction for research. Our conception of the nature of meaning was derived in large measure from Wittgenstein's view (1958, p. 20) that 'the meaning of a word is its use in the language'. Equation of meaning and use suggested that the basic problem was to identify the distinctive functions language actually serves in the verbal interplay between pupils and teachers.

In searching for the meaning of what teachers and students communicate in the classroom, we found it helpful to identify (a) what the speaker was doing *pedagogically* with the words he spoke at a given time; (b) *what* he was saying (i.e. the content of his statement); and (c) the *feeling tone* or emotional meaning conveyed by the communication. That is, in analysing the utterance of a teacher or of a student at a given point in class discussion, we were first of all concerned with the pedagogical significance of what the speaker was saying – whether, for example, he was structuring the class discussion by launching or focusing attention on a topic or problem, eliciting a response from a member of the class, responding to a question posed by a previous speaker, or reacting to a comment previously made. Second, we were interested in identifying the content of the communication – what topic was under discussion, what information the question called for, what explanation was being offered, or what assignment was being made. Furthermore, in addition to the pedagogical function of the language and the content of the message, we were concerned with both the explicit and the implicit emotional aspects of the speaker's vocal expression.

The basic methodological problem was to devise the means whereby these three dimensions of meaning could be defined operationally. In dealing with this problem, we were again influenced by Wittgenstein's approach to language. In his view, 'the *speaking* of language is part of an activity, or a form of life' (1958, p. 11). Language is adaptable to many uses and functions in carrying on activities that are essentially linguistic in nature. Wittgenstein refers to these activities as 'language games', a metaphor used to point up the fact that linguistic activities assume different forms and structures according to the functions they come to serve in various contexts. A game has a definite structure, and there are certain moves that a player is bound to make insofar as he is playing the game at all. These are some of the verbal activities that he identifies as language games (1958, pp. 11–12):

Giving orders and obeying them
Reporting an event
Forming and testing a hypothesis
Play acting
Making a joke and telling it
Making up a story and reading it

Carrying the game metaphor a step further, Wittgenstein observes that verbal activities in various contexts follow language rules that govern the use of words in these activities. Learning to participate in various types of language activities is therefore very much like learning to play a game. Participants have to learn the rules, the purpose of the rules, and how the various parts of the game are related; only if one learns these rules can one play the game successfully.

Viewing classroom discourse as a kind of language game was a useful approach for purposes of this research, in that it suggested a framework for analysis within which the various dimensions of meaning could be defined in operational terms. Teaching is similar to most games in at least two respects. First, it is a form of social activity in which the players – teachers and pupils – fill different but complementary roles. Furthermore, teaching is governed by ground rules of play which guide the actions or moves made by participants. We reasoned that if we could identify the various types of verbal moves teachers and students make in playing the game of teaching and the rules they implicitly follow in making these moves, we would be in a position to investigate the functions these verbal actions serve in classroom discourse and hence the meanings which are communicated.

Examination of the transcripts of classroom discussions suggested that the actions that characterize the verbal interplay of pupils and teachers could be classified in four major categories. We labeled these basic verbal actions *pedagogical moves* and classified them in terms of the functions they serve in classroom discourse:

Structuring. Structuring moves serve the pedagogical function of setting the context for subsequent behavior by launching or halting – excluding interaction between pupils and teachers and by indicating the nature of the interaction. For example, teachers frequently begin a class period with a structuring move in which they focus attention on the topic or problem to be discussed during that session.

Soliciting. Moves in this category are designed to elicit a verbal response, encourage persons addressed to attend to something, or elicit a physical response. All questions are solicitations, as are commands, imperatives and requests.

Responding. These moves bear a reciprocal relationship to soliciting moves and occur only in relation to them. Their pedagogical function is to fulfil the expectation of soliciting moves. Thus, students' answers to teachers' questions are classified as responding moves.

Reacting. These moves are occasioned by a structuring, soliciting, responding, or another reacting move, but are not directly elicited by them. Pedagogically, these moves serve to modify (by clarifying, synthesizing or expanding) and/or to rate (positively or negatively) what has been said previously. Reacting moves differ from responding moves, in that while a responding move is always directly elicited by a solicitation, preceding moves serve only as the occasion for reactions. Rating by a teacher of a student's response, for example, is designated a reacting move.

As we proceeded with the analysis of the data in terms of pedagogical moves, it became evident that these moves occur in certain cyclical patterns or combinations which we designated *teaching cycles*. A teaching cycle begins either with a structuring move or with a soliciting move, both of which are *initiating* maneuvers; that is, they serve the function of getting a cycle underway. In contrast, responding and reacting moves are *reflexive* in nature; a responding move is elicited by a soliciting move and a reacting move is occasioned by a preceding move and therefore they cannot begin a cycle. A cycle frequently begins, for example, with a soliciting move by the teacher in the form of a question, continues with a responding move by the student addressed, and ends with a rating reaction by the teacher. A cycle might also get underway with a structuring move by the teacher in which he focuses attention on the topic to be discussed, continues with a question related to this topic, and ends with responding moves by one or more pupils. The concept of teaching cycles makes it possible to identify patterns in the verbal exchange between teachers and students and thus to describe the ebb and flow of the teaching process as it develops over time.

In addition to meaning from the viewpoint of the pedagogical significance of what teachers and students communicate, we were also interested in the dimension of meaning represented by the content of the messages communicated. Analysis of the classroom protocols from this point of view revealed that teachers and students communicate four functionally different types of meanings: (*a*) *substantive meanings* with associated (*b*) *substantive-logical* meanings; and (*c*) *instructional meanings* with associated (*d*) *instructional-logical* meanings.

Substantive meanings refer to the subject matter discussed in the class; that is, specific concepts such as multilateral trade and generalizations involving, for example, the relation between specialization and the factors of production. Substantive-logical meanings refer to the cognitive processes involved in dealing with the subject matter, such as defining, explaining, fact stating, interpreting, opining and justifying. Instructional meanings refer to the social-managerial aspects of the classroom, such as assignments, materials and routine procedures which are part of the instructional process. Instructional-logical meanings refer to distinctively didactic verbal processes such as those involved in rating negatively and positively, explaining procedures, and giving directions.

As we developed techniques for analysing classroom discourse in terms of pedagogical units, we attempted to develop parallel methods for dimensions of meaning suggested by Osgood, Suci and Tannenbaum (1957): however, this did not prove feasible; instead, a procedure utilizing larger time samples of the discourse was developed. This provided a reliable basis for characterizing the emotional style of the discourse in terms of dimensions of meaning suggested by Osgood, Suci and Tannenbaum: (*a*) valence; (*b*) strength; and (*c*) activity.

Analysis of the data
Coding system

The four types of pedagogical moves described above were the basic units of analysis. Within each pedagogical move the four types of meanings described in the preceding section were identified when they appeared in the discourse and were coded according to categories 3 through 8 summarized below.[1]

1. SPEAKER: indicates source of utterance
Teacher (T); *Pupil* (P); *Audio-Visual Device* (A)

2. TYPE OF PEDAGOGICAL MOVE: reference to function of move.
Initiatory moves
Structuring (STR): sets context for subsequent behavior, launches, halts/excludes.
Soliciting (SOL): directly elicits verbal, physical, or mental response; coded in terms of response expected
Reflexive moves
Responding (RES): fulfils expectation of solicitation; bears reciprocal relation only to solicitation
Reacting (REA): modifies (by clarifying, synthesizing, expanding) and/or rates (positively or negatively); occasioned by previous move but not directly elicited; reactions to more than one previous move coded REA
Not Codable (NOC): function uncertain because tape inaudible

3. SUBSTANTIVE MEANING: reference to subject matter topic (Based on a content analysis of the pamphlet by Calderwood)
Trade (TRA)
  Domestic and international (TDI)
  Money and banking (TMB)
  Who trades with whom (TWH)

1. Italics indicate actual coding terminology.

Factors of production and/or specialization (FSP)
   Natural resources (FNR)
   Human skills (FHS)
   Capital equipment (FCE)
   Factors other than natural resources, human skills, and capital equipment occurring in discussion of reasons for trade (FRE)
Imports and/or Exports (IMX)
Foreign investment
   General (FOR)
   Direct (FOD)
   Portfolio (FOP)
Barriers to Trade (BAR)
   Tariffs (BAT)
   Quotas (BAQ)
   Exchange control (BAE)
   Export control (BAX)
   Administrative protectionism (BAA)
Promoting free trade (PFT)
Relevant to trade (REL)
Not trade (NTR)

4. SUBSTANTIVE – LOGICAL MEANING: reference to cognitive process involved in dealing with the subject matter under study
Analytic Process: use of language or established rules of logic
Defining-general (DEF) defining characteristics of class or term with example of items within class explicitly given
Defining-denotative (DED) object referent of term
Defining-connotative (DEC) defining characteristics of class or term
Interpreting (INT) verbal equivalent of a statement, slogan, aphorism, or proverb
Empirical Process: sense experience as criterion of truth
Fact stating (FAC) what is, was, or will be without explanation or evaluation; account, report, description, statement of event or state of affairs
Explaining (XPL) relation between objects, events, principles; conditional inference; cause-effect; explicit comparison-contrast; statement of principles, theories or laws

Evaluative Process: set of criteria or value system as basis for verification

Opining (OPN) personal values for statement of policy, judgment or evaluation of event, idea, state of affairs; direct and indirect evaluation included

Justifying (JUS) reasons or argument for or against opinion or judgment

Logical process not clear (NCL) cognitive process involved not clear

5. NUMBER OF LINES IN 3 AND 4 ABOVE

6. INSTRUCTIONAL MEANING: reference to factors related to classroom management

Assignment (ASG) suggested or required student activity; reports, tests, reading, debates, homework, etc.

Material (MAT) teaching aids and instructional devices

Person (PER) person as physical object or personal experiences

Procedure (PRC) a plan of activities or a course of action

Statement (STA) verbal utterance, particularly the meaning, validity, truth or propriety of an utterance

Logical process (LOG) function of language or rule of logic; reference to definitions or arguments, but not presentation of such

Action-general (ACT) performance (vocal, non-vocal, cognitive, or emotional) the specific nature of which is uncertain or complex

Action-vocal (ACV) physical qualities of vocal action

Action-physical (ACP) physical movement or process

Action-cognitive (ACC) cognitive process, but not the language or logic of a specific utterance; thinking, knowing, understanding, listening

Action-emotional (ACE): emotion or feeling, but not expression of attitude or value

Language mechanics (LAM): the rules of grammar and/or usage

7. INSTRUCTIONAL–LOGICAL MEANING: reference to cognitive processes related to the distinctly didactic verbal moves in the instructional situation

Analytic Process: see 4 above

Defining
   General (DEF)
   Denotative (DED)
   Connotative (DEC)
Interpreting (INT)
Empirical Process: see 4 above
Fact stating (FAC)
Explaining (XPL)
Evaluative Process: see 4 above
Opining (OPN)
Justifying (JUS)
Rating: reference to metacommunication; usually an evaluative reaction (REA)
Positive (POS) distinctly affirmative rating
Admitting (ADM) mild or equivocally positive rating
Repeating (RPT) implicit positive rating when statement (STA) is repeated by another speaker; also for SOL to repeat vocal action (ACV)
Qualifying (QAL) explicit reservation stated in rating exception
Not admitting (NAD) rating that rejects by stating the contrary; direct refutation or correction excluded
Negative (NEG) distinctly negative rating
Positive/negative (PON) SOL requesting positive or negative rating
Admitting/not admitting (AON) SOL asking to permit or not permit procedure or action
Extralogical Process: SOL expecting physical action or when logical nature of verbal response cannot be determined
Performing (PRF) asking, demanding, explicit directive or imperative
Directing (DIR) SOL with or without stated alternatives; asking for directive, not permission for specific action
Extralogical process not clear (NCL) extralogical process involved not clear

8. NUMBER OF LINES IN 6 AND 7 ABOVE
Each pedagogical move is coded as follows:
1/2/3/4/5/6/7/8
1. Speaker
2. Type of pedagogical move

3. Substantive meaning
4. Substantive-logical meaning
5. Number of typescript lines in 3 and 4
6. Instructional meaning
7. Instructional-logical meaning
8. Number of typescript lines in 6 and 7

Coding the protocols

The following excerpt from one of the coded protocols illustrates the coding procedures and interpretation of the coded information.[1]

Excerpt from protocol. Teacher (Move#1): Now, in order to pacify, or help satisfy, certain groups in American industry and American politics who want high protective tariffs, or who are clamoring for protection, we have inserted into our reciprocal agreements two – what you might call – safeguards which are coming up now as President Kennedy looks for greater authority in the tariff business. (Move#2): What have we inserted in here to give an element of protection or to stifle the outcries of American businessmen who want protection? Two clauses which we call ...? Yes?

Pupil (Move#3): The peril point and the escape clause.

Teacher (Move#4): Right. The peril point and the escape clause.

Code

Move#1 T/STR/BAT/XPL/5/-/-/-
Move#2 T/SOL/BAT/FAC/2/-/-/-
Move#3 P/RES/BAT/FAC/1/-/-/-
Move#4 T/REA/BAT/-/-/STA/POS/1

Interpretation. The teacher focuses on a substantive area by explaining something having to do with tariffs to the extent of five lines (Move#1). He then solicits for two lines with the expectation that a factual response on tariffs will be given (Move#2). A pupil gives a one-line response by stating a fact about tariffs (Move#3). The teacher positively evaluates the statement by the pupil (Move#4).

The entire segment of discourse is an example of a teacher-initiated cycle (STR SOL RES REA).

1. For a full one-page excerpt see the addendum to this article.

Reliability

The results . . . indicate a consistently high degree of reliability for all major categories of analysis; agreement ranged from 84 to 96 per cent (between pairs of coders). Thus, the data strongly support the conclusion that the system devised in this research for a content analysis of classroom discourse is highly reliable.

Emotional meanings

The semantic differential technique was used to describe each teacher's emotional style in terms of the meanings he conveyed along three dimensions: valence, activity, and strength (Osgood, Suci and Tannenbaum, 1957). Since it seemed reasonable to assume that our interpretations of the emotional meanings expressed by teachers would be quite different from those of the typical high school students who participated in the research, it was decided that emotional meanings should be analysed from the point of view of student observers. Judges in this part of the study were 11th grade students in a communications class in a senior high school similar to those who participated in the experimental classes. Because of the confidential nature of the tape recordings, ratings were obtained only for thirteen teachers who consented to have recordings of their classes played for persons other than regular members of the research staff. These ratings served as the basis for analysing the emotional meanings communicated by the teachers. The correlations (of reliability between sets of judges) obtained are valence, $r = 0.81$, activity, $r = 0.75$, and strength, $r = 0.84$. The results thus indicate adequate internal consistency.

Results

Perhaps the most striking aspects of the results are the remarkable similarities among many of the teachers and classrooms and the stability of individual classes over the four sessions. The data reveal a consistent and generally stable pattern of pedagogical discourse.

1. Teachers dominate the verbal activities of the classrooms studied. The teacher-pupil ratio in terms of lines spoken is approximately 3 to 1; in terms of moves, the ratio is about 3 to 2. The

volume of total verbal output is thus considerably greater for the teacher than for the pupil.

2. The pedagogical roles of the teacher and the pupil are clearly defined in terms of the frequency of behavior in each category of pedagogical moves. The teacher is responsible for structuring the lesson, for soliciting responses from pupils and for reacting to pupils' responses. The pupil's primary task is to respond to the teacher's solicitation. Occasionally the pupil reacts to preceding moves, but he rarely uses the reacting move to rate previous action. Only infrequently does the pupil solicit a response from the teacher or from another pupil. Seldom does the pupil spontaneously structure the discourse; when he uses a structuring move he frequently presents it as the fulfilment of a specific assignment made by the teacher, which usually involves a debate or a report.

Pedagogical move		Total	Percentage of moves by teachers	Percentage of moves by pupils	Percentage of moves by audio-visual devices
Soliciting	SOL	100	86·0	14·0	0
Responding	RES	100	12·0	88·0	0
Structuring	STR	100	86·0	12·0	2·0
Reacting	REA	100	81·0	19·0	0

N (SOL) = 5,135
N (RES) = 4,385
N (STR) = 854
N (REA) = 4,649

3. Structuring moves account for about six per cent of the discourse in terms of moves spoken. Soliciting, responding and reacting each account for approximately 30 per cent of the moves. The classes vary somewhat from this pattern, but for the four moves the distribution of variations is fairly restricted, with most classes clustering within a few percentage points of each other. Furthermore, in each of the classes the proportion of moves devoted to each of the pedagogical moves tends to be generally stable over the four sessions. This reflects a consistent style of play within each class.

4. Analysis of teaching cycles centers on the dimensions of

initiator (teacher or pupil) of the cycle, pattern of pedagogical moves within the cycle, and the rate at which cycles occur. Classes vary in the extent to which teachers initiate teaching cycles; generally, teachers initiate about 85 per cent of the cycles. Analysis of cycle pattern indicates that the basic verbal interchange in the classroom is the soliciting-responding pattern. Teachers often shape and frame this basic pattern with reacting moves and occasionally with structuring moves, although teachers differ in the extent to which they use the structuring and reacting moves. Classes also differ in the rate at which verbal interchanges take place; the average rate is slightly less than two cycles per minute.

5. In approximately two-thirds of the moves and about three-fourths of the lines speakers refer to or talk about substantive material, that is, the subject matter of international trade. Of all the categories of analysis, classes vary most widely in the substantive meanings expressed. This finding was not anticipated, since the major restriction imposed on the teachers by the research procedure was specification of the substantive material to be covered.

6. With respect to the substantive-logical meanings, approximately one-half of all moves involve empirical meanings (fact stating and explaining). Speakers use the analytic mode (defining and interpreting) and the evaluative mode (opining and justifying) much less frequently; each of these two modes accounts for about one-tenth of the moves in any class. Thus, a major proportion of the discourse in the classes studied is devoted to stating facts about and explaining principles and problems of international trade, while considerably less of the discourse is concerned either with defining terms and interpreting statements or with expressing and justifying personal opinions about economic issues.

7. In almost one-half of the moves and approximately one-fourth of the lines of the discourse, speakers convey instructional meanings. It is chiefly the teacher who expresses the instructional meanings. A large proportion of these meanings might be viewed as metacommunications, in that they involve teacher comments about preceding comments by pupils. Other instructional categories that occur with relative frequency are procedures, materials,

and assignments. All other instructional categories account for very little of the discourse.

8. The instructional-logical meanings that occur most frequently involve fact stating, usually about procedures, assignments, and other instructional matters. A substantial proportion of statements in this area also deal with teachers directing pupils to perform various actions. Almost all of the remaining instructional-logical entries involve some form of rating reaction by the teacher.

9. With respect to the analysis of emotional meanings, teachers maintain a relatively stable emotional style, insofar as the dimensions of potency and activity are concerned, and, to a lesser degree, in terms of valence. Teachers thus tend to be consistent over time in the kinds of emotional meanings they convey to students.

The language game of teaching

These results provide a description of the language game of teaching. Despite the fact that the rules of this game are not explicitly stated for any of the players, teachers and students in the classrooms under study obviously follow a set of implicit rules with few deviations. These rules define the teaching game. Although classes differ somewhat in details, for the purpose of an initial description of the classroom game, the results indicate that common elements underlie much of the teaching game, in that pupils and teachers follow a consistent set of language rules.

The classroom game involves one player called the teacher and one or more players called pupils. The object of the game is to carry on a linguistic discourse about subject matter, and the final 'payoff' of the game is measured by the amount of learning displayed by the pupils after a given period of play. In playing the game, each player must follow a set of rules. If one plays the role of teacher, he will follow one set of rules; if one plays the role of pupil, he will follow a somewhat different, though complementary, set of rules. In fact, the first rule, which might be called 'the rule of rules', is that if one is to play the game at all, he will consistently follow the rules specified for his role.

Within the general set of rules defining the game, there are individual differences among teachers and classes in style of play. In one classroom, the teachers or pupils may specialize in one kind of move or sequence of moves, while in another class the players may specialize in a slightly different pattern of discourse. Notwithstanding these variations in style and differences in specialization of moves, the game is played by a consistent set of general rules. These rules are rarely made explicit during the course of play: more often, they are defined implicitly by the ways in which teachers and pupils use these moves. It follows then that if one is to understand the rules of classroom behavior, he must study the functions that the pedagogical moves actually serve in the discourse of teachers and pupils.

Another way to interpret these data is to consider the sequence of pedagogical moves that occurs most commonly in the typical game. This sequence is, essentially, the solicitation-response teaching cycle which is shaped and framed by structuring and reacting moves. The most common type of verbal interchange in the classroom involves a teacher's solicitation and a pupil's response, which is usually followed by an evaluative reaction by the teacher. If this sequence does indeed define a general pattern of classroom discourse, it would seem to be important to investigate this sequence of moves in greater detail, to evaluate its pedagogical effectiveness, and to devise methods of increasing the effectiveness and efficiency of both teachers' solicitations and teachers' reactions.

A one-page excerpt from a protocol

T However, to get back to our main point once more, in talking about the US role in, in all this international trade. Our export trade is vital to us. Our import trade is vital to us, and it would upset and shake American economy to a tremendous extent if we were to stop importing or stop exporting.   T|*REA*|IMX|XPL|6|PRC|FAC|2
Let's turn to American investments abroad.   T|STR*|FOR|-|-|PRC|FAC|1
You suppose we do invest much money, outside of the US?   T|SOL|FOR|FAC|2|-|-|-|

P Yes.   P|RES|FOR|FAC|1|-|-|-|

T In what ways, in what fields? How would it be done?   T|SOL▲|FOR|XPL|2|-|-|-|

P Well, a lot of the big companies here in the US will set up companies over in other countries, and that way they can give the workers over there a chance to work and to sell their products and the foreign countries can get the tax off that.   P|RES|FOD|XPL|7|-|-|-|

T I think you put the most important thing last, but that's true.
T|REA|FOD|-|-|STA|QAL|2
The branch office in a foreign country, which involves the exportation of American capital, is so often done to avoid paying what?
T|SOL■|FOD|XPL|3|-|-|-|

P Taxes.   P|RES|FOD|XPL|1|-|-|-|

   * This move begins a STR-SOL-RES teaching cycle.
   ▲ This move begins a SOL-RES-REA teaching cycle.
   ■ This move begins a SOL-RES teaching cycle.

References

CALDERWOOD, N. D. (1961), *International Economic Problems*, Curriculums Resources Inc.

OSGOOD, C., SUCI, J., and TANNENBAUM, P. H. (1957), *The Measurement of Meaning*, University of Illinois Press.

WITTGENSTEIN, L. (1958), *Philosophical Investigations*, Blackwell.

Part Three
Preparation for the Classroom

Studies of the professional training and socialization of teachers may be divided into two broad categories: those concerned with describing changes which typically occur during training and first experiences of teaching; and those concerned with the effectiveness of particular techniques aimed at influencing students' behaviour in predetermined ways.

Research of the first type has tended to focus on attitudes, values and conceptions of the teacher's role. Results in this area have been fairly consistent; both the trend towards more 'progressive' attitudes during training which McIntyre and Morrison found, and the opposing trend during the first year of teaching found by Hoy are in line with the results reported by most other investigators.

Very little research has been reported into the effectiveness of such traditional training procedures as teaching practice. More effort has been made, however, to assess some of the analytic approaches increasingly used in recent years. The article by Jecker and his associates reports one such investigation. Micro-teaching procedures, in particular, have been the subject of quite extensive research, the results of which are reviewed in McKnight's article.

8 D. McIntyre and A. Morrison

The Educational Opinions of Teachers in Training

From D. McIntyre and A. Morrison, 'The educational opinions of teachers in training', *British Journal of Social and Clinical Psychology*, vol. 6, 1967, pp. 32–7.

Introduction

Little information is as yet available on the effects of professional training upon the educational opinions of students in colleges of education and university education departments in Britain. In studies carried out in the USA and elsewhere the Minnesota Teacher Attitude Inventory (Cook, Leeds and Callis, 1951) has commonly been used to make assessments of opinions, but the inventory has frequently been criticized on both theoretical and practical grounds (e.g. Heikkinen, 1962; Evans, 1958). More recently, the Manchester Scales of Opinions about Education have been constructed (Oliver and Butcher, 1962) and these appear to meet some of the more general criticisms of the MTAI as well as being more obviously relevant to the practices and policies of British educational systems.

So far, only one study (Butcher, 1965) using the Manchester scales has been published. This investigated changes in opinions during training and some correlates of opinions in samples of students in training in England, and compared results with those obtained from a sample of experienced teachers. Results indicated fairly consistent changes during training in the direction of increased naturalism, radicalism and tendermindedness in educational opinions, with some tendency towards reversal after experience of full-time teaching. Also, the study suggested that 'attitudes to educational practice are more closely related to the effects of education, indoctrination and experience than to sex or age . . .' and that 'changes on the scale of radicalism–conservatism in education are associated with changes in political opinions during the course of training . . .' (Butcher, 1965).

The present investigation, some of the primary findings of which are reported here, was partly designed to replicate Butcher's study, but has the further purposes of providing comparisons between Scottish and English students and giving follow-up data on some of the students after experience of full-time teaching in Scottish schools.

Method
Subjects

Unlike the English system, the training of all categories of teachers in Scotland is centralized in colleges of education.[1] The only student teachers attending university are those who wish to study concurrently with training for the diploma of education, and in these cases education and psychology are studied in the relevant university departments instead of those departments in the colleges.

The samples of student teachers were drawn from various year groups attending courses in one college of education. A further sample, of university undergraduates, was taken from members of a first year class studying psychology. In all, 430 students were involved, drawn from the following categories:

1. 73 women non-graduates in the first year of the three year college diploma course.

2. 125 women non-graduates from the third year of the three year college diploma course.

3. 189 men and women graduates attending a one year course of teacher training in the college.

4. 43 first year university undergraduate women.

Of the graduates, more than half were concurrently attending diploma of education classes in the university departments of Education and Psychology. Also, for the entire graduate group there were approximately equal numbers of men and women.

1. Since this article was published the University of Stirling has established first degree courses combined with concurrent professional training for teachers [eds].

Administration of measures

All the students participating in the study were asked to complete the three Manchester scales of opinions about education. In addition, they were requested to provide the following information:

1. Father's occupation.

2. Political party affiliation.

3. Ratings, on five-point scales, for opinions on the quality of the school education they received, church attendance, and their opinions of the importance of belief in God.

For the student teachers, marks or grades for education, psychology and practical teaching were obtained from college records.

Since it was intended that the third year non-graduate women and the graduate students would be retested on the opinion scales it was necessary for students in these categories to provide their names to the questionnaire. These groups were first tested, as were the others, at the beginning of the session (October 1963), and were then retested at the end of the year (May–June 1964). For both groups approximately 50 per cent were retested. Examination of the first occasion scores of the retest groups showed, however, that in no case were they significantly different from those of the whole groups, though for both sexes the diploma of education students retested had consistently lower mean scores than those of the whole group on all three scales.

Results
Mean scores of samples on the opinion scales

The means and standard deviations for all samples on the first testing are shown in Table 1 below.

Changes in opinions during teacher training

Examination of the test–retest scores for the third year non-graduate women and for the four graduate groups showed changes in the direction of increased scores on all three scales. A comparison between non-graduate women in the first and third years of their college training gave a similar result. These changes were greatest for the non-graduate women and for the graduate women who were not taking the diploma in education: in these cases

Table 1 High scores are given to the naturalistic, radical and tenderminded ends of the three respective scales

	Idealism – Naturalism		Conservatism – Radicalism		Tough – tendermindedness		N
	M	s.d.	M	s.d.	M	s.d.	
1st yr non-graduate women: single	84·81	7·96	134·26	13·79	133·76	12·75	54
1st yr non-graduate women: married	83·95	5·17	132·00	7·47	131·05	11·89	19
1st yr undergraduate women	83·77	9·28	135·02	14·65	133·47	15·16	43
3rd yr non-graduate women: single	89·54	7·75	139·49	9·49	136·95	13·53	106
3rd yr non-graduate women: married	88·16	9·01	142·31	13·65	141·21	17·63	19
Graduate women: non dip. ed.	88·08	9·23	134·45	11·97	143·37	13·23	49
Graduate men: non dip. ed.	83·17	11·70	135·83	13·00	131·28	15·26	29
Graduate women: dip. ed.	84·30	11·00	135·59	12·27	141·39	16·56	46
Graduate men: dip. ed.	83·58	10·13	132·51	12·47	135·98	15·62	65

changes on the naturalism and radicalism scales were highly significant ($p < 0.001$), and significant on the tendermindedness scale ($p < 0.05$) for the non-graduate women.

Comparisons between samples

While there were no significant differences between the samples of women in their first year at the university or at the college beginning the three year non-graduate course, the non-graduate women at the end of their three year course had significantly higher scores on the naturalism and radicalism scales than did graduate women who had completed their degree course and had started college training.

There were no significant initial differences between those graduates who took the university diploma in education course and those who did not. At the end of the course, however, those women who took the diploma course were significantly less naturalistic and less radical, the difference for radicalism applying to the men also.

Thus, while the university, at the diploma of education level and during undergraduate education, appears to influence students towards higher scores on tendermindedness, the effects of college training appear to be in the direction of greatly increased naturalism and radicalism, with a rather smaller influence towards tendermindedness than the university.

Finally, for the graduates it was possible to examine the scores made by the sex groups against a common background of professional training. For those graduates doing their entire training in college the women were throughout more tenderminded ($p < 0.01$) and naturalistic ($p < 0.05$); however, there were no significant differences between men and women doing the concurrent diploma of education course, either at the beginning or end of training.

Comparisons with English samples

On the basis of results already published by Butcher (1965) on samples of students in England, it was possible to compare some groups of English and Scottish students on both initial scores and changes in scores on the three scales. The results are given in Table 2.

Table 2

	Mean scores on first testing			Mean differences between first and second testing		
	N	R	T	N	R	T
Graduates in English university education dept.	80·81	123·95	136·96	+3·62	+ 6·00	+4·85
Scottish graduates dip. of ed.	83·94	133·79	138·20	+3·37	+ 4·60	+8·51
Scottish graduates non dip. of ed.	86·26	134·96	139·00	+9·27	+10·50	+3·87
English training college, 1st yr initial testing	80·95	128·66	127·35			
Scottish non-graduate women, 1st yr initial testing	84·59	133·67	133·05			

Comparisons of mean scores of students entering the two year English training course in 1957 and the three year Scottish course in 1963 show that the Scottish students have significantly ($p < 0.05$) higher scores on all three scales. A similar comparison of graduates entering training in the two countries shows that the Scottish students are significantly ($p < 0.01$) more naturalistic and more radical. These differences are maintained and, indeed, increased for those Scottish graduates whose training was entirely in college, but those who took the diploma of education course were not, at the conclusion of training, different in any significant respect from the English graduates.

College assessments and educational opinions

Results from the opinion scales for non-diploma graduates and third year non-graduate women students were examined in relation to college assessments of their performance in education and psychology examinations and of their practical teaching. All correlations were negligible between opinions and examination marks. Relationships between teaching assessments and opinions were examined by *t*-tests: again no significant relationships were found.

Further variables

Information obtained from the students on their social class background, as assessed by the father's occupation (Moser and Hall, 1954), on their opinions about religion, politics and personal schooling, was compared with their scores on the three scales. Social class was generally not related to scores, although there was a tendency for social classes 1 and 2 to be the least radical; and opinions on school had a short-lived influence on girls entering college from school, but this had disappeared later in college training.

Relationships between opinions and political allegiance, religious opinions and habits were markedly stronger, although variable in significance across the groups. Thus, for all student samples the higher scores on all three scales were made by the least religious and by Labour supporters. Although there were inconsistencies the naturalism scale appeared to be the one most closely associated with religious beliefs and habits, and the radicalism scale the most closely related to political allegiance. No clear pattern of associations was apparent for the tough–tenderminded-ness scale.

Conclusions

The principal findings reported on here clearly corroborate those obtained from the earlier English study by Butcher on the general trend during training towards increased naturalism, radicalism and tendermindedness in educational opinions, and on the differential effects of training courses upon the type and degree of opinion change. In the latter respect the results are of particular interest concerning the particular effects of university and college upon students.

A noteworthy feature of the results is the finding of higher scores on the scales for the Scottish groups as compared to the scores made by the English students some seven years earlier. There is no study at present available which presents simultaneous results for Scottish and English students, the only partly relevant study being that made with samples of teachers of science in the two countries by Pollock (1964) in which he found no significant differences on any of the scales. Thus, as far as students in training are concerned it cannot be conclusively determined whether there are systematic differences present as a result of the differences in training or whether there has been a fairly rapid change in the general climate of educational opinion in recent years. This latter explanation seems far more likely, but it is a matter of considerable general interest which deserves to be examined on a wider scale with student and other samples.

The results obtained for the further variables included in the study are largely what might have been expected; thus, the expressed religious attitudes and behaviour and the political affiliations generally bear a close relation to educational opinions expressed on the naturalism and radicalism scales respectively. However, the scale of tough–tendermindedness appears more specific to education and less clearly associated with wider areas of social attitudes. Butcher (in a personal communication) has suggested that this scale might better be described as a theoretical–practical one, and such an interpretation seems consistent with the present results, with the major influence of the university on students' opinions being to encourage a more theoretical position on educational issues and with the college trained students being relatively more practical.

References

BUTCHER, H. J. (1965), 'The attitudes of student teachers to education', *Brit. J. soc. clin. Psychol.*, vol. 4, pp. 17–24.

COOK, W. W., LEEDS, C. H., and CALLIS, R. (1951), *The Minnesota Teacher Attitude Inventory*, The Psychological Corporation, New York.

EVANS, K. M. (1958), 'An examination of the Minnesota teacher attitude inventory', *Brit. J. educ. Psychol*, vol. 28, pp. 374–84.

HEIKKINEN, V. (1962), 'Educational attitudes of teachers under training and in the first in-service years', *Annales Academiae scientiarium fennicae.*

MOSER, C. A., and HALL, J. R. (1954), in D. V. GLASS (ed.), *Social mobility in Britain*, Routledge & Kegan Paul.

OLIVER, R. A. C., and BUTCHER, H. J. (1962), 'Teachers' attitudes to education: the structure of educational attitudes', *Brit. J. soc. clin. Psychol.*, vol. 1, pp. 56–9.

POLLOCK, G. J. (1964), 'The opinions of science teachers on the objectives of teaching science', unpublished M. Ed. thesis, University of Manchester.

9 J. D. Jecker, N. Maccoby and H. S. Breitrose

Improving Accuracy in Interpreting Non-Verbal Cues of Comprehension

From J. D. Jecker, N. Maccoby and H. S. Breitrose, 'Improving accuracy in interpreting non-verbal cues of comprehension', in *Psychology in the Schools*, vol. 2, 1965, pp. 239-44.

In general, it is a difficult task to gear classroom teaching to achieve optimal student comprehension. This problem could be largely avoided if the teacher were able to make accurate judgments of student comprehension at various critical points during the lesson.

The present investigators, in a previous article (in press), have shown that such judgments can be made with significant accuracy when verbal feedback from the students is available. During the ordinary classroom presentation of a lesson, however, the teacher must rely predominantly on non-verbal feedback – facial expressions and various bodily movements. The previous research referred to above found no evidence that such non-verbal feedback is being currently used successfully in judging student comprehension.

It was our belief that non-verbal feedback should provide some useful cues for making such judgments. The present article reports an attempt to discover useful non-verbal cues and train teachers to use them.

Method

Sound-film recordings were made of individual students while they were being taught by their regular teachers. The teachers were our subjects. These films were then scored for student comprehension and used as test materials in testing our subjects' ability to judge student comprehension. The procedure followed was one of pre-test, followed by training, followed in turn by post-testing.

Subjects

Twenty graduate students doing their supervised teaching under the direction of the teacher training program in the School of Education at Stanford University served as subjects.

Collecting the film materials

Since it was necessary to collect films in twenty different classrooms during instruction by twenty different teachers, it seemed desirable to reduce the variability of some aspects of the lesson being taught. Also, since the films were to be used as test materials for judging student comprehension, we needed some method of independently assessing the degree of actual student comprehension. To satisfy these two needs, all teachers were provided with a standard program of instruction to present to their students while we filmed. This program consisted of thirty-five items of instruction in the field of anthropology, on the concept of familial structure. By and large, this material had not been taught previously to any of the students being filmed, and the level of difficulty was appropriate for our purposes. The information was presented verbally by the teacher in a manner approximating normal classroom teaching techniques. Immediately after the teacher presented each item of information, she posed a question to the students concerning that item. The students were provided with answer sheets and recorded their own answers.

Each question was presented on one of a set of large cards mounted on an easel at the front of the class. Students were requested to reserve any questions they had until the lesson had been completed, thus minimizing verbal feedback from students to teacher. Each question card had a set of multiple-choice type answers, the last of which was 'I don't know'. Students were instructed to answer each question as best they could, and to use the last answer whenever they really had no idea which was the correct answer. As the teacher finished each item on instruction, she would reveal the question card concerning that item and read the question. She would pause twenty to thirty seconds for the students to answer the question, and then step in front of the question card to present the next instruction item.

Two sixteen mm. Auricon cameras with thirty-three minute film magazines were used to obtain continuous photographs of individual students as they responded to the lesson. The cameras were equipped with variable focal length lenses, so that the size of the student on the actual film frame could be kept reasonably constant despite variation in distance from camera to student. Cameramen were instructed to pick individual students in the class and photograph them for a period of either five or ten instruction items. (The purpose of this variation will become apparent during discussion of the construction of the post-test.) A synchronous sound recording was made of the teacher's instruction.

These films were then broken down into 'clips'. A clip consisted of the film footage on one student from the beginning of one instruction item up to the beginning of the next item, usually about forty-five seconds. Each clip thus included the period of time during which the student was expected to answer the question for that item. Through the use of the synchronous sound recording, each clip on a student could be identified as to the specific instruction item presented during that clip. By consulting the student's answer sheet, we scored each clip 'right' or 'wrong' depending on whether the student answered the question on that item correctly or incorrectly. Thus each clip was identified by teacher, student, instruction item number, and right or wrong answer. Once identified, the clips could be assembled into test films in any order.

The pre-training test

Our first experimental objective was to assess the ability of the teachers to judge student comprehension accurately before any training. To this end, pre-training test films were constructed in the following manner. From the films of each teacher's class, 25 clips distributed evenly over 5 students, were drawn.[1] These clips were drawn from students filmed for 10 consecutive items so that a post-training test could include new clips on these same students. Since the teachers were aware that the instructions and accompanying questions grew increasingly difficult during the lesson period, each set of five clips on any one student was randomized to eliminate item difficulty as a cue in judging student comprehension.

Groups of four teachers were assigned to five pre-training test groups. Approximately twenty randomized sets of five clips on

1. Due to incomplete films, fewer than 25 clips were drawn for six teachers. For these six, we drew 24, 24, 24, 30, 15, and 13 clips.

single students were presented in each pre-training test film by following a fixed order of teachers to which the student in each set belonged. Thus each teacher saw one set on one of her students, and then three sets, one of which belonged to each of the other three teachers in the test group. This fixed order of five-clip sets was repeated throughout each test film.

The test films were shown silent. This procedure was followed for two reasons. First, we were interested in judgments based on non-verbal cues only. Second, since the sound track contained the teachers' instruction, it could provide cues concerning the difficulty of each item. Before beginning the test, all teachers were instructed that each clip they would see would show a student during the instruction of one item and the time allotted to answer the question on that item, and that the clips would not necessarily be shown in the order in which they were photographed. They were instructed to judge whether the student answered the question in each clip correctly or incorrectly, and were to judge all clips, those of their own students and those of others. An answer sheet was provided for this purpose. Each teacher made from 84 to 100 such judgments during the pre-training test.

Isolating useful non-verbal cues

The films were next viewed by the investigators in an effort to select non-verbal cues which might prove useful in judging student comprehension. The films allowed us to investigate many relationships between specific non-verbal behaviors and the student's actual performance on the question answered for each clip. Facial movements and expressions, as well as various other specific behaviors of a non-verbal nature were considered for their utility in assessing comprehension. After many revisions the investigators agreed on a set of specific non-verbal cues as being related to comprehension, including such body and facial movements as orienting oneself towards the source of information, frequency and speed of movement to and away from such sources, brow furrowing and raising, chin rubbing, and the like. For each of these cues, a set of scoring categories was designed so that a score could be given on every cue for any clip. The cue items were then assembled into a single-sheet coding form which could be completed for each clip viewed. Thus the completed cue-coding form resembled those used in standard interviewing techniques. Although our initial attempts at agreement among independent coders varied and were not uniformly satisfactory, we had the means at our disposal for improvement. By comparing disagreements and rerunning any given film clip, we could either redefine the category so as to sharpen it or discover problems in the

Table 1 Items analysed from code form 'Mark 8'

1. Clip Number
2. Amount of time looked at source
(a) Little or none
(b) Somewhat
(c) A great deal
(d) Virtually all the time
3. Number of times looked away from source
(a) Many times (more than 4)
(b) Some (3 or 4)
(c) Little (1 or 2)
(d) None
4. Speed of eye movements away from and returning to the source
(a) Slow
(b) Fast
(c) None away from source
5. Amount of blinking
(a) More than normal
(b) Normal
(c) Less than normal
6. Grouping of blinking
(a) Spaced
(b) Clustered
(c) Virtually no blinking
7. Duration of lowering eyebrows
(a) A lot
(b) A little
(c) None
8. Strength of lowering eyebrows
(a) Strong
(b) Weak
(c) No eyebrow lowering

9. Duration of raising eyebrows
(a) A lot
(b) A little
(c) None
10. Strength of raising eyebrows
(a) Strong
(b) Weak
(c) No eyebrow raising
11. Movement of hands on face
(a) A lot
(b) Some
(c) A little
(d) None
12. Frequency of general body movement
(a) A lot
(b) Some
(c) A little or none
13. Extent of general body movement
(a) A lot
(b) Some
(c) A little or none
14. Amount of mouth movement
(a) A lot
(b) Some
(c) A little or none
15. Chewing gum or candy
(a) Yes
(b) No

16. My guess of student's answer
(a) Wrong
(b) Right
17. Student's actual answer
(a) Wrong
(b) Right

observation process that required special attention. After a long series of revisions based on such a procedure, we developed a version of the code that provided adequately reliable items (Mark 8 – see Table 1). The first item is an identification number. The last item is a judgment of student comprehension. On the whole, agreement ratios approximated those normally attained in the coding of open-ended verbal material. Coding reliability was measured in the usual way; namely, the ratio of agreements among independent coders coding the same material to the total number of possible agreements. When the film clips were coded independently by either four or five members of the research team, such ratios ranged from a low of 0·67 agreement (where 0·40 would be the chance base line) to 0·99 agreement (where 0·50 would be chance). The overall mean ratio was 0·78. Of course, some of the categories are quite easy to score reliably in that the behavior being coded occurred only rarely, and coders could easily agree that it did not occur in a particular clip. Such items were retained, however, because when such behavior does occur, it may be highly indicative of the degree of comprehension.

The training procedure

The 20 teachers were next assigned to one of two groups by the toss of a coin. One restriction was placed on this assignment: males and females were distributed as evenly as possible between the groups. One of these groups was designated as the experimental training group. Their training procedure was as follows: Four separate sessions of one and a half to two hours each were conducted. At each training session, teachers viewed from 15 to 30 clips, completing a Mark 8 form for each clip. Open discussion occurred in all training sessions as to the correct scoring, interpretation and meaning of non-verbal cues, and feedback was provided on the student's actual performance, right or wrong.

The other group of ten teachers was designated as the control group. They also met for four one and a half to two hour sessions. During each session, they were shown a film concerning interpersonal communication and discussed those aspects of each film which were relevant to the student–teacher communication process.

The post-training test

Following the training session, the teachers were assigned to post-training test groups. New test films were prepared, each containing 90 clips. These test films were constructed so as to contain clips of three types: 30 repeats of clips shown in the pre-test and used in experimental training sessions, 30 clips on students shown in the pre-test clips, but specific clips which did not, themselves, appear in the pre-training test or in training; and 30 new clips on students not shown in the pre-training test. Some variation in the exact number of clips of each type occurred due to incomplete films in some classes. Those students who had been photographed for ten consecutive items supplied clips of each of the first two of the above types. Students photographed for five consecutive items supplied clips in the last category. These three types of items were deliberately included to check on two types of practice effects which might occur in the experimental training group. It might occur that teachers in the experimental condition simply learned, from feedback in the training sessions, the correct judgments for some of the clips used in training. A comparison of accuracy in judging clips of types I with clips of types II and III provides a check on such a practice effect. It might also occur that the teachers in the experimental condition may have learned to judge the students shown during training. A comparison of accuracy in judging clips of types I and II with clips of type III provides a check on this kind of practice effect.

The clips were presented in the post-training tests in pairs of clips of each student. The order of presentation of these pairs was again fixed so as to rotate through the teachers viewing each test film. The order of original occurrence of the items was not randomized within each pair of clips, but the order of the type of clip was randomized within each set of three pairs, i.e., within each rotation through teachers. Thus each teacher saw one set of two clips on one of her students, and then two additional sets, one of which belonged to each of the other teachers in the test group; and each set of three pairs of clips contained one pair of each type of clip.

Completion of the post-training test marked the end of the experiment.

Results and discussion

The pre-training test scores were analysed first. Each teacher was given a 'per cent accurate' score by dividing the number of correct judgments of student comprehension by the total number of judgments made. As mentioned above, our previous research found no evidence that visual cues were being successfully used to judge student comprehension. The result obtained on the pre-training test in this study is consistent with the earlier finding. The mean per cent score obtained here for all twenty teachers was 56·7 per cent accurate. This is not significantly different from a chance accuracy score of 50 per cent ($t = 1·12$).

It will be recalled that following the pre-training test, teachers were assigned by the flip of a coin to experimental and control groups. Ideally, performance on the pre-training test should not differ between the two groups. Unfortunately, comparison of these scores reveals that teachers assigned to the control group had a significantly higher mean per cent accurate score (59·8 per cent) than did the experimental teachers (53·7 per cent): $t = 2·68$, $p < ·02$.

Assessing the training effect must therefore take into account this difference in pre-training accuracy. To accomplish this, an improvement score was obtained for each teacher by subtracting pre-training per cent accurate from post-training per cent accurate. Comparing these per cent improvement scores, we find that the experimental training group had a mean gain in accuracy of +7·2 per cent, while the control had a mean of −0·5 per cent. These means are significantly different: $t = 2·12$, $p < ·05$.

It is obvious that the absolute gains obtained in the experimental training group are relatively small. We are encouraged, however, for a number of reasons. First of all, the training technique used here can be unequivocally and objectively evaluated. This is seldom the case with standard teacher training programs. Secondly, the effect of the experimental training is demonstrated and significant. Thirdly, this statistically significant improvement was achieved with only six to eight hours of training, possibly the most encouraging feature of the study.

Thus we have significant evidence that the experimental training procedure employed improved accuracy in judging student comprehension. However, there are several ambiguities concerning the ability to make such judgments and the exact nature of the training effect. First of all, we must consider whether or not there is a pattern of non-verbal cues related to comprehension which is common across students. Our basic assumption has been that there is such a common set of cues, but until now we have had no data suitable for testing such an assumption. One of the interesting results of the earlier study referred to above was the lack of any evidence to suggest that teaching experience improves ability to use non-verbal cues to assess comprehension. However, teachers taking part in the earlier study had no opportunity to judge comprehension in clips of their own students. If there are very few, or no common cues of comprehension, they could not be expected to develop any generalized ability, even though they might become very adept at judging students whom they had taught. The previous study thus allowed no comparison of a general versus a student-specific ability to judge comprehension. The present data do allow for such a comparison since teachers' pre-training test performance can be broken down by accuracy in judging their own students (Own) versus accuracy in judging students with whom they are unfamiliar (Others). Table 2 presents mean per cent accurate scores when they are broken down by Own students versus

Table 2 Comparison of experimental and control
pre-training mean per cent accurate scores broken down by
own versus others' students

	own	other	
E	55·6	53·0	E v. C $F = 4·94, p < 0·05$
			OW v. OT $F < 1$
C	60·0	59·7	Interaction $F < 1$

Others' students. The only significant effect is the one reflecting the fact, reported above, that controls had a higher pre-training mean than experimentals. There is no evidence that teachers judge their own students more accurately than they judge others' students. Per cent improvement scores were also broken down by Own versus Others' students, with similar results. The analysis of variance main effect of Own versus Others' students yielded

$F < 1$. Thus there is no basis in either of these analyses to reject our assumption that the visual cues useful in judging student comprehension are common across students.

In the description of the post-training test films, it was pointed out that three types of clips were used in order to be able to check on two possible 'practice effects' of the experimental training procedure. Actually, these effects can be thought of as alternative interpretations to a general training effect. They suggest task specific learning rather than improvement in general ability. The first practice effect suggested was that experimental teachers were simply learning the correct answers to the type I clips because they were given right-wrong feedback during training. Controls, of course, were never given any such feedback and could not have 'learned' correct judgments.

Table 3 **Post-training per cent accurate scores broken down by previous exposure**

	Training clips on training students	New clips on training students	New clips on new students
E	67·8	63·0	56·9
C	65·6	59·8	57·9

E v. C $F < 1$; Type of Clip $F = 4·10$, $p < 0·05$; Interaction $F < 1$.

The second practice effect suggested pertains to the question raised above concerning general versus student-specific cues of comprehension. This practice effect suggests that possibly experimental teachers are learning several sets of comprehension related cues, one for each student shown in the training sessions, again due to right-wrong feedback during training. If this were true, we would expect post-training performance to be better, for experimental subjects only, on all clips showing these students, regardless of whether the specific clips had been shown in training sessions. Table 3 presents post-training per cent accurate scores when broken down by previous exposure to students shown in the film clips. Those clips shown in training; new clips on students shown in training, and new-student clips not previously shown. It is evident that when we do not take into account pre-training differences in accuracy between experimentals and controls, no significant difference obtains in a post-training experimental versus control comparison. It is also evident that there is a 'previous exposure' effect, suggesting both the effects discussed immediately above. Inspection of the means reveals, however, that the effect is equally present in experimental and control data, and thus cannot be the result of the experimental training procedure. The interaction effect is entirely absent. An explanation of this 'previous exposure' effect is lacking, but it cannot be invoked as an alternative to the interpretation that the experimental training procedure improves general ability to judge student comprehension.

Through this research, we have made the assumption that the situation in which the students were originally filmed closely approximates a 'normal', or typical classroom learning situation. We have little direct evidence to support such an assumption. Clearly, there are some differences. The effect of the presence of movie cameras, sound recording equipment, and the necessary technical crew has been judged negligible for our purposes, and is discussed in our previous work (in press).

The fact that a program of instruction was employed undoubtedly produced something of an unusual situation for the student, as did the props used in connection with that program. Essentially, it had the characteristics of a highly organized audiovisual presentation. We feel that the students enjoyed the lesson, were interested in the material, and responded satisfactorily, in spite of the fact that they were instructed that performance on the lesson would have no effect on their grade in that class. It was true that most students attended sufficiently to answer all the questions during instruction.

The criticism may be raised that for the above reasons, and primarily because the lesson constituted a test situation, this basic assumption is subject to question. To the contrary, we believe that typical classroom learning is a self-test situation for at least the interested student, and given the instruction that performance on this lesson (and its accompanying test) would not affect the student's grade, the uninterested student should remain uninterested. The only feature of our procedure which is essentially different, as far as the test nature of the situation is concerned, is that students were requested to record their answers to formally stated questions. We do not feel that this difference constitutes a drastic or meaningful change from the typical classroom learning situation.

To summarize, evidence has been obtained to support the hypothesis that the ability to judge student comprehension on the basis of non-verbal cues, while largely undeveloped in the normal classroom teacher, can be significantly improved by training in the recognition and interpretation of such non-verbal cues. Further, the obtained improvement in this ability cannot be dismissed as a transient, task-specific effect.

Reference

JECKER, J., MACCOBY, N., BREITROSE, H. S., and ROSE, E. (1964), 'Teacher accuracy in assessing cognitive visual feedback', *J. App. Psychol.*, no. 48, pp. 393–7.

10 P. C. McKnight

Microteaching in Teacher Training:
A Review of Research

From P. C. McKnight, 'Microteaching in teacher training: A Review of Research', *Research in Education*, vol. 6, 1971, pp. 24–38.

The following discussion is concerned with describing the essential characteristics of microteaching, a new design for teacher training, and with describing the results and implications of studies of the effectiveness of several combinations of microteaching components.

Description

Microteaching is a scaled down but realistic classroom context which offers a helpful setting for a teacher (experienced or inexperienced) to acquire new teaching skills and to refine old ones. It does so by reducing the complexity and scope of such classroom components as the numbers of pupils and length of lessons, and by providing trainees with information about their performance immediately after completion of their lesson.

The first microteaching programme began in 1963 as part of a pre-service training programme at Stanford University under the leadership of professors Allen, Bush and McDonald. In a recent survey of American colleges and universities, Ward (1968) found that 176 institutions were using microteaching in their teacher training programmes. In their book *Microteaching*, Allen and Ryan (1969) cite a survey of student teaching programmes by Johnson which showed that microteaching was being used by 53 per cent of such programmes.

Microteaching has been introduced in Great Britain by several institutions including the University of Stirling, where a five-year research programme sponsored by the Leverhulme Trust is seeking information about the usefulness of microteaching to teacher training in Britain. In both the Stirling and Stanford programmes, microteaching has been used for the initial training programme of teachers, and has been planned around the following training pattern: after teaching a brief lesson (usually five to ten minutes), the trainee and his supervisor (usually a more experienced teacher) critique the lesson. If videotape recordings are made of the lessons, they are played back at this time. After the critique the trainee revises his lesson and teaches it again, usually to a different group of pupils. The second teaching session is also followed by a critique. There are many variations possible to this pattern due to the flexibility of the components. For example, if skills training is involved, it may occur before the initial teaching session when, for example, videotapes of teachers 'modelling' the teaching skill are shown to trainees who then practice the skill in their lesson. In another variation, the reteach may be held much later, giving the trainee longer to revise his lesson. From this description, four components of the microteaching process emerge: setting and equipment; participants; specified teaching skills (often called the 'technical skills' of teaching); and a programme for imparting these skills. Most of the research into microteaching has been concerned with this last component and it is therefore with this component that most of the present paper is concerned. The other three components are discussed briefly below.

Setting and equipment

A normal classroom setting, with a teacher's desk, blackboard, and student desks, provides the necessary space and equipment for a microteaching station. Special rooms or equipment may be needed for certain subject areas (e.g. physics, gymnastics). If the clinic is held in a school, it should be possible to provide appropriate teaching settings for all subject-matter areas. If videotape recordings are used, there will be additional equipment and an operator in the room. However, many videotape recorders are compact, easily manoeuvrable, and operable by non-technical staff.

There are several advantages to using videotape recordings in microteaching.

For training purposes, videotape recordings provide supervisors and trainees a common, objective frame of reference for critiquing a teacher's performance immediately after it is completed. The advantages of such attributes are pointed out by extensive psychological research on the effects of feedback, including work on knowledge of results, trial and error learning, and reinforcement. A discussion of some of this research is found in a report by McDonald and Allen (1967), on the 'Training effects of feedback and modelling procedures on teacher performance'.

For research purposes, videotape recordings provide objective data which can be stored and replayed almost indefinitely so that a data bank of teaching behaviours and situations can be accumulated. Longitudinal studies benefit especially from such data banks. The portability of the equipment allows recordings to be made in natural as well as experimental environments, and the equipment's size and ability to record under standard lighting conditions helps to obtain unobtrusive, yet valid samplings.

It is important to note that while videotape recordings are an extremely useful adjunct to the microteaching setting, they are not the essence of the concept. Their frequent use in microteaching contexts has led some to assume that there cannot be microteaching without videotape recording. Because they lack the resources to provide such technical contexts, many would-be contributers to the development of microteaching have declined to investigate its potential.

Participants

Trainees are individuals given the opportunity to become more proficient at teaching, usually with reference to a certain skill or group of skills, through a programme of focused presentation, practice and feedback. Feedback may come from pupils and supervisors in written and/or verbal form and possibly from playback of a videotape recording of the performance. The trainee is then given a chance to revise his performance strategy and to teach a second lesson, usually with a different group of students. The task of microteaching pupils, usually selected to represent a variety of socio-economic backgrounds, subject-matter interests and competencies, and age levels, is twofold: to provide realistic classroom interaction for trainees, and to help provide them with accurate information about their teaching performances.

Supervisors play a key role in microteaching, particularly in pre-service training programmes. Experienced in the skills emphasized in the training, it is their responsibility to help trainees relate such skills to both the theory underlying the skills and to the practical conditions of the classroom.

The role of supervisor is one of continuous consultation. It should be continuous so that the supervisor can help the trainee transfer the skills learned in the microteaching setting to the actual classroom. With his understanding of the trainee's teaching characteristics, the supervisor is the appropriate person to help the trainee to adapt his microteaching learning to the classroom.

Supervision should be consultative because the type of assessment a trainee receives affects the amount of freedom he feels he has to innovate in his microteaching performances; i.e. the supervisor's role is to provide information about trainees' performances which will help them to acquire the appropriate teaching skills.

The technical skills of teaching

In the initial microteaching clinic at Stanford, it was found that some sort of systematic exposure to teaching strategies was needed to help acquaint trainees with a repertoire of useful behaviours and also to help provide a focus for critiquing trainees' microteaching lessons. Instead of being limited to overall and individual impressions about teaching performances, supervisors could concentrate on helping trainees acquire strategies previously identified as helpful to teachers.[1] One such skill is that of reinforcement. As with many of the technical skills of teaching identified thus far, it is based on psychological rationale and research, in this case about the importance to learning of receiving positive feedback about one's previous actions.

A more cognitive skill is that of asking 'probing' questions. A probing question requires a pupil to go beyond his initial response to a teacher's comment or question. This usually entails some sort of clarification or elaboration upon his previous response.

It is clear from the number and diversity of these components

1. Although the technical skills are not an essential part of the microteaching process, they have become an integral component in most training involving microteaching.

that planning a microteaching programme is a demanding task administratively. Still, this is perhaps an advantage in that it forces a training programme to analyse and to evaluate the bases for, and consequences of, its plans. In this way, microteaching encourages discussion and debate about these issues, as well as providing a setting for observing and assessing the decisions made.

Research on micro-teaching programmes[2]

The majority of research to date has been concerned with assessing the effects of various elements within microteaching programmes, rather than with evaluations of microteaching as a whole. One general evaluation conducted by Allen and Fortune (1966) during the initial microteaching programme at Stanford compared the effectiveness of a twenty-five-hour-a-week student teaching programme of observation and work as an aide in a summer school with the effects of a ten-hour-a-week microteaching programme which utilized videotape recordings in supervision. Using the Stanford Appraisal Guide assessment instrument, comparison of initial and final microteaching sessions of the groups indicated that trainees with microteaching experience received significantly higher ratings for teacher effectiveness than teachers in the observation-aide programme. The study also indicated that performance in the microteaching situation was a valid prediction of subsequent classroom performance, and that 89 per cent of the trainees felt that microteaching had been a valuable experience. The appraisal guide used in this study, and in the microteaching clinic generally, is a general assessment instrument of twelve items (each with a seven point forced-choice scale) covering various aspects of a lesson such as the beginning and end of a lesson and various teaching behaviours such as reinforcement. Studies on this instrument have been made by Allen and Fortune (1966) and by Fortune, Cooper and Allen (1967). The earlier study indicated adequate reliability over the twelve items. For the second study, significant differences were found for nine of the items on comparisons between trainees' initial (diagnostic) video recorded performance and their final videotaped lesson. Further work on such rating guides led to the development of specific evaluation

2. For a bibliography of the research conducted to date on microteaching, see McKnight and Baral (1969).

forms for the various technical skills to complement the more general purpose of the Appraisal Guide.[3]

Studies on components of the microteaching process itself have concentrated on the techniques of presentation of technical skills to trainees (modelling research) and on the way in which trainees are given information about their attempts to learn and apply these and other teaching skills (research on feedback), because these two variables have been identified by many concerned with microteaching to be the most important in skills training. The research has also supplied information about the combinations of various modelling and feedback arrangements and about the role of the supervisor in such training procedures. Some of this research is described below.

Modelling

Modelling has been described (Borg, Kelley, Langer and Gall, 1970) as a two-step process where the learner first observes a model (e.g. an expert teacher) demonstrating a skill or skills and then tries to shape his own behaviours after those of the model.

Theoretical background to modelling

Theoretical rationale for using models comes from several sources. The work of Sheffield (1967) on a contiguity theory of vicarious learning supports the idea that a trainee could

acquire through the contiguous association of sensory events, perceptual and symbolic responses possessing cue properties that are capable of eliciting at some time after demonstration, overt responses corresponding to those that have been modelled (McDonald and Allen, 1967, p. 10).

A review of research on observational learning in personality development by Bandura and Walters (1963) 'has shown that complex social behaviour may be acquired almost entirely through imitation', and that 'the provision of face-to-face models accelerates the learning process . . .' (McDonald and Allen, 1967, p. 83). Work by Bandura, Ross and Ross (1963) showed that filmed

3. The General Learning Corporation has produced a series of instructional packages (films, supervisor's manuals, and teacher's manuals) which illustrate another refinement on the Appraisal Guide concept (Allen and Ryan, 1969).

models are as effective as real life models in transmitting behaviours.

Modelling has been seen to be important to teacher education because trainees are able to discern from deliberately planned models distinctive characteristics of teaching skills.

Constructed audiovisual demonstrations are assumed to be more effective than 'live' classroom observations which are usually uncontrolled in the sense that the trainee may not observe the correct behaviours or correctly interpret what he has been told to observe. Also, as McDonald and Allen point out,

the method of live observation does not provide for successive examinations of the teaching performance, nor for careful analysis of it. The same difficulties plus the effects of forgetting and selective remembering characterize the trainee's recollections of teaching performances he has observed during his own schooling. Obviously, descriptions of how to teach are fraught with all the problems of verbal description (p. 3).

Research on modelling in teacher training

In teacher training, effective modelling requires that the skills which trainees observe and imitate be described in terms of specific behaviours, that competent models be used, and that trainees have practice opportunities on which they will receive immediate feedback.

After providing for these conditions, several experiments have investigated the relative effects of these conditions on teachers' acquisition of several of the technical skills of teaching. In the modelling techniques investigated, trainees view short video-recordings of master teachers performing lessons to demonstrate various teaching strategies[4] and then practice the skill in a lesson of their own. They then view a videotape recording of the lesson with or without a supervisor to critique their attempt to emulate the skill previously modelled.

A model tape might be an outstanding lesson selected from the microteaching classes or a prepared tape planned and constructed according to specific criteria. Such tapes can be constructed to highlight positive and negative teaching behaviours by exaggeration or repetition and with the help of role playing students.

Young (1967) studied the effectiveness of self instruction using

4. Techniques of model preparation have been discussed by McDonald, Allen and Seidman (1967).

modelling and videotape feedback to train teachers in the use of lecturing skills (use of examples, etc.) and in techniques of class management. During the first phase of the study, treatment alternatives focused trainees' attentions on the skills with the use of contingent focus (comments recorded on a second sound track of the videotape parallel to the occurrence on the model tape of the behaviour to be learned) or the use of a non-contingent focus provided by a written guide. The third treatment consisted of a written explanation of the behaviour (the 'symbolic' model). Classroom control techniques were modelled on a sixteen mm. film which showed eleven problematic classroom situations, each with three alternative teacher reactions, a videotaped lesson with one alternative to each of six situations, and a symbolic model.

In the second phase of training, which took place several months later, trainees were exposed to three different modelling protocols for the lecturing skills. The 'specific illustration' model simply showed a teacher giving examples of the skills in front of the camera. The 'complete' model displayed the behaviours in a lesson context with pupils, and was presented with either a contingent or non-contingent focus. Self feedback procedures involved trainees viewing their own performance with a contingent focus (with a supervisor's critique dubbed on to the videotape) and a non-contingent focus.

Results indicated that the most effective training procedure was a combination of a 'complete' model with contingent focus, a specific illustration model, and a self viewing of performance with a contingent focus.

Koran (1968) studied the relative effects of using positive and/ or negative training models of student and/or teacher behaviours. Koran assumed that

by using student or teacher behaviours alone, or negative instances of these, a problem-solving situation is produced which broadens a trainee's perception of what the stimulus condition (teacher question) on the response condition (student answer) might be, and also suggests to him what it is not. It was predicted that this method would produce more variety in questioning behaviour (dependent variable) and responsiveness to student answers than the rather narrow range of skills which might be acquired by imitating a model (p. 500-a.).

None of the treatment groups produced significant results, although there was a tendency for training methods which used student models, alone or in combination with teacher models, to be more effective. Koran suggests that the student dimension is an important one in the use of videotape models.

Claus (1969) continued the research on modelling procedures, assessing their effect on teachers' higher order questioning behaviours. Her independent variables were the presence or absence of cueing by a supervisor of the essential characteristics of the skill during presentation of a videotaped model or during the playback of the trainee's own videotaped microteaching performance. Results showed that cued modelling procedures were more effective than non-cued modelling, and that modelling in general was significantly more effective than feedback procedures, with or without cueing, in the acquisition of a complex teaching skill.

Thus, in addition to showing the overall value of model techniques to teacher training, the studies conducted thus far have indicated that some sort of accompanying commentary (e.g. cueing and contingent focus) is a useful adjunct to the model tapes. Written commentaries are also useful but perhaps not as valuable by themselves as are the model tapes. In sum, videotape models are an efficient and effective addition to microteaching training techniques.

Feedback

Research on the feedback component of microteaching has concentrated on assessing various possible means of providing trainees with helpful information about their microteaching performances so that they can improve upon their teaching behaviours in subsequent microteaching sessions and/or actual classroom performance. The need to develop new modes of providing feedback stemmed from the inadequacy of the subjective, limited feedback possible from self or supervisory observations. 'The difficulties in this procedure are that it invites heavy reliance on private frames of reference, the communication requires a high order of psychological skill, and it stimulates defensiveness.' (McDonald and Allen, 1967, p. 1). Videotape recordings were seen as potentially viable adjuncts to supervision because of their desirable feedback properties; i.e. they reproduce the teaching performance immediately, and in a complete, objective and reliable manner.

Thus the teacher and his supervisor can view the teacher's performances as they actually happen, thereby avoiding the pitfalls of traditional supervisory sessions.

Research on feedback in teacher training

Olivero (1964) studied various methods of providing feedback in the microteaching context. There were three training variables: source of supervision (from university or school supervisors or through self analysis by the trainee); type of feedback (from supervisors who saw a videotape recording versus those who had seen the performance 'live'); and the conditions of observation (with verbal and video feedback versus verbal feedback only). Hypotheses dealt with which combination of variable would produce the greatest change in trainee behaviour as indicated by pupils using the Stanford Appraisal Guide to evaluate five-minute microteaching lessons.

Results indicated that trainees benefit more from some kind of feedback than from self analysis, that university supervisors were able to produce greater changes on selected behaviours than did school supervisors, and that video plus verbal feedback is more effective than verbal feedback alone.

Acheson (1964) compared the relative effectiveness of videotape feedback with various forms of supervisor feedback on decreasing teacher's monologues and increasing pupil participation (Borg, Kelley, Langer and Gall, 1970, p. 43). Independent variables included the presence or absence of supervisory feedback, as accompanied by videotape recorded feedback or no such feedback. Results indicated that a combination of videotape feedback with supervisory conferences produced significantly greater changes in teacher verbal behaviour than supervisory conferences without videotape feedback.

Acheson also compared the relative effects of pupil, supervisory, and videotape feedback on teaching behaviour, as measured by pupil and teacher evaluations of teaching performance before and after a six week period. During this time, each intern taught eighteen microteaching lessons. Interns who received pupil feedback made significant gains over those in the control group, and interns who received videotape as well as pupil feedback made the greatest gains of any group. Consideration of these results should take account of the fact that, unlike the treatment groups, the control group did not receive instruction related to the criterion appraisal form. It received experience in classroom observation and experience as teacher aides. Thus, the differences between the treatment and control groups could be attributed to differences in training experiences rather than to different feedback conditions.

McDonald and Allen (1967) also studied the effects of feedback procedures in two related investigations conducted in the Stanford microteaching clinic. In the first experiment, 'effects of self-feedback and reinforcement on the acquisition of a teaching skill', the objective was to 'compare the effects of self-evaluation of a teaching performance with feedback provided by a supervising instructor' (McDonald and Allen, p. 19). The dependent variable was the relative frequency with which the teacher positively reinforced pupils' participatory responses during teacher–pupil interaction in the classroom. The treatment groups received training involving either self-feedback only, reinforcement only, or reinforcement plus discrimination (where they were given cues to pupil behaviours to which reinforcements should be made). Results indicated that reinforcement plus discrimination training had the most effect on subsequent teacher performance.

The objective of the second experiment was 'to compare the effects of delay of reinforcement and the kind of reinforcement provided' (McDonald and Allen, p. 19). Trainees' use of probing questions constituted the dependent variable. Following initial written instructions about probing, treatment groups provided trainees with either immediate feedback with massed practice (three teaching and feedback sessions held together on successive days); immediate feedback with distributed practice (the next teaching session, following immediate feedback on the previous session, took place one or two weeks later); delayed feedback (one week after a performance) with distributed practice (where the feedback on, for example, performance one, was given a week later, at which time the next practice performance took place also); or reinstated feedback (supervision based on a tape recording of the performance) and distributed practice. No significant differences were found between groups, though results suggested that distributed practice and delayed feedback groups kept relatively higher probing response rates when measured on a post test seven weeks after initial training. The lack of significance between the conditions of practice is contrary to most experimental results on the spacing of practice, where distributed practice has proven superior to massed practice. Replications of this study should be made to check the validity of its findings. If valid, they suggest that training might be scheduled in a variety of ways to satisfy administrative and personnel requirements.

To summarize: the research on feedback to date indicates that videotape recordings are a valuable adjunct to supervisory critiques. Though there is evidence that, if the two procedures are compared, videotape recordings may be a more effective feedback mode in technical skills training than supervisory critiques alone, it would be dysfunctional to use such evidence as indicative of any general superiority of videotape records. The two modes are complementary, and the most effective procedure involves supervisory use of videotape recordings in the critiques. The results of the studies on feedback in microteaching do, however, suggest possible redefinitions of the supervisory role.

Relative effectiveness of modelling and feedback

In the third of McDonald and Allen's experiments, different combinations of modelling and feedback procedures were compared. Within the modelling training, data was gathered to help determine which was more efficient: *symbolic modelling* (where desired behaviours are transmitted to the learner by means of written or verbal instructions) or *perceptual modelling* (where behaviours are transmitted by means of a filmed or videotape recorded model portraying the behaviours). The study also investigated combinations of these presentation techniques with a feedback process which included reinforcement and discrimination training on relevant cues. The dependent variable was the number of probing questions initiated by the trainee. Results suggested that Perceptual and Symbolic modelling procedures proved more effective than Symbolic modelling treatments alone. Supervisory feedback, in relation to Perceptual modelling, did not lead to significantly greater increases in performance. The optimal combination was that of the combined symbolic and perceptual modelling procedures in the presentation phase plus prompting and confirmation feedback conditions.[5]

Concerning the overall results of their three studies, the authors concluded that the power of videotape recordings to recreate the original teaching experience made the feedback phase of supervision more relevant and effective. Further, and perhaps because of these same attributes, the delay of feedback did not seem to be a critical factor. Videotapes were also effective when used to present models of teaching performance. The third, and perhaps most important, aspect of the studies was the comparative effectiveness of the complementary modelling and feedback procedures. This question was seen by McDonald and Allen as having both theoretical and practical significance. Assuming that modelling variables affect acquisition of a behaviour (i.e. the attainment of a level of satisfactory performance after training) while feedback procedures affect performance (i.e. the ability to adapt a skill appropriately to various kinds of complex situations after training), assessing their relative importance would help to provide effective and efficient combinations of the procedures. If modelling techniques do assist acquisitions of a technical skill to the point where subsequent feedback can be reduced in scale and in depth, more efficient training schedules can be planned.

In an experiment in a non-microteaching context, Bandura and McDonald (1963) had previously demonstrated that modelling procedures had a significantly greater effect on behaviour than reinforcement alone. And another microteaching study by Salomon and McDonald (1969) lends further support to the comparative importance of modelling, this time from the point of view of the model's ability to provide trainees with an idea of the criterion performance required. Salomon and McDonald found that without a prior conception of criterion behaviour, the videotape playback of a lesson only gave a trainee information

5. Observations about such differences must be made cautiously because of the complexity of the variables involved in such studies. Several of these are listed by Borg, Kelley, Langer and Gall (1970) including personal characteristics (age, sex, experience, etc.), the lesson content, the attributes of the modelled skill, and the nature and quality of the videotape production. Borg feels that both symbolic and perceptual models are useful, but that perceptual models may be more motivating.

about how much his behaviour departed from his own pre-dispositions about a skill, so that subsequent performance would be unlikely to be productively changed. As indicated by the McDonald and Allen studies, when the learner knows what behaviours are expected of him, he can utilize the feedback sessions to compare his performance with the criterion by assessing the amount of departure (as perceived from the videotape playback) of his performance from the desired performance. He can then make the necessary changes. Annett (1969) would call such a process that of giving the trainee proactive feedback. Proactive feedback is seen by Annett as giving both knowledge of results about previous performance and information which will help in the choice of subsequent responses, possibly by the kind of comparison process discussed by McDonald and Allen. In microteaching, because of the reconstructive attributes of videotape used in the playback sessions, the trainee may not require extensive supervisor feedback to help him compare his performance with the possibly more appropriate behaviour demonstrated in a model tape.

Claus (1969) also found that, with Perceptual modelling, supervisory feedback did not lead to any greater increase in learning than did self view of videotapes.

Borg, after a review of the studies on these variables, concludes that it appears that if perceptual modelling and videotape feedback are present, supervisory feedback is unnecessary. This apparent ineffectiveness of the supervision in such training situations is an important finding of such studies which needs to be explored.

Redefinition of the role of the supervisor

One reason why supervision has little demonstrable effect may be that there have not been enough time and/or supervisory sessions for trainees' performances of the skills to improve past the initial level of achievement reached after modelling training. With sophisticated teaching strategies like higher order questioning or probing, more practice and feedback may be required for a trainee to adapt the skill to his own personality, subject area, teaching situation, etc. The process of refinement is unlikely to show marked behaviour change over the short run. As Allen has said, once past an initial acquisition state, the performance of a newly learned skill may show signs of regression for some time, but eventually a more competent level of performance will be reached. To test this possibility, studies of a longitudinal nature need to be performed. The post-training tests reported to date may not be a fair reflection of the importance of the supervisor, as they may have measured initial improvement only. It is possible that supervisors' talents are more appropriate for helping teachers adapt newly learned strategies to their particular subject and situation, as in the Young study. The role of the supervisor should, therefore, be studied to try to identify the unique advantages of supervisory assistance so that this scarce resource may be more effectively utilized.

Results of unpublished pilot studies at the University of Stirling suggest an additional factor which needs to be considered further. Results of these studies (on the acquisition of various technical skills) support the idea that improvement in performance is not significantly increased by the presence of a supervisor; however, the great majority of trainees expressed a strong preference for supervisory assistance. Research is needed to find if these opinions had been generalized from training on certain skills or whether trainees saw the need for supervision on all skills.

The research carried out in the microteaching context to date has shown the value of various modelling and feedback procedures which promise to increase the effectiveness of aspects of pre-service teacher training. It has also indicated the need for a redefinition of the role of the supervisor in such training programmes. Although the studies reviewed here need to be replicated, results obtained thus far about microteaching procedures have been substantial and fairly consistent. There are, however, several problematic areas of microteaching training which need to be studied.

One such consideration involves developing a framework for classifying the technical skills of teaching according to their place in the overall teaching process. Such a framework might help trainees to see the nature and importance of the technical skills more clearly, thereby making their training more effective. The framework might also make training more efficient if complementary skills could be trained for at the same time, and might provide a guide for the most efficient utilization of resources; i.e. in light of experimental research evidence to date, some technical skills such as reinforcement might not require as much time and/or supervisory assistance.

The technical skills themselves need to be validated with reference to their hypothesized effects on pupils' learning. To date, research has concentrated on finding how they can best be imparted to teachers, assuming their relevance and value in the classroom. Exploratory research is also needed on individualizing technical skills training. Finally, development of microteaching as an effective training procedure for classroom teaching would be aided by investigations of the effects of trainees' attitudes towards the technical skills approach, and by investigation of the problems encountered by teachers of different subjects and with different personal characteristics in transferring to the classroom the skills they have acquired in the microteaching context.

Research on these and other aspects of microteaching is currently being conducted at institutions such as the Universities of Stirling, Kansas, Massachusetts and Chicago, the Stanford Center for Research and Development in Teaching, and the Far West Laboratory for Educational Research and Development.

References

ACHESON, K. (1964), 'The effects of feedback from television recordings and three types of supervisory treatment on selected teacher behaviour', doctoral dissertation, Stanford University, University Microfilms, no. 64–13542.

ALLEN, D. W., and FORTUNE, J. C. (1966), 'An analysis of microteaching: new procedure in teacher education', in *Microteaching: A Description*, Stanford University.

ALLEN, D. W., and RYAN, K. A. (1969), *Microteaching*, Addison-Wesley.

ALLEN, D. W., RYAN, K. A., BUSH, R. N., and COOPER, J. M. (1969), *Teaching Skills for Elementary and Secondary School Teacher*, General Learning Corporation.

ANNETT, J. (1969), *Feedback and Human Behaviour*, Penguin.

BANDURA, A., and MCDONALD, F. J. (1963), 'The influence of social reinforcement and the behaviour of models in shaping children's moral judgements', *J. abnorm. soc. Psychol.*, vol. 67, pp. 274–81.

BANDURA, A., and WALTERS, R. H. (1963), *Social Learning and Personality Development*, Holt, Rinehart and Winston.

BANDURA, A., ROSS, D., and ROSS, S. (1963), 'Transmission of aggression through imitation of aggressive models', *J. abnorm. soc. Psychol.*, vol. 66, pp. 3–11.

Borg, W. R., Kelley, M. L., Langer, P., and Gall, M. (1970), *The Minicourse: A Microteaching Approach to Teacher Education*, Macmillan.

Claus, K. E. (1969), 'Effects of modelling and feedback variables on questioning skills', Technical Report no. 6, Stanford Center for Research and Development in Teaching.

Fortune, J. C., Cooper, J. M., and Allen, D. W. (1967), 'The Stanford summer microteaching clinic, 1965', *J. Teacher Education*, vol. 18, pp. 389–93.

Koran, J. J. (1968), 'The relative effectiveness of imitation versus problem solving in the acquisition of a complex teaching skill', doctoral dissertation, Stanford University, University Microfilms, no. 68–11314.

McKnight, P. C. and Baral, D. P., (eds) (1969), 'Microteaching and the technical skills of teaching: a bibliography of research and development at Stanford University, 1963–69', Research and Development Memorandum no. 48, Stanford Center for Research and Development in Teaching.

McDonald, F. J., Allen, D. W., and Seidman, E. (1967), 'Televised models for teacher training', Paper presented at the meeting of the American Educational Research Association, New York, February.

McDonald, F. J., and Allen, D. W. (1967), 'Training effects of feedback and modelling procedures on teacher performance', final Report of United States Office of Education Project OE–6–10–078. Stanford University, 1967. (EO 017 985). Also issued as Technical Report no. 3, Stanford Center for Research and Development in Teaching.

Olivero, J. L. (1964), 'Video recordings as a substitute for live observations in teacher education', doctoral dissertation, Stanford University, University Microfilms, no. 65–2866.

Orme, M. E. J. (1966), 'The effects of modelling and feedback variables on the acquisition of a complex teaching strategy', doctoral dissertation, Stanford University, University Microfilms, no. 67–4417. (ed. 014 441).

Salomon, G., and McDonald, F. J. (1969), 'Pre- and post-test reactions to self-viewing one's teaching performance on videotape', Research and Development Memorandum no. 44, Stanford Center for Research and Development in Teaching.

Sheffield, F. O. (1967), 'Theoretical considerations in the learning of complex sequential tasks from demonstration and practice', in A. A. Lumsdaine (ed.), *Student Response in Programmed Instruction*, Washington: National Research Council, pp. 117–40.

Ward, B. E. (1968), 'A survey of microteaching in secondary education programmes of all NCATE accredited colleges and universities', unpublished doctoral dissertation, University of South Dakota.

YOUNG, D. B. (1967), 'The effectiveness of self-instruction in teacher education using modelling and videotape feedback', doctoral dissertation, Stanford University, University Microfilms, no. 68–6518. (ed. 019 883.)

11 W. K. Hoy

The Influence of Experience on the Beginning Teacher

From W. K. Hoy, 'The influence of experience on the beginning teacher', *School Review*, vol. 76, 1968, pp. 312-23.

Since a primary task of the teacher is to define and evaluate student levels of accomplishment, some restraint upon individual student behavior is inevitable. In fact, the political organization of the school has been described as a despotic structure which emphasizes dominance of teachers and subordination of students (Waller, 1932).

The problem of pupil control is not new, nor is there any lack of opinion or prescription on the subject, but unfortunately there is little systematic study of pupil control in schools, much less study which begins from the perspective of the school as a social system. Such a view calls attention to both the structural and the normative aspects of the school. Studies which have focused upon the school as a social system have described antagonistic student subcultures and attendant conflict and control problems (see Coleman, 1932; Willower and Jones, 1967; Gordon, 1957; Waller, 1932).

Control of students – 'discipline' – is a major concern of all teachers, but it is especially acute for beginning teachers. Likewise, teaching experience has impact upon all teachers, but for new recruits, initial teaching experience may be a sudden confrontation with conflicting role demands of teaching, especially with regard to pupil control and learning goals of the school. Teachers' orientations toward pupil control may be studied in terms of behavior or in terms of ideology. The present inquiry focuses upon the relationship between teaching experience and the pupil control ideology of beginning teachers.

A conceptualization of pupil control ideology[1]

The importance and centrality of pupil control in the organizational life of the school should not be surprising, especially in light of the involuntary nature of student participation. In fact, selectivity in the relationship between the organization and the client has been used to develop a useful typology of service organizations (Carlson, 1964, pp. 262–76). Public schools fall into the same category of organizations as prisons and public mental hospitals, in that clients have no choice in their participation in the organization; and conversely, the organization has no control in the selection of clients. A word of caution seems necessary when comparing schools to prisons and public mental hospitals. Most prisons and public mental hospitals are coercive organizations, while most public schools are normative organizations (Etzioni, 1961, pp. 3–66). Further, prisons and public mental hospitals are 'total institutions' and schools are not (Goffman, 1961). Nevertheless, the similarity of the selectivity in the client–organization relationship should have important consequences for certain aspects of organizational life.

Relevant conceptualization is a necessary prerequisite for fruitful analysis and study of pupil control ideology. A classification of client control ideology employed by Gilbert and Levinson (1957, pp. 20–34) to study staff ideology in mental hospitals has been adapted for use in the study of pupil control ideology in public schools. Prototypes of custodial and humanistic orientations toward pupil control were developed, and a brief schematic formulation of each ideological orientation is presented below.

The model of the custodial orientations is the traditional school which provides a rigid and highly controlled setting concerned primarily with the maintenance of order. Students are stereotyped in terms of their appearance, behavior, and parents' social status. Teachers who hold a custodial orientation conceive of the school as an autocratic organization with a rigid pupil–teacher status hierarchy; the flow of power and communication is unilateral downward. Students must accept the decision of their teachers without question. Teachers do not attempt to understand student behavior,

1. For a more complete discussion of pupil control ideology and the development of an operational measure for pupil control ideology, see Willower, Eidell and Hoy (1967).

but instead view misbehavior as a personal affront. Students are perceived as irresponsible and undisciplined persons who must be controlled through punitive sanctions. Impersonality, pessimism, and 'watchful mistrust' pervade the atmosphere of the custodial school[2] (Powelson and Bendix, 1961, pp. 73–86).

The humanistic orientations, on the other hand, conceive of the school as an educational community in which students learn through cooperative interaction and experience. Learning and behavior are viewed in psychological and sociological terms, not moralistic terms. Self-discipline is substituted for strict teacher control. Humanistic orientations lead teachers to desire a democratic atmosphere with open channels of two-way communication between pupils and teachers and increased self-determination. In brief, a humanistic orientation is used in the socio-psychological sense suggested by Fromm (1948); it indicates an orientation which stresses the importance of the individuality of each student and the creation of an atmosphere to meet the wide range of student needs.

The teacher and organizational socialization

The particular part of the learning process which deals with the acquisition of the requisite orientations for satisfactory functioning in a role is referred to as the process of socialization (Parsons, 1951, p. 205). Socialization is an ongoing process which begins early in childhood and continues throughout life. Primary socialization, the formation of the 'basic personality structure', usually is well completed by adulthood; that is, the major value-orientation patterns of an individual are not, on a large scale, subject to drastic change in later life (Parsons, 1951, pp. 208, 236–48). However, as Etzioni (1961, p. 142) indicates, 'Learning of specific skills and role orientations continues with every change of status, in particular with membership in new social units, such as organizations.'

Organizational socialization is concerned with the processes by which requisite role orientation of offices, statuses, and positions is acquired by participants in the organization. Formal organizations

2. It is of interest to note that a genotypically similar prototype of the custodial orientation in the prison setting is given by Powelson and Bendix (1961).

are partial systems in that they do not affect all the basic needs of their members; however, few members can escape the formative influence of the values, expectations, incentives, and sanctions of the organization. Organizations mold role ideology and role performance of personnel through a variety of procedures and mechanisms designed to make individual beliefs, values, and norms correspond with those of the organization. The period before and/or shortly after new participants join an organization is highly significant in terms of socialization; it is a time 'when efforts to induce consensus between newcomers and the rest of the organization are comparatively intense' (Etzioni, 1961).

Public school teachers go through a double socialization process. Initial socialization to professional norms and values occurs during college preparation, where teaching and learning are likely to focus on ideal images and practices. The second phase of the socialization process begins as new teachers enter the 'real' teaching world as full-time members of a school organization. Here neophytes may suddenly be confronted with a set of organizational norms and values at variance with those acquired in formal preparation; that is, the internalized ideal images of the teacher role may be in conflict with the norms and values of the school subculture.

During socialization, both before and after entrance into the profession, each teacher forms his own version of the necessary orientations for effective pupil control. It appears likely that as the new, idealistic teacher comes to his first position, he will be confronted with a conflicting set of norms and values concerning the control of students. During the initial phase of the socialization of the prospective teacher, professors of education stress the desirability of permissive pupil control, while 'discipline' as it is actually practiced in the public schools emphasizes the need for more authoritarian controls (Asubel, 1961, pp. 26–8). More experienced teachers tend to oppose permissiveness and embrace a more custodial pupil control ideology than do inexperienced teachers (Willower, Eidell and Hoy, 1967 and Willower and Jones, 1967). In fact, in some schools, the ability to control is often equated with the ability to teach. Willower (Willower, Hoy and Eidell, 1967, pp. 228–34) furnishes a few illustrations of this kind of conflict experienced by newer teachers in one school:

Newer teachers reported that a major problem was to convince the older, more experienced teachers that their younger colleagues were not soft on discipline. The older teachers, dominant in the informal structure of the school, seldom hesitated to communicate their views to the younger, newer teachers whom they often thought of as being lax about maintaining sufficient social distance with regard to pupils. Teachers viewed as weak on control had marginal status among their colleagues and others. Situations of high visibility such as the assembly or school library furnished special testing grounds where teachers made valiant efforts to 'look good'. Thus, in assemblies, some of the most striking performances emanated from the audience.

The significance of the attitudes of experienced teachers for beginning teachers, during a period when the latter are especially vulnerable to formal and informal organizational demands, is succinctly described by Waller (1932, p. 389): 'The significant people for a school teacher are other teachers, and by comparison with good standing in that fraternity, the good opinion of students is a small thing and of little price. A landmark in one's assimilation to the profession is that moment when he decides that only teachers are important.'

If beginning teachers are confronted with a relatively custodial pupil control ideology on the part of experienced teachers and if these experienced teachers constitute a group of 'significant others', then it seems reasonable to predict a positive relationship between teaching experience and a change toward a more custodial pupil control ideology. More specifically, two major hypotheses guided the empirical phase of this study:

1. The pupil control ideology of beginning public school teachers will be significantly more custodial after one year of teaching.

2. The pupil control ideology of prospective teachers who do *not* teach the year after graduation will *not* be significantly more custodial after one year.

Procedures

Instrument (Willower, Eidell, Hoy, 1967) – Pupil control ideology was measured by a twenty-item instrument, the Pupil Control Ideology form (hereafter called the PCI form). Responses to each item were made on a five-point Likert-type scale and are scored from 5 ('strongly agree') to 1 ('strongly disagree'); the higher the overall score on the instrument, the more custodial the ideology of the respondent.

Examples of items used include: 'A few pupils are just young hoodlums and should be treated accordingly', 'It is often necessary to remind pupils that their status in schools differs from that of teachers', and 'Pupils can be trusted to work together without supervision' (score reversed).

Split-half reliability coefficients, in two samples, were 0.95 ($N = 170$) and 0.91 ($N = 55$) with application of the Spearman–Brown formula. Validity of the measure was supported by principals' judgments of certain of their teachers. Teachers judged to be most custodial by their principals had significantly higher ($P < 0.01$ using t-test procedures) PCI form scores than a like number of teachers judged to be most humanistic. Further evidence of the validity was established by a comparison of PCI form scores of personnel from schools known by reputation to be humanistic with scores of personnel from other schools at the same grade levels.

Subjects. Eighty-two elementary and ninety-three secondary teachers comprised the original sample of this study. These 175 subjects represented virtually the entire set of student teachers who completed their practice teaching during the 1966 spring semester at Oklahoma State University. All subjects completed the PCI form in group meetings on campus just prior to the commencement of their practice teaching. Upon the conclusion of their eight weeks of practice teaching, again on campus and in group sessions, the subjects responded to the PCI form for the second time. Approximately one year later, in the spring of 1967, the same 175 subjects were contacted by mail and asked to respond to the PCI form once again. One hundred and sixty-two of the 175 participants (92·57 per cent) returned usable PCI forms and other information concerning their present status. Of these 162 respondents, all fifty-eight elementary teachers returning usable forms were female, while forty-two of the fifty-eight (73·4 per cent) secondary teachers were female; twenty-eight out of thirty-nine (71·8 per cent) respondents who had not taught during the 1966–67 year were female, and seven female respondents were graduate assistants.

Findings

The major hypotheses of this study were confirmed by *t*-tests for the difference between means of correlated samples. The pupil-control ideology of beginning teachers was significantly more custodial after their first year of teaching. Separate tests of this hypothesis were made and confirmed on both elementary and secondary levels, since previous research had indicated that the pupil control ideology of secondary teachers was significantly more custodial than pupil control ideology of elementary teachers (Willower, Eidell and Hoy, 1967). In addition, as predicted, there was no significant custodial change in the pupil control ideology for individuals who did not teach during the first year after graduation. The results of the *t*-tests are summarized in Table 1.

It is also instructive to examine the progressive changes in pupil control ideology of subjects in the present sample as they began and completed student teaching[3] and then completed their first year of teaching. Groups of teachers at both the elementary and secondary levels showed significantly more custodial pupil control ideology after each successive period of teaching experience; however, the PCI mean scores for the group of thirty-nine teachers who did not teach the year subsequent to graduation remained virtually the same during that year, although a significant change in the custodial direction had occurred during student teaching.[4] Further-

3. Earlier research, using a larger sample of participants, indicated that a significant change in the pupil control ideology of student teachers also occurred during student teaching; student teachers were significantly more custodial in their pupil control ideology after student teaching. See Hoy (1967, pp. 153–5).

4. All elementary teachers in the present sample were female; however, there were sixteen men and forty-two women in the group of secondary teachers. A comparison of mean PCI scores indicated that both men and women become increasingly more custodial in their orientation after each successive period of experience. Their respective mean scores as they began and completed student teaching and then completed their first year of teaching were 45·024, 50·286, and 53·524 for the women and 51·313, 56·375, and 58·563 for the men. A separate analysis of male and female respondents who did not teach the year subsequent to graduation indicated similar patterns of change regardless of sex. The before student teaching, after student teaching, and after one year PCI means were 43·393, 45·643, and 45·821, respectively, for twenty-eight women respondents and 48·364, 51·545, and 50·182, respectively, for eleven men respondents.

Table 1 A comparison of the pupil control ideology of teachers before and after student teaching and after the first year of teaching

Position	N	Experience	PCI form mean score	Standard error	t
Public school teacher	116	Before student teaching	44·56	0·560	
		After student teaching	48·93	0·704	6·569*
		After first year teaching	51·48	0·766	3·783*
Elementary teacher	58	Before student teaching	42·36	0·593	
		After student teaching	45·90	0·759	4·336*
		After first year teaching	48·05	0·950	2·446*
Secondary teacher	58	Before student teaching	46·76	0·862	
		After student teaching	51·97	1·050	4·971*
		After first year teaching	54·91	1·026	2·871*
Graduate assistant	7	Before student teaching	43·86	1·471	
		After student teaching	48·00	1·363	2·008
		After first year teaching	43·14	2·283	2·303
Not teaching	39	Before student teaching	44·80	0·982	
		After student teaching	47·31	1·553	2·404*
		After first year teaching	47·05	1·278	0·270

* P < 0·01.

more, the pupil control ideology of a group of seven participants became substantially more custodial during student teaching but returned to nearly the prior level when they returned to college the following year as graduate assistants. The results of this statistical analysis are also summarized in Table 1.

Participants teaching during the 1966–7 school year were also asked to respond to several other statements concerning their preparation and teaching. In response to the statement, 'Teacher education programs tend to focus on ideal images and situations rather than the "harsh" realities of teaching', 71·14 per cent of the secondary teachers and 67·24 per cent of the elementary teachers agreed. In addition, 81·03 per cent of the secondary teachers and 84·48 per cent of the elementary teachers agreed with the statement, 'In the school in which I am teaching, good teaching and good classroom control tend to be equated.' In brief, approximately 94 per cent (109 out of 116) of all the teachers completing their first year of teaching agreed with one of the above two statements. It is also of interest to note that none of the 116 teachers planned to leave the profession permanently, although thirteen planned a temporary departure. Most teachers claimed they were relatively satisfied with teaching after one year; in fact, only thirteen teachers expressed dissatisfaction.

Discussion

Although the hypothesis that teacher socialization results in the adoption of a more custodial pupil control ideology has been tested using cross-sectional data (Willower, Eidell and Hoy, 1967), the results of this study are based on longitudinal data. The findings suggest that the pupil control ideology of beginning teachers is affected by teaching experience. The process of socialization within the school subculture seems important in reshaping the control ideology of organizational newcomers. New, idealistic teachers appear to be confronted with a relatively custodial control orientation as they become a part of the organization; in fact, the vast majority of teachers in the present study at both elementary and secondary levels described their school subculture as one in which good teaching and good discipline were equated. Again, the saliency of pupil control in public schools, organizations in which participation is mandatory and clients are unselected, is underscored. Although only seven graduates returned to college as graduate assistants, it is interesting to note an increase in the custodialism of their pupil control ideology during student teaching but a return to a relatively humanistic control ideology as they returned to the university subculture, a setting described by most respondents as one which focused on ideal images and situations rather than the 'harsh' realities of teaching. In brief, the significant increase in custodialism of first-year teachers along with a virtually constant pupil control ideology for non-teaching graduates supported the theoretical formulation from which these predictions were generated.

Student teaching is strategically located in terms of the socialization of teachers. Usually occurring at the conclusion of formal classroom education and immediately preceding the first field assignment, practice teaching provides a transitional phase in the socialization process. The student-teaching experience appears to be functional for prospective teachers in terms of mitigating the potential role strain with respect to control of students that tends to be created as they become official members of a school faculty. Recall that student teachers become significantly more custodial during practice teaching as they are confronted with the realities of teaching and the relatively custodial teacher subculture of the public schools. This kind of anticipatory socialization, that is, adopting the norms and values of the teacher subculture to which practice teachers aspire but do not fully belong, should facilitate their acceptance by teachers and make for easier adjustment to the teacher group.[5]

Since the concept of socialization refers to learning specific skills and orientations associated with various status positions, a change from teacher to principal or teacher to counselor implies further resocialization. Although the socialization of beginning teachers is stressed in the present study, the resocialization of public school professional personnel as they change status positions within public schools is an area for further research.

It seems appropriate to raise the question as to what extent the concepts of custodialism and humanism are useful in identifying different types of schools. If student control is central in the

5. For a more detailed discussion of anticipatory socialization, see Merton (1957), pp. 262–80.

organizational life of public schools and if statements concerning ideology correspond relatively well with behavior, then the pupil control ideology of a school may be an important first step in identifying the 'social climate' of the school.

The results of this study should be interpreted with some care. The entire sample of subjects completed their formal education at one university. Moreover, the proportion of female teachers in the group of teachers completing their first year of teaching was relatively high. This was in part due to the world situation; many of the young men were drafted into the armed services upon graduation. Nevertheless, all predictions were confirmed and the findings of this study complement well the results of earlier research which dealt with status relations, role, personality, and pupil control ideology of public school professional personnel (Willower, Eidell and Hoy, 1967).

References

AUSUBEL, D. P. (1961), 'New look at classroom discipline', *Phi Delta Kappa*, vol. 93, October.

CARLSON, R. O. (1964), 'Environmental constraints and organizational consequences: the public school and its clients', in E. Griffiths (ed.), *Behavioral Science and Educational Administration*, University of Chicago Press.

COLEMAN, J. S. (1961), *The Adolescent Society*, Free Press.

ETZIONI, A. (1961), *A Comparative Analysis of Complex Organization*, Free Press.

FROMM, E. (1948), *Man for Himself*, Holt, Rinehart & Winston.

GILBERT, D. C., and LEVINSON, D. V. (1957), 'Custodialism and Humanism', in M. Greenblatt (ed.), *Mental Hospital*.

GOFFMAN, E. (1961), *Asylums*, Doubleday.

GORDON, W. C. (1957), *The Social System of the High School*, Free Press.

HOY, W. K. (1967), 'Organizational socialization: the student teacher and pupil control ideology', *J. educ. Res.*, vol. 111, December.

MERTON, R. K. (1957), *Social Theory and Social Structure*, Free Press.

PARSONS, T. (1951), *The Social System*, Free Press.

POWELSON, H., and BENDIX, R. (1961), 'Psychiatry in prison', *Psychiatry*, vol. 14.

WALLER, W. (1932), *The Sociology of Teaching*, Wiley.

WILLOWER, D. J., and JONES, R. G. (1967), 'Control in an educational organization', in J. D. Raths (ed.), *Studying Teaching*, Prentice-Hall.

WILLOWER, D. J., EIDELL, T. L., and HOY, W. K. (1967), *The School and Pupil Control Ideology*, Pennsylvania State University Studies Monogr. no. 24.

WILLOWER, D. J., HOY, W. K., and EIDELL, T. L. (1967), 'The counselor and the school as a social organization', *The Personnel and Guidance Journal*, vol. 94, November.

Part Four
The Teacher's Role

Of the many studies of the norms which various groups hold for the teacher's role, two are included in this section. In both cases, the roles which teachers or student-teachers themselves conceive teachers should fulfil are compared with the norms held by others whose behaviour can directly affect the teacher's role; and in both cases, potential sources of conflict or misunderstanding are made apparent. Musgrove and Taylor review research into what pupils value in teachers and report an investigation of different weights attached by pupils and teachers to various areas of teacher behaviour. Finlayson and Cohen, in an article which could equally well have been included in the previous section, compare the conceptions of the teacher's role held by student-teachers and by headmasters.

It is not easy to isolate the effects of others' norms and expectations upon teachers' behaviour. Several studies, however, have attempted to assess the effects of different institutional contexts on teachers' role-behaviours; for example, different patterns of teacher behaviour have been demonstrated in schools designed for pupils of different assessed levels of ability, and in schools whose pupils differ in their social class backgrounds. The article by Hargreaves discusses differences in the observed behaviour of teachers dealing with different streams in a secondary school.

12 F. Musgrove and P. H. Taylor

Pupils' Expectations of Teachers

From F. Musgrove and P. H. Taylor, *Society and the Teacher's Role*, 1969, chapter 2.

Pupils expect teachers to teach. They value lucid exposition, the clear statement of problems, and guidance in their solution. Personal qualities of kindness, sympathy and patience are secondary, appreciated by pupils if they make the teacher more effective in carrying out his primary, intellectual task. At least in our day schools, there appears to be little demand by pupils that teachers shall be friends or temporary mothers and fathers. They are expected to assume an essentially intellectual and instrumental role.

This appears to be broadly true for all stages of education from the infants' school to the university. Enquiries carried out in England and America over half a century have pointed to this conclusion. At the end of the nineteenth century Kratz (1896) reported an investigation which showed that schoolchildren demanded first and foremost of their teachers 'help in study'. In the 1930s Hollis conducted research with over 8,000 children of different ages in both mixed and single-sex schools: the characteristic of teachers which they valued most highly was the ability to explain difficulties patiently. Other teacher characteristics in descending order of importance were: sympathy; fairness; humour; readiness to accept children's questions; wide interests; firm discipline (Hollis, 1935).

In a study of the expectations of the older adolescent pupil in America, Michael found that the teacher's method of teaching was judged to be his most important attribute. Of less importance were the teacher's 'personality' and his mode of enforcing discipline (Michael *et al.*, 1951). These findings are in line with research carried out by Allen in English secondary modern schools. Both boys and girls were found to value most highly the teacher's competence as an instructor, his pedagogical skills. But they also wanted their teachers to make lessons interesting, to take a joke, and to be friendly and approachable (Allen, 1959).

Comparatively little work has been done on the expectations of university students, but one study of English science undergraduates indicates that they demand first and foremost of a lecturer that he 'presents his material clearly and logically'. The students who took part in this inquiry rated forty lecturer characteristics. At the top of the list were: 'Enables the student to understand the basic principles of the subject' and 'Makes his material intelligibly meaningful'. Far less weight was attached to a lecturer's more 'human' characteristics: 'Has a sympathetic attitude towards students' came thirty-second in order of importance, 'Is spontaneous and friendly' came thirty-fourth, and 'Appears to enjoy teaching' came thirty-sixth (Cooper and Foy, 1967).

More indirect approaches to the study of pupils' expectations have produced similar results. American high school pupils have been asked to say which of their classes they have found especially good, satisfying and worthwhile, and then to describe what went on in these classes, what they got out of them, and what they found enjoyable. First in importance was subject matter, second the type of classroom activity that the lesson required, and third the teacher's pedagogical ability. Far less weight was attached to the teacher's personal and social qualities: only 9 per cent of the pupils' responses referred to these, while 27 per cent referred to subject matter. 'Evidently, high school juniors do attribute their plus and minus experiences to more than the personal and social variables of their teachers' (Gump, 1964).

There is little evidence that pupils are expecting their teachers to take on a less specialized role with reduced emphasis on pedagogical functions. Home rather than school is still the main source of expressive, emotional satisfactions. The school and its teachers are expected to meet instrumental (mainly intellectual) needs. A study of adolescents' demands of home and school in England has shown this sharp contrast in expectations. When young people between fourteen and eighteen years of age were asked what they expected of their homes, 77 per cent of their statements referred to 'expressive' needs: feeling wanted, secure, appreciated, and the like. Approximately 50 per cent of the statements about school were in expressive terms. Thirteen categories of demand were distinguished (six 'instrumental' and seven 'expressive'). By far the greatest demand of school fell in the 'intellectual' category. Approximately a quarter of all the statements about school referred to the need for intellectual activity and achievement (Musgrove, 1966, parts 1 and 2).

Teachers are often conceived as models for the young, sources of values, attitudes, styles of behaviour, as well as intellectual stimulus and enlightenment. The studies we have of this modelling process do not testify to its effectiveness. Inquiries into the nature and source of the socio-moral values of sixteen-year-old boys and girls in 'Prairie City' revealed parents rather than teachers as the moulders of the character of the young. Indeed, teachers appeared to have a negligible influence. The report on this study concludes:

Another clear implication is that parents cannot reasonably expect to turn over very much of the character training of their children to other people, whether in school, church, or youth organizations. By the very nature of character formation, no one other than parents can ordinarily have one-tenth of their influence; and if the parents are continually re-inforcing their own influence by their day-to-day treatment of the child, other adults can have little expectation of outweighing the parents' influence. Dramatic exceptions to this rule are known, to be sure; but they are dramatic precisely because they are so rare and so hard to achieve. No such exceptions occurred in the Prairie City group, during the study (Peck and Havighurst, 1960, p. 190).

When the teacher is taken as a model of social attitudes and behaviour, this may be because he is failing to communicate knowledge and promote understanding. Modelling may, in fact, be a retreat from skill acquisition to style acquisition. The more peripheral and irrelevant qualities of the teacher may be seized upon precisely because the intellectual content of his work is difficult to grasp (see Adelson, 1962).

The process of modelling is often discussed in terms of 'identification'. An attempt to discover the extent to which English secondary school children 'identify' with their teachers has led to the same conclusion as the American 'Prairie City' inquiry. Wright investigated the self concepts and the perceptions of parents and teachers among 105 last-year secondary modern school boys and girls. He concluded that 'in their last year at school, secondary modern pupils are a good deal less identified with their teachers than with their parents'. Pupils value their teachers mainly for their intellectual abilities; they are little concerned with their more general, human qualities: 'In so far as the pupils do identify with teachers, it is restricted to those aspects of personality which relate to academic achievement. They admire teachers for their cleverness and knowledge. But they do not seem to value them highly as persons' (Wright, 1962).

Like the report on Prairie City's adolescents, Wright emphasizes the influence of parents rather than teachers: 'It is of interest to note that the opinion sometimes expressed that adolescents are, in general, rejecting parental influence, receives no confirmation here.' Wright is sceptical about the efficiency of the wider, less specialized role that is today ascribed to teachers. He points out that 'there has been a tendency in recent years to place increasing responsibility on the teacher for such things as mental health, attitudes, values and social awareness of adolescents'. There are no indications that pupils expect these services from their teachers or that when they are rendered they have much effect.

In order to explore further pupils' expectations of teachers in the classroom situation, one of the authors conducted an inquiry with some nine hundred children in junior, secondary modern and grammar schools (Taylor, 1962, part. 3). The purpose of the investigation was to see whether children of different ages, in different types of school, and in schools differently organized, had different expectations of teachers' behaviour. The views of 131 teachers and of 43 college of education students were also obtained on the relative importance of different aspects of the teacher's task.

The nature of the inquiry

Eight hundred and sixty-six children in twelve junior schools, 401 in four secondary modern schools, and 112 children in one grammar school were asked to write two short essays on 'A good teacher' and 'A poor teacher'. Between twenty and thirty minutes were allowed for both essays.

The 1379 essays were analysed for content by twenty-one teachers. Each teacher analysed a separate batch of essays. Every independent statement made about 'good' and 'poor' teachers was then assigned to one of four categories considered to be descriptive of mutually exclusive areas of a teacher's classroom behaviour. The four categories were: Teacher (T), Discipline (D), Personal Qualities (P), and Organization (O). The meaning to be attached to these categories was clarified in a general discussion with the twenty-one teachers after a sample of the essays had been read. In the later stages of the inquiry use was made only of the analysis of essays about a 'good' teacher.

The 5664 statements about a good teacher which had been collected and sorted were used to construct five scales and a check-list of twenty words and phrases. The first scale (A) consisted of six statements: the two most frequently used by children to describe a good teacher's teaching, the two most frequently used to describe his methods of discipline, and the two most frequently used to describe his personal qualities. These six statements were presented in random order for pupils to rank in order of importance. (The items in the scales were not numbered and no headings were given to the scales.)

Scale A
Teaching, Discipline and Personality
1. A good teacher is fair and just about punishment and has no favourites.
2. A good teacher explains the work you have to do and helps you with it.
3. A good teacher is patient, understanding, kind, and sympathetic.
4. A good teacher is cheerful, friendly, good-tempered, and has a sense of humour.
5. A good teacher is firm and keeps order in the classroom.
6. A good teacher encourages you to work hard at your school work.

The second scale (B) consisted of the six statements which most often occurred in the children's essays to describe a good teacher's manner and method of maintaining discipline.

Scale B
Manner and Method of Discipline
1. A good teacher is firm and keeps order in the classroom.
2. A good teacher is fair and just about punishment.

3. A good teacher praises you for behaving well and working hard.
4. A good teacher has no favourites.
5. A good teacher lets you have some of your own way.
6. A good teacher uses the cane or strap when necessary.

Again the scale was to be used without a heading for pupils to rank the items in order of importance.

The third scale (C) consisted of the six statements most frequently used to describe a good teacher's manner and method of teaching.

Scale C
Manner and Method of Teaching
1. A good teacher encourages you to work hard at school.
2. A good teacher explains the work you have to do and helps you with it.
3. A good teacher knows a great deal about the subject he is teaching.
4. A good teacher gives interesting lessons.
5. A good teacher gives you time in the lesson to finish your work.
6. A good teacher marks your work regularly and fairly.

The fourth scale (D) was constructed in a similar manner from statements about a good teacher's personal qualities.

Scale D
Teachers' Personal Qualities
1. A good teacher is cheerful and good-tempered.
2. A good teacher looks nice and dresses well.
3. A good teacher is well-mannered and polite.
4. A good teacher is patient, understanding, kind, and sympathetic.
5. A good teacher has a sense of humour.
6. A good teacher is friendly with children in and out of school.

The last scale (E) related to a good teacher's organizing abilities.

Scale E
Teachers' Organizing Abilities
1. A good teacher makes certain that the classroom is tidy and attractive.

2. A good teacher has work ready for you as soon as you get into the classroom.
3. A good teacher makes sure you have the pens, paper and books you need.
4. A good teacher lets children help to give out books, pencils and paper.
5. A good teacher knows where to find the things he wants.
6. A good teacher is able to organize all kinds of activities in the classroom.

The check-list consisted of twenty words and phrases which children had used in their essays to describe a 'good' teacher, e.g. 'young', 'has children of his own', 'is like my mother', 'joins in'. The check-list carried the instruction to tick only the words or phrases which describe a good teacher.

The five scales and the checklist were administered in booklet form to 897 schoolchildren: 500 in the fourth year of the junior school, 230 in the second and 167 in the fourth year of the secondary school. Fourteen junior schools, six secondary schools and two grammar schools took part in the inquiry. The schools were in urban and rural areas, and all came under the same local education authority which organizes its schools in the conventional manner and uses orthodox eleven-plus selection procedures.

Scale A was also completed by 131 teachers and forty-three first-year students in a mixed college of education. Seventy-seven of the teachers were men, fifty-four women; 105 were nongraduates, twenty-six were graduates. Seventy of the teachers taught in junior schools, sixty-one in secondary schools.

Results of the inquiry

The 897 schoolchildren showed the importance they attached to the three aspects of a teacher's behaviour (T, D and P) by ranking the statements on Scale A. In the analysis of results, the rankings were inverted, so that the highest score (6) was given to an item ranked first, and the lowest score (1) to an item ranked sixth. The rankings (thus inverted) for each pair of items representing the three areas of the teacher's behaviour were added together. In this manner the weight attached to each pair of items was obtained.

The following table shows the weight attached by the school-children to the three areas of behaviour.

Table 1 Weight attached by children to three areas of teacher behaviour (sum of ranks)

Scale A items	Area		4year J.	Children 2year S.	4year S.
$b+f$	Teaching	(T)	4187	1929	1385
$a+e$	Discipline	(D)	3701	1624	1134
$c+d$	Personality	(P)	2612	1277	988
		N	500	230	167
Percentage		T	39·9	39·9	39·5
Distribution		D	35·2	33·6	32·3
		P	24·9	26·4	28·2
Value of X^2				5·6	2·6
and				N.S.	N.S.
Level of P				17·7	
				***	

All children gave most weight to the good teacher's teaching, least weight to his personal qualities. The only differences among the children were that junior schoolchildren placed more emphasis than secondary schoolchildren on the good teacher's discipline; and secondary schoolchildren placed more weight than juniors on the good teacher's personal qualities, particularly on his being cheerful, good-tempered, and having a sense of humour. Roughly 40 per cent of the 'weight' was given to 'teaching', a third to 'discipline', and a quarter to 'personality'.

The formal organization of the school appeared to influence children's notions of a good teacher. Children in unstreamed junior schools were significantly more concerned with the good teacher's personal qualities, and those in streamed schools were more concerned with his discipline. It is possible that in the relatively informal situation of the unstreamed class, in which the needs of children differing widely in ability must be met, the personal qualities of the teacher are of especial importance.

There was a striking contrast between the children's view of a good teacher and the teacher's view. Whereas the children emphasized 'teaching', the teachers emphasized 'personality'. The graduate teachers gave greater emphasis to teaching, but the college of education students gave even greater emphasis to 'personality' than the nongraduate teachers. The following table shows the weight given by the different groups of teachers and by the college students to the three areas of teacher behaviour.

Table 2 Weight attached by teachers to three areas of teacher behaviour (sum of ranks)

Scale A items	Area	Jun.	Sec.	Teachers Men	Women	N'Grd.	Grad.	Students Jun.	Sec.
b+f	T	457	390	502	345	658	189	127	130
a+e	D	442	397	479	360	667	172	93	172
c+d	P	571	494	636	429	880	185	179	202
	N	70	61	77	54	105	26	19	24
Percentage	T	31·1	30·3	31·1	30·4	29·8	34·6	31·8	25·8
Distribution	D	30·1	31·1	29·6	31·8	30·3	31·5	23·3	34·1
	P	38·8	38·6	39·3	37·8	39·9	33·9	44·9	40·1
Value of X^2 and level of P		2·0 N.S.		1·5 N.S.		7·6 *		12·9 †	

Men and women teachers did not differ significantly in their emphasis, nor did teachers in primary and secondary schools. There were no differences among teachers according to the length of their teacher experience.

The small sample of students from a college of education took up a more exaggerated position than practising teachers. They placed the greatest emphasis on a good teacher's personal qualities. The group training to become junior school teachers placed least weight on 'discipline', those training to become secondary teachers placed least weight on 'teaching'.

In analysing the remaining four scales, the weight attached by the different groups of children to the scale items was obtained by summing their rankings. From these 'weights' a rank order of the items in each of the scales was obtained for the various pupil groups. The extent to which one group of children agreed with another in the value they attached to the items in a scale was calculated by using Spearman's rank correlation coefficient (*rho*).

There was a high level of agreement among all the children in their rankings of the items in Scale B (manner and method of discipline). All children ranked first either item (1) 'A good teacher is firm', or item (2) 'A good teacher is just and fair about punishment'. They ranked sixth item (5) 'A good teacher lets you have some of your own way'.

There were some differences in emphasis among girls at different stages of education. Fourth-year secondary school girls differed from younger girls in placing weight on the good teacher's having no favourites (ranked first) rather than on being firm (ranked third). The converse was true for younger girls.

In ranking the items on Scale C (manner and method of teaching) secondary schoolchildren were in close agreement, but differed markedly from junior children. The latter ranked first item (1), the good teacher encouraging them to work hard, while secondary schoolchildren ranked this item third or fourth. Secondary schoolchildren placed greatest weight on the teacher explaining work. All children ranked item (3), the good teacher knowing his subject, second. They ranked sixth item (5), the timing of the lesson.

Fourth-year secondary schoolchildren differed from all the rest in ranking the statements on Scale D (Teachers' Personal Qualities). All children agreed in ranking item (2), the good teacher's appearance, as least in importance, and in placing item (6), the good teacher being friendly, first or second. The main difference was in the emphasis fourth-year secondary children placed on the good teacher being cheerful and good tempered. This item was ranked second by fourth-year secondary children, but only fourth by younger children. Junior school girls placed particular emphasis on the manners and politeness of the good teacher, placing this item first.

Scale E (teachers' organizing abilities) was analysed for junior schoolchildren only. Boys and girls were in close agreement in their rankings ($r_s = 0.99$ $P < 0.01$). They both ranked first the good teacher's making sure they had material to work with, and last his willingness to let pupils give out books, pencils and paper.

The items in the checklist which were ticked by more than 50 per cent of at least one group of children were: 'young', 'married', 'has own children', 'man', 'joins in', 'doesn't use the cane', and 'gives little homework'. Only one item, 'joins in', was checked by 50 per cent or more of the children in all the groups. Items checked by fewer than 15 per cent of the children in each of the groups were: 'old', 'women', 'is like my father', 'is like my mother', 'fat', and 'doesn't join in'. This suggests that children's stereotype of the good teacher is a young, married man with children who gives little homework and no corporal punishment. They may reject as 'good' teachers women, elderly teachers, and those inclined to behave towards them as their parents might.

This inquiry highlights the discrepancy between children's notions of a good teacher, and teachers' notions of a good teacher. Particularly if they were nongraduates, teachers placed great emphasis on the personal qualities of a good teacher; children at all stages placed emphasis on his teaching skills. The need which pupils want teachers to satisfy is above all the need to be taught and to learn.

The contemporary emphasis on 'good personal relationships' in teaching, and on close and sympathetic contact with children, may actually interfere with the teacher's performance of his task as an instructor. In his classic, *The Sociology of Teaching* (1932), Waller maintained that the effective teacher should maintain a marked social distance from his pupils, that he must be 'relatively meaningless as a person'.

Waller's dictum doubtless requires some modification. Yet there is probably a 'curvilinear' relationship between teachers' friendliness to pupils and their effectiveness. When 'expressive' relationships are emphasized unduly, whether in a school or factory, 'instrumental' relationships may be impaired. Insistence on getting the job done might put at risk the friendliness between subordinates and those in authority. Too little friendliness between teachers and taught may well provoke resistances to learning; too much concern with friendliness may mean that more difficult tasks are never seriously attempted.

References

ADELSON, J. (1962), 'The teacher as model', in N. Sandford (ed.), *The American College*, Wiley.

ALLEN, E. A. (1959), 'Attitudes to school and teachers in a Secondary Modern school', unpublished M.A. thesis, University of London.

COOPER, B., and FOY, M. (1967), 'Evaluating the effectiveness of lecturers', *Universities Quarterly*, no. 1, p. 21.

GUMP, P. V. (1964), 'Environmental guidance of the classroom behavioral system', in B. J. Biddle and W. J. Ellena (eds.), *Contemporary Research on Teacher Effectiveness*, Holt, Rinehart and Winston.

HOLLIS, A. W. (1935), 'The personal relationship in teaching', unpublished M.A. thesis, University of Birmingham.

KRATZ, H. E. (1896), 'Characteristics of the teacher as recognized by children', *Pedagogic Seminar*, 3.

MICHAEL, L. B., *et al.*, (1951), 'Survey of student–teacher relationships', *J. educ. Res.*, vol. 44.

MUSGROVE, F. (1966), 'The social needs and satisfactions of some young people', *Brit. J. educ. Psychol.*, vol. 36.

PECK, R. F., and HAVINGHURST, R. J. (1960), *The Psychology of Character Development*, Wiley.

TAYLOR, P. H. (1962), 'Children's evaluation of the characteristics of the good teacher', *Brit. J. educ. Psychol.*, vol. 52.

WALLER, W. (1932), *The Sociology of Teaching*, Wiley.

WRIGHT, D. S. (1962), 'A comparative study of the adolescent's concepts of his parents and teachers', *Educ. Rev.*, vol. 14.

13 D. S. Finlayson and L. Cohen

The Teacher's Role: A Comparative Study of the
Conceptions of College of Education Students and
Head Teachers

From D. S. Finlayson and L. Cohen, 'The teacher's role: a comparative
study of the conceptions of college of education students and head teachers',
British Journal of Educational Psychology, vol. 37, 1967, pp. 22-31.

Research procedure

The few empirical studies which have been done in this country
of the role of the teacher (Musgrove, 1961, pp. 167–80; Taylor,
1962, pp. 258–66; Musgrove and Taylor, 1965, pp. 171–8) have
assessed the values which teachers might be expected to have in
relation to educational aims. This study utilized expectations of
their actual behaviour in school situations. The aim was to examine the changes which took place in student teachers' conceptions of the teacher's role as they progressed through their course
of professional training, and to compare the expectations of the
student teachers with those of head teachers.

A role is defined by Gross, Mason and McEachern (1958) as a
set of expectations applied to an incumbent of a position in a social
system. In this study such expectations were measured by a role
definition instrument (RDI)[1] which contained a number of statements about teacher behaviour derived from the literature and
students' essays. To reduce response set, desirable and undesirable
statements were used. The statements related to four role sectors
discussed by Fleming (1958) which were judged suitable for initial
exploration:

Organization. These items included expectations about the way
children were grouped in the school, and about the clerical and
supervisory duties of the teacher.

General Aims. These items included expectations for the teacher's
work in such areas as teaching the three Rs, inculcating attitudes

1. A copy of the RDI, with the items categorized into these sectors, is
given in the appendix.

and values, and helping children to acquire good manners and correct speech. Controversial curriculum content areas such as sex instruction and religious education, were also included in this sector.

Motivation. These items included expectations for teacher behaviour as the motivator of children's learning, e.g. by comparing the work of different children in the class. The extent of belief in the 'discipline' of uninteresting work was also assessed.

Classroom behaviour. These items included expectations about the teacher's personal relationships with the children, his approach to individual children, the kind of social climate he sought to establish, and the mode of leadership that he favoured.

Respondents were required to indicate for each item which of five modes of response best expressed their own expectations about that particular item, viz., that the teacher absolutely must, preferably should, may or may not, preferably should not or absolutely must not behave in this way. These response categories were weighted with scores from 1 to 5.

The RDI was submitted to the entire student population (268 females) of a college of education. It was also given to a sample of 183 head teachers, made up of almost equal numbers from primary and secondary schools. The primary head teachers were selected from school lists of five divisions of one county authority, and three county boroughs. The secondary head teachers were selected from the school lists of one county authority, from four county boroughs and two excepted districts. Sixty-one per cent of the primary, and 55 per cent of the secondary head teachers returned completed schedules.

Statement of results
Differences between types of students

Initially, the mean scores of students preparing to teach infant children were compared with those of students training to teach junior and secondary children. Of all the items on the RDI, the *t*-test showed significant differences above the 5 per cent level on only four. These were concerned with classroom management. The students training to teach older children showed more authoritarian attitudes. They stressed the need for children to acquire better manners and correct speech, favoured more punitive methods of control, and expected to maintain a more distant and formal relationship with their pupils than did the teachers of infant children.

Differences between year-groups

The responses to each of the items by the three year-groups of students were treated by analysis of variance. Table 1 shows the means of each of the three groups on the items grouped according to role sectors. F ratios have been calculated only where the mean sum of squares between groups is larger than the mean sum of squares within groups, and only for those items which produced significant F ratios are the differences between the means shown. Where the subsequent application of the t test showed these not to be significant this is indicated.

Of the items in the organizational category, only in relation to the peripheral duties expected of teachers such as the collection of savings and the supervision of school meals is any significant change noted. There is an increasing trend to reject these expectations as teacher functions as the students progress through college. There is, too, a growing opposition to the notion that children should be grouped by academic attainment, but the differences do not reach the 0·05 level of significance.

Of the items dealing with the general aims of education, again only one item shows differences large enough to be significant. This is the item dealing with the relative importance of the basic subjects. As the students progress through college, they tend to regard these as increasingly important. Another item which just fails to reach the level of significance is that dealing with the acquisition of correct speech and manners, where the second-year students appear less mandatory in their expectations than either the first or third year students.

Neither of the items dealing with the motivation of children shows any significant changes throughout the course of training.

Of particular interest are the items dealing with classroom behaviour. In this section eight out of the twelve items showed differences large enough to be significant, half of them at the 1 per cent level. Not only are there more items recording significant

Table 1 Item means, F ratios and differences between student year groups

Item no.	1st year mean ($\overline{X}_1$)	2nd year mean ($\overline{X}_2$)	3rd year mean ($\overline{X}_3$)	F Ratio	Difference between means $\overline{X}_1 - \overline{X}_3$	$\overline{X}_2 - \overline{X}_3$	$\overline{X}_1 - \overline{X}_3$
1	3·206	3·413	3·651	5·683†	−0·207	−0·238	−0·445
2	3·686	3·835	4·000	1·365			
3	1·618	1·450	1·512	<1			
4	1·324	1·525	1·407	2·911			
5	2·824	2·875	2·756	<1			
6	3·265	3·125	2·721	4·149*	0·140 NS	0·404	0·544
7	1·490	1·438	1·628	1·495			
8	2·382	2·325	2·233	<1			
9	2·693	2·788	2·894	<1			
10	3·832	4·013	3·953	<1			
11	2·382	2·588	2·186	3·250*	−0·206	0·402	0·196
12	3·725	4·063	3·826	1·632			
13	2·775	3·538	2·872	13·549†	−0·763	0·666	−0·097 NS
14	2·970	3·487	2·907	4·945†	−0·517	0·580	0·603 NS
15	1·765	2·544	1·942	11·426†	−0·779	0·602	−0·177 NS
16	2·363	2·400	2·291	<1			
17	2·275	1·913	2·023	4·571*	0·362	−0·110 NS	0·252
18	2·455	2·650	2·776	1·434			
19	1·647	1·575	1·477	1·544			
20	2·470	2·975	2·791	3·932*	−0·505	−0·184 NS	−0·321
21	2·931	3·713	3·209	9·258†	−0·782	0·504	−0·278
22	3·343	2·963	3·198	4·088*	0·380	−0·235	0·415 NS

* Significant at the 5 per cent level.
† Significant at the 1 per cent level.

changes, but also these changes conform to a consistent pattern. A study of the group means suggests that, in the second year, the students hold beliefs that indicate less authoritarian views about the pupil–teacher relationship and give stronger support to practices promoting the mental and emotional health of their pupils, than either first or third-year students. The items which significantly demonstrate this attitude of growing liberality which then gives way to more traditional views are those in which the second-year students see themselves as:

1. Less of a judge of right and wrong for the children.
2. Less punitive towards the aggressive child.
3. More consistent in their classroom behaviour.
4. More approachable.

5. More prepared to allow children to learn from their own experience.
6. Less concerned with immediate obedience.
7. More prepared to create warm, harmonious relationships in the classroom.

Item 12 shows the same trend towards a peak of permissiveness in the second year, but the differences do not reach the level of significance. Amongst the remaining three items in this category, item 16 shows scarcely any differences at all between years, and both items 18 and 19, although not sufficient to be significant, show a growing acceptance throughout the three years of a supportive role for the teacher, in which she sees herself more as a confidante and more prepared to show affection towards children in her class. Both of these items, however, deal with relationships with individual children rather than with the class *en masse*.

Students and head teachers

A comparison of the mean responses of students, the three year-groups being taken together, with those of the head teacher sample was now carried out and the results are shown in Table 2.

As the mean responses of the primary and secondary head teachers were very similar, they have been combined for purposes of comparison with the students. The *t*-test showed that 82 per cent of the differences between head teachers and students were significant.

Each of the three organizational items showed a significant difference, the head teachers being much more in favour of teachers performing peripheral duties, more in favour of grouping children by academic attainment and less in favour of the teacher having access to children's records.

In the general aims category, the only item on which the head teachers and students showed a similar level of agreement was that concerned with helping children to acquire attitudes and values not fostered in their homes. On all the other items in this category, highly significant differences are shown. The head teachers are, on the one hand, more in favour of teachers giving religious education and, on the other, less in favour of their giving sex instruction than the students. In relation to manners, dress and speech, the head teachers hold more mandatory views than the

Table 2 Item means, variances and differences between student and head teacher groups

Item no.	Students		Head teachers		Difference between means	Level of significance
	$\bar{X}$	a^2	$\bar{X}$	a^2		
1	3·410	0·839	2·697	1 375	0·713	0·001
2	3·831	0·957	3·038	1·070	0·793	0·001
3	1·534	0·682	1·764	0·793	−0·230	0·01
4	1·411	0·317	1·094	0·114	0·317	0·001
5	2·817	0·993	2·175	0·590	0·642	0·001
6	3·049	0·1777	2·551	1·672	0·498	0·001
7	1·519	0·585	1·458	0·399	0·061	NS
8	2·317	0·784	3·535	0·939	1·218	0·001
9	2·786	1·580	2·112	0·769	0·674	0·001
10	3·925	1·197	3·406	0·996	0·519	0·001
11	2·381	1·042	1·425	0·518	0·956	0·001
12	3·858	1·603	3·324	1·958	0·534	0·001
13	3·034	1·495	2·077	1·028	0·957	0·001
14	3·102	1·722	2·980	1·583	0·112	NS
15	2·052	1·346	1·863	0·763	0·189	0·05
16	2·351	0·675	2·953	0·760	−0·602	0·001
17	2·086	0·713	2·762	1·029	−0·676	0·001
18	2·617	1·703	2·639	1·702	−0·022	NS
19	1·571	0·439	2·287	0·903	−0·716	0·001
20	2·726	1·537	1·894	0·998	0·832	0·001
21	3·254	1·577	3·068	1·358	0·186	NS
22	3·183	0·817	3·024	0·594	0·159	0·05

students and also give greater importance to the teaching of the three Rs.

Both the motivational items show highly significant differences, the head teachers believing more in the alleged discipline of uninteresting work and being less opposed to the comparison of one child's work with another.

In the behaviour item comparisons, those which did not reach the 0·05 level of significance related to expectations about a consistent classroom discipline, the showing of affection to children, and the giving of praise. On all the other items, significant differences are demonstrated. Head teachers are much more strongly in favour of teachers interpreting right and wrong for the child, using punishment, being stricter in their discipline, and insisting on immediate conformity from children than are the students. On the other hand, they are more inclined to reject activities in which children formulate their own rules of behaviour, opportunities for children to learn from their own experiences and for them to discuss their personal difficulties with teachers. In all of these items, the head teachers' greater concern for good order and discipline and outward conformity is clearly manifested.

The disparity which has been demonstrated between the role conceptions for the teacher held by the students and the head teachers is extremely widespread. It exists in all four role sectors, and to some extent, is a measure of possible conflict for these students as they move into the schools as teachers.

In an endeavour to clarify those areas in which conflict is most likely between students and head teachers, the items were listed in rank order of mean score for each group separately and grouped according to whether the mean responses placed them in the 'agree' category, the 'uncertain' category or the 'disagree' category. By comparing the groupings of head teachers and students separately, it is possible to pick out those items which the two groups place in different categories. These items are listed in Table 3 below.

Table 3 **Grouping of items according to responses of head teachers and students**

	Agree	Uncertain	Disagree
Head teachers	9, 13, 5, 20	16, 17, 12, 2	8
Students	16, 17, 8	9, 13, 5, 20	12, 2, 10

As will be seen, these items represent all the four role sectors but two general types of items can be distinguished. There are the items having motivational implications and those which involve considerations of authority, discipline and value judgement. In the motivational group of items, the head teachers are uncertain about placing slow learners with slow learners and about comparing one child's work with that of another child, whereas the students disagree with these statements. In the set of items concerned with the use of authority the students are uncertain about the discipline of uninteresting work, the punishment of aggressive children, the teaching of religious education, and seeking to get children to unquestioningly obey orders whereas the head teachers agree that these things should be done by a teacher. The head teachers are uncertain about caning, about the formation of class councils and allowing children to act upon what teachers consider to be wrong decisions, whereas the students reject caning, and are positively orientated towards class councils and allowing children the opportunity to learn from their own mistakes. The item involving sex instruction is particularly conflicting, the students feel that the teacher should do this, the heads do not.

An interesting point can be made about the relative importance of educational aims held by teachers. The only item which students regarded as mandatory related to helping children to acquire correct manners and speech. The head teachers also placed this item first in their responses. Along with it in the mandatory category was their view that teachers should help children acquire attitudes and values not fostered in their own homes and this item came second in the students' rank order. Thus, both groups regard the function of social training very highly indeed. In fact, they regard it as more important than giving first priority to teaching the three Rs. This finding is in contrast to that of Musgrove and Taylor (1965) and the explanation may well lie in the differences in the samples, or, more likely, in the way in which the general aims were presented for evaluation. In Musgrove and Taylor's study the teachers were required to rank the general aims in order of importance, whereas in this study, specific behavioural descriptions tend to be used. In this way, our results probably convey the popular notion that, until a class accepts a certain measure of social conformity, no formal instruction is possible.

The variance of the responses from any group is an indication of the consensus amongst the individuals. The two items on which the two groups were in greatest agreement amongst themselves were those just discussed, relating to social training. To study consensus further, the items were arranged in rank order, according to variance, each group being treated separately. A median split in the rank order of both groups was made to distinguish low from high variance items. The items which had low variance in both groups were those statements which contained general aims or dealt with organizational matters. Thus, there was greatest consensus amongst the groups about the extent to which teachers should encourage children to acquire good manners, correct speech, and appropriate attitudes and values, teach religious knowledge, group friends, allow the formation of a class council, have access to record cards, and give sex instruction. There was also high consensus about the pupil–teacher relationships which would encourage child confidences. The items for which both groups had high variances were generally those dealing with face-to-face classroom situations, such as comparing the work of children, obedience, punishment, the use of praise, consistent classroom behaviour, the showing of affection, and the priority to be given to the teaching of the three Rs, which presumably would depend on a number of factors in any particular class.

Discussions and conclusions

When a student begins a three-year course of teacher-training, it might be hoped that this would be the start of a growth process in which the student becomes increasingly aware of all the aspects of the teacher's role and makes these expectations part of his own conception of teacher behaviour. The data discussed in this paper suggest that no matter how gratifying such a view might be to those engaged in teacher training, it is not tenable on several grounds:

1. Firstly, when one looks at the table of differences between the first- and third-year groups of students what stands out is not the number of differences but the number of similarities in mean responses of the first and third years. In 72 per cent of the items there are no significant differences. In the six items in which there are differences, one is an increasing resistance to peripheral duties which, presumably, is not the result of college influence, and another is an increasing tendency to give the three Rs a higher priority. There are, too, some surprising absences of changes. For example, there is no relinquishing of the faith in the discipline of performing uninteresting tasks, no increasing awareness of the need to maintain a consistent pattern of classroom behaviour, and no reduction in the comparison of work belonging to children. One would have expected that students would have become increasingly aware of motivational considerations and of the necessity of classroom consistency during their training and that

this awareness would have produced some changes of expectancy. Thus, the general impression that one takes away from this first- and third-year comparison is the relative absence of difference between them.

2. A second reason for maintaining that teachers in training do not acquire growing insight into the teacher's role can be found in changes which take place between the first and second years of the course and the second and third years. As was pointed out, the role sector in which there is the greatest change is that dealing with the classroom expectations for the teacher. The nature of the changes in the student's conceptions of the teacher's role suggests that there is a high-peak of understanding and insight which occurs during the second year. Less authoritarian attitudes and pupil–teacher relationships which pay more regard for practices and beliefs concerned with the mental health and emotional wellbeing of the children characterize this period but, by and large, these trends give way in the third year to beliefs and expectancies similar to those which students had at the beginning of their course of training, and which they gained, no doubt, from being pupils at school. The second year of training is, in fact, the time during which the student is furthest away from the school situation as pupil or teacher, and the findings of this study suggest that this time coincides with the students' maximal liberality.

3. The third reason for rejecting the notion of steady growth in understanding arises from a consideration of the head teachers' conceptions of the teacher's role. When their conceptions are compared with those of the students, what is obvious is the very high percentage of significant differences, most of them at a high level. The direction of these differences show that the head teachers' conception of the teacher's role is generally in a contrary direction to the changes noted in the first two years of the students' training. In fact, the head teachers' conceptions go beyond the mean responses of the student-teachers' conceptions towards a relatively organizationally-orientated, child-dominating, and conformity-desiring point of view. A hypothesis is suggested that this predominantly organizational focus of the head teachers' expectations for his staff may well stem from his occupancy of the position of ultimate responsibility for these matters, but this hypothesis

would require to be tested. Mention has already been made of the possible conflict areas which face the student-teacher as he enters school as a teacher. As the disparity between the students' and head teachers' conceptions of the teacher's role is maximal during the second year of training, it could be that the regressions in expectations which take place during the third year of training are evidence of the students' growing awareness of these disparities and that they are seeking to narrow the gap in the conceptions of what is thought desirable teacher behaviour by the college and what they see will be expected of them in schools.

Further support to this argument is given by the fact that the role sector in which these regressions of conception occur is that of classroom behaviour. This is the role sector in which expectations are most obviously reflected in behaviour and hence most open to observation and evaluation by others. The fact that the extent of change in any of the other role sectors is very slight indeed, perhaps suggests that in these other sectors beliefs are less subject to pressure from the organizational demands made by the head teacher. A teacher can, for example, hold beliefs about school organization and curricular content without ever disclosing them for they will not be reflected in his behaviour as these areas of decision-making tend to be the responsibility of the head teacher, not the individual teacher. Regarding expectations about motivating children, these may be reflected in a teacher's behaviour but their implementation need not necessarily affect the good order or organizational efficiency of the classroom: their effects would rather be detected in the feelings of individual children, and hence not open to the judgement of the head teacher.

Tentatively, a second hypothesis can be formulated which might be tested further, viz., that tutors in colleges of education may have one frame of reference[2] from which to view the teacher's position while head teachers in schools have another.

1. *College of Education frame of reference.* The college staff and students are detached from the everyday workings of school. Their positions do not have associated with them any responsibilities

2. Krech, Crutchfield and Ballachey (1962) define a frame of reference as the contextual system with respect to which an object is judged. The object in this study is the teacher's position.

for running a school and for dealing with the variety of problems which arise in it. Their concern is perhaps more with learning about children and teaching rather than working with children in face-to-face relationships. The student thus, when asked to respond to the RDI, probably does so in terms of this contextual system.

2. *School frame of reference.* Teachers in schools are involved in dealing with children often under very adverse conditions, in which large classes, overcrowded conditions and lack of appropriate material are often featured. The head teacher has responsibility for the educational results of these teachers and there is little need to reiterate the complaints of too few teachers, untrained teachers and the frequent changes of staff which occur in many schools. It is in this context that the head teachers probably make their judgements of expected teacher behaviour. It is hardly surprising, therefore, that they tend to give high place to those aspects of teacher behaviour which emphasize the maintenence of good order and discipline rather than the individual growth and mental wellbeing of individual children.

Some evidence which supports this hypothesis of the two frames of reference has come from a comparison of the responses of a national sample of college of education tutors with the responses of the student group and those of the head teachers. Broadly speaking, the differences between the groups indicate a greater measure of agreement between tutors and students on the one hand, than between tutors and head teachers on the other.

This hypothesis of the two frames of reference appears closely related to Gross's (1965) idea that taking up a professional appointment in schools should be considered as part of a two-phased process of socialization. The first or preparatory phase is the period of formal training when the skills, knowledge, values and attitudes prescribed for entry into the post are taught. Presumably, during this time, students will have internalized an ideal conception of their role as a teacher. The second phase of training, that of organizational reality, begins when the student confronts the complex realities of organizational life and finds that theory and practice are rather different things.

While it may be necessary to think of teacher training in such terms, it has been pointed out that differences beyond a certain point in the role conceptions of these two aspects of the training process may imply conflict for the new teacher. Further implications stemming from these differences could be drawn relating to school–college relationships, to the role of inspectors and advisers, and to the rate and direction of change within the educational system.

In addition to these social implications, it is important to bear in mind the large variances reported for many of the items, particularly those relating to face-to-face classroom situations. This indicates the absence of any real consensus of opinion within groups about these expectations of teacher behaviour. Further work is obviously necessary to investigate the personality and other factors contributing to these differences. Another area which would require further investigation is the relationship between role conception and actual teaching behaviour in the classroom.

These comments indicate the limited nature of the present study of which various criticisms might be made. A longitudinal study would be preferable to a cross-sectional one. It would be preferable to draw a sample from a number of colleges and to include males as well as females. The response rate of the head teachers might have been improved. What is maintained, however, is that the results are of sufficient interest, and the implications which might be drawn of sufficient importance, to justify a much bigger and more broadly based inquiry which seeks to integrate personality assessment, role conception, and classroom behaviour.

References

BURNHAM, P. S. (1964), 'The role of the deputy head in secondary schools', M.Ed. dissertation, University of Leicester.

BUTCHER, H. J. (1959), 'The opinions of teachers and student teachers about education', Ph.D. dissertation, University of Manchester.

CANNON, C. (1964), 'Some variations in the teacher's role,' *Education for Teaching*, no. 64.

COHEN, L. (1965), 'An exploratory study of the teacher's role as perceived by head teachers, tutors, and students in a training college', M.Ed. dissertation, Liverpool University.

FLEMING, C. M. (1958), *Teaching – A Psychological Analysis*, Methuen.

GROSS, N., MASON, W. S., and MCEACHERN, W. B. (1958), *Explorations in Role Analysis: Studies in the School Superintendency Role*, Wiley.

GROSS, N., and HERRIOT, R. E. (1965), *Staff Leadership in Public Schools*, Wiley.

HOLLINS, T. H. B. (1955), 'Teachers' attitudes to childrens' behaviour', M.Ed. dissertation, University of Manchester.

KISSACK, M. (1956), 'The attitude of training college students towards corporal punishment', M.Ed. dissertation, University of Manchester.

KRECH, D., CRUTCHFIELD, R. S., and BALLACHEY, E. L. (1962), *Individual in Society*, McGraw-Hill.

MUSGROVE, F. (1961), 'Parents' expectations of the junior school', *Soc. Rev.*, vol. 9, pp. 167–80.

MUSGROVE, F., and TAYLOR, P. H. (1965), 'Teachers' and parents' conception of the teacher's role', *Brit. J. educ. Psychol.*, vol. 35, pp. 171–8.

SHARMA, C. L. (1963), 'A comparative study of the processes of making and taking decisions within schools in the UK and USA', Ph.D. dissertation, University of London.

TAYLOR, P. H. (1962), 'Children's evaluations of the characteristics of the good teacher', *Brit. J. educ. Psychol.*, vol. 32, pp. 258–66.

WEBB, J. (1962), 'The sociology of a school', *Brit. J. Soc.*, vol. 13, pp. 264–72.

WILSON, B. R. (1962), 'The teacher's role – a sociological analysis', *Brit. J. Soc.*, vol. 13, pp. 15–32.

Appendix
The Role Definition Instrument[1]

1. Supervise school meals, collect savings, etc.

2. Put 'slow' learners with 'slow' learners in all academic work.

3. Have access to the children's personal record folders and to all information contained there.

4. Help children acquire good manners, correct speech.

5. Teach Religious Knowledge.

6. Teach the three Rs as his primary responsibility as a teacher.

7. Help children acquire attitudes and values not fostered in them in their own homes.

8. Give sex instruction to pupils.

9. Alternate interesting work with less interesting so that the pupils will appreciate the former yet gain by the discipline of the latter.

1. The items above have been grouped according to role sectors. At the time of presentation, their order was randomized.

10. Use the comparison of one child's work with that of another as a method of motivation.

11. Interpret 'right' and 'wrong' for children.

12. Cane those children who need it.

13. Punish the aggressive child for his attacks on other children.

14. Never allow children to know how he will react to classroom situations.

15. As a newly-qualified teacher, start as a strict disciplinarian and gradually become 'approachable' as his class respects his authority.

16. Encourage children to form a class council to make rules for their own classroom behaviour.

17. Allow children at times to act upon what he thinks are wrong decisions on their part.

18. Guard against showing affection to children in his class.

19. Allow children to confide in him with personal problems that they may not wish to discuss with their parents.

20. Teach children to obey orders at once and without question.

21. Give praise sparingly lest it lose its effectiveness.

22. Group friends together for work in Mathematics and English.

14 D. Hargreaves

Teacher–Pupil Relations in a Streamed Secondary School

Abridged from D. Hargreaves, *Social Relations in a Secondary School*, Routledge and Kegan Paul. 1967, chapter 5.

Lumley Secondary Modern School for Boys draws its pupils from a working-class district of a highly industrialized and densely populated town in the North of England. On entry to the school, pupils are streamed on the basis of their scores in the secondary school selection examinations; and during their four years at the school they change streams, on average, slightly less than once. At the time of this investigation, which was largely concerned with fourth-year classes, 4A consisted of pupils who intended, and were thought sufficiently able, to stay on for a fifth year to take Certificate of Secondary Education Examinations. Other pupils were allocated to 4B, 4C or 4D on the basis of their achievements on tests at the end of the third year.

In many respects the relations between teachers and pupils in the school were friendly, sympathetic, cooperative, and constructive. Most of the teachers were genuinely concerned about the lives, careers, and prospects of the boys in their care, even of those boys whose attitudes and behaviour in school were antagonistic and rarely a source of teacher satisfaction. For many teachers and most pupils, however, life at school was a necessary evil. Life was directed towards a reduction of potential conflict by a minimal imposition of demands upon one another. If the upper streams passed their examinations and the lower streams did not riot, the school was, for most teachers, succeeding.

The attitudes of fourth-year pupils to school and to teachers differed according to their streams. The higher the stream, the more favourable the attitudes to school tended to be, and the greater the pupil preference for teachers who made the boys work, who kept the class under control, and who punished 'messers'. The boys in lower streams not only regarded the teachers less favourably, but also perceived their relationships with teachers as much less adequate. When asked to complete the statement 'Teachers here think of me as . . .', 73 per cent of the D stream gave negative replies such as '. . . a big bully, and a great big long-haired nit' and '. . . hopeless', whereas only 10 per cent of the A stream did so.

In short, the higher the stream, the more favourably the pupils regarded the teachers, and the more positively they assessed their relationships with the teachers. This pattern is consonant with the different norms of the dominant pupil groups in the various streams. In the A stream, the pupils were positively orientated towards the teachers' values, and so tended to like the teachers and to have good relationships with them. In the lower streams, the pupils were orientated against the teachers' values and tended to dislike the teachers, who, they believed, regarded them as villains and trouble-makers. [. . .]

Why is it that by the fourth year at Lumley School the pupils' attitudes to the teachers and their conception of the teacher–pupil relationship have diverged so fundamentally? To indicate that such attitudes are consistent with the normative structure of different forms tells us little about *the process* by which both of these develop. A definite answer cannot be attempted here; it must suffice if we indicate some of the ways in which the teachers influence the process.

One element we must consider is the bias of the teachers towards members of the A streams, for these boys were, in the first place, most likely to take examinations successfully in the fourth year: they were the academic elite, the boys who were in ability, achievement, and values closest to the teachers. The staff were thus anxious to create an academic atmosphere in the form.

The form teacher of the first-year A stream felt a need to establish as early as possible an awareness amongst these pupils of being an A stream, and regretted that the boys seemed to resist these pressures for the first two years in school.

I've tried several times to make them feel like an A stream, but it's not much use at this stage.

Invidious comparisons were frequently made by teachers between the different streams. Most frequently this occurred when an A class misbehaved. On one form blackboard I found the notice:

We must always remember to behave as an A class.

On one occasion a teacher left the room to investigate some noise in the corridor. 'Who are you lot?' he cried. '3B, sir,' came the reply. 'You sound more like 1E than 3B!' was the master's crushing retort. The point is that he did not compare their behaviour with that of a first form, but with the *E* stream of the first year. On another occasion a teacher took a number of boys to visit the local Courts. As his numbers had to be limited, he selected the prefects out of 4A and made up the party with those who had the highest positions in the history examination. The rest were placed in the charge of another teacher, who decided that they would clean up his room. At this news the boys groaned and protested. The teacher softened the blow by saying:

You're the only form in the school that I can trust. I wouldn't dare let 4E do a job like this. They'd make a complete mess of it. You ought to be complimented.

The favourite saying of another teacher was:

We like to think the A stream have more common sense than the rest. Do you want to let us down?

One teacher, when members of 4B were misbehaving, said:

This is 4B. You wouldn't believe that this was next to the top class. Does B stand for blockheads?

Some teachers felt that not only were the A stream to be made conscious of their superiority, but that they should also maintain a certain social distance from other forms. One teacher, for example, told me that if he saw a member of the A stream going with a boy from the lower stream, he would discourage the friendship.

I tell him to go round with the lads in his own form. 'They're not for you,' I tell him.

The tendency towards favouritism of the A stream becomes evident in more concrete ways. The selection of prefects, for example, shows a very heavy bias, since it is predominantly A and B stream pupils who are considered most suitable for appointment by the Headmaster and staff. During the academic year 1964–5, fifteen of the prefects came from 4A, seven from 4B, two from 4C, and three from 4D. Thus half the 4A boys were elected prefects and gained considerable status in their own and younger boys' eyes. Further, since prefects' duties are a delegation of staff authority, appointment led to an intensification of their sense of unity with the teachers.

Most important of all, the organization of the school time-table reflected this concern with the higher streams at the expense of the lower ones.

Mr A and Mr B taught 4A and 4B for nearly half the school week. Mr A was the Deputy Headmaster. Mr B was a graduate who left the school at the end of 1965 to become the head teacher of another school. Both were noted as two of the most strict disciplinarians of the school. Mr C, who taught 4C and 4D for sixteen periods each, was by no means a strict disciplinarian; most would judge him to be the reverse.

This was no accidental process. It seems to have been part of the school policy to put younger, less experienced teachers with junior forms, and although the teachers of senior forms were older and more experienced, the men with lower qualifications and/or weaker discipline were given the lower streams.[1] (This is not to say that teachers with lower qualifications are poorer teachers.) The resulting variation in experience of the teaching situation for boys in different streams cannot be ignored, for although all the fourth-year boys shared the same teachers for half of their periods, the C- and D-stream boys in the third and fourth years tended to be taught by teachers with lower qualifications, lower status in terms of allowances and weaker discipline than in the case of A and B stream boys. This allocation could be justified by the Headmaster on the grounds that the A and B stream boys take external examinations and must therefore be taught by the better teachers.

Since all teachers are 'tested out' by pupils to see 'how far they can go', pupils with less strict teachers will build up different concepts of acceptable behaviour to boys with more strict teachers. The policy of placing lower streams under the supervision of less competent and less strict teachers has the effect of giving these

1. A similar point is made by Partridge (1966).

pupils extended expectations about the kind of behaviour which will be tolerated from them, and thus of granting the high status pupils even greater control over the deviant behaviour which in any case becomes normative in lower streams by the fourth year. The school's method of allocating teachers may thus reinforce those processes by which lower stream pupils deviate increasingly from the school's expectations as they progress through their four years at Lumley.

The significance of the allocation of teachers becomes more clear when we examine the background to 4A and 4D in the *third* year. The form teacher of 3A (now the 4A in this study) was extremely proud of his class. In his opinion they were the best form he had ever had. Under his guidance, they developed a strong *esprit de corps*. He admitted to me that on occasions he may have exceeded normal bounds in fostering this in-group loyalty, but he felt that basically the achievement of some sense of unity was beneficial to the boys and to the school. This in-group loyalty was further increased by the sense of rivalry between 3B and 3A over such matters as football, house-points, contributions to the school fund, the Attendance Shield, and so on.[2] In the words of the 3A teacher,

They couldn't bear not being on top in everything.

During the year of the study, this teacher became very nostalgic about his old form. Several times during the year he compared his present 3A very unfavourably with their predecessors. On one occasion, when a member of his present 3A was standing outside the Headmaster's study for being late, he said:

Last year it was completely unknown for a boy in 3A to be standing against that wall. It just shows you the different standards. I'm disgusted.

On another occasion he mused sadly about the record his old 3A had achieved – winning the Attendance Shield for nine consecutive weeks.

2. The form teacher of 3B, an enthusiastic, able and progressive young teacher, encouraged 3B boys to emulate 3A boys. He, too, was anxious to imbue his pupils with a strong corporate spirit and a sense of achievement.

It is of course, impossible to measure the extent of this or any other teacher's influence on the normative structure of 4A; but it is important to consider this influence. The third year background of the present 4D sharpens our understanding of the importance of the teacher.

Whereas 3A were moulded into a form with strong group loyalties and an internalized wish to excel, 3D seems to have been subjected to depressing and inhibiting forces. In the words of their form teacher, who took them for nearly half the lessons,

You just can't afford to trust that lot.

In practice he carried out this policy to the letter. In order to reduce theft – which did occur with less strict teachers – all the equipment was kept locked in the cupboard. The teacher distributed all the equipment himself and then locked the cupboard. If a boy required a new pencil or rubber, the teacher would go through the process of locking and unlocking the cupboard. Occasionally the boys would ask needlessly for materials simply to watch the master performing this extensive ritual. The boys were thus given no responsibility – he even sharpened their pencils himself.

The policy of this teacher in mathematics was based on the correct assumption that most of the pupils in 3D were far from expert at the theory or practice of simple mathematical calculations, and had not fully memorized the multiplication tables. His method was thus to take each pupil back to the most basic mathematical computations and allow him to progress from that point. This meant that few of the pupils were doing the same work at the same time, wheras in 3A the slow boys were forced to keep up with the rate the teacher imposed. Most of the boys worked from text books which gave endless lists of repetitive exercises. Any mistake was penalized by repetition of the page of work. Thus, one slight error would lead to a considerable delay in the boy's progress. It is hardly surprising that most of the boys failed to make progress, became bored and tried to undermine the lessons.

If you didn't like working with Mr — all you had to do when he was giving the books out was to, 'Tut, tut, tut,' and he'd go, 'Right, that's it!' and collect all the books in and you'd have to sit there while he talked to you. And then about five minutes before the end of the lesson he'd give the books out and you'd just put the title and the bell would go.

Mr — wasn't like other teachers. He used to just let us sit there without doing our work. He wouldn't give you any work unless you were quiet. He used to give [two low status boys] all the privileges, you know what I mean? If he had an errand he used to send them. He used to give them books as well. He gives them books to take home with them for a test and we didn't get none so they used to come top.

I don't like the work here. In the first year we was doing addition and all that and we're still doing that now. We can do it, but we're still doing it. It's not worth it, is it? if you're doing nowt. When we was in third year we had Mr — for the first time. We started again from first year with all these simple add-ups and that. Addition, it's easy that. But if you did owt wrong you had to do it all again. We'd have done harder work better.

We should have learnt more in third year, but we didn't. We learnt nowt off Mr —.

Of course, the boys in these lower streams were much more difficult for teachers than boys in higher streams, especially by the third or fourth years. Discipline becomes an important problem and most of the boys make a show of not being interested in the lessons. Attempts to sabotage the lesson would result in lessons where the teacher was not firmly in control and prepared to take firm action. But the point here is that the teachers unknowingly contribute to this process by their rejection of these lower stream boys as 'unintelligent louts'. Dave, who held the top position on the informal status ranking in 4D, was described by this teacher in his report to the Headmaster at the end of third year as:

Mediocre; untidy in every way; lazy; doesn't care two pins for anyone except himself; vicious; sly; smoker; uncooperative; liar; paranoiac; moaner; bully; hates anyone intelligent; trouble-maker.

A less favourable report is hardly possible. Yet much of it was true. Whenever possible, he would shout wildly and distract or provoke others boys. Most of his time at school was spent in a search for distractions. He would laugh openly if a teacher told him that his school work would help him to get a good job. Most of his actions were directed to 'getting a laugh' and he would revel in the guffaws that emanated from the rest of the class when a prank was successful or a teacher fell into his trap. When rebuked or punished he would sulk if he could not lie himself out of the situation.

Yet this behaviour represents an adaptation to a situation. In part it is a necessary adjustment to a situation in which he is a member of a stream whose members are penalized in favour of upper and especially A streams. He has learned to be seen as a relative failure. His relationships with teachers deteriorated steadily over the four years until he was totally rejected by many. He made virtually no progress at his work. In short, the allocation of teachers, the tendency for teachers to favour higher stream boys, and the kind of relationships teachers made with the boys contribute in a fundamental way to the values of the boys. Whilst the A stream boys progress in all the ways which the teacher regards as important, and thus create a teaching situation which is rewarding to both, the D stream boys become increasingly slow and difficult and create a situation which becomes mutually dissatisfying.

The boys were, of course, not unaware of the privileges conferred on high stream boys by the teachers.

I think we've more privileges than 4C and 4D have. There's more prefects from our class and from 4A than from them. They've been treated different to us, you know, we've been treated kindly and they've been treated rough. It's perhaps only slightly, but it makes a big difference. You know, the teachers pick on them 'cos they've got long hair and dirty shoes and dirty clothes. They don't see why they're picked on. If they was to watch themselves doing things they'd know they was doing wrong (B stream boy).

I just don't like [4A and 4B] getting treated better than us, you know what I mean? They call them by their first name and everything. They just treat us as though we're not there. One or two call me by my first name, but not many. But I'm not really bothered about that. I've got that all through school (D stream boy).

I'd drop dead if they called me [by my first name].

They're [teachers] not interested in us. It's all 4A and 4B. 'Cos they never take us out [on school visits] do they? I admit there's a few that's scruffy in our class and you can't take them all out but if they just picked the ones that aren't so scruffy it would be different (D stream boy).

It's dead cushy at this school. You don't do owt. You're supposed to do writing but they don't check the books so you don't have to do it (D stream boy).

I don't think they bother about us here. They can't do 'cos they don't mark our books. If [the Headmaster] saw our books he'd go mad 'cos of all the things wrote over them. Mr — doesn't say owt (D stream boy).

[The Head] calls you, don't he? He calls you rotten and gives you a lecture. He tells you you're a layabout and all that and tells you to get your hair cut. And if you don't you won't get a reference. But I don't want a reference (C stream boy).

This paper has been primarily concerned with the ways in which the allocation and attitudes of teachers are related to the differentiation between streams of the pupils' attitudes to teachers. Whilst it is true that boys in different streams are faced with different problems of adaptation to the teaching situation, it is also important to consider the variety of modes of adaptation of the teachers themselves. We are not so much concerned with how *new* teachers adapt to their careers, but with how the *experienced* teachers who taught the third and fourth year pupils adapted to the forms they taught daily. The Headmaster at Lumley allocated the more competent teachers to the higher streams and the less competent ones to the lower streams. The argument here is that this system of allocation reinforces the teacher's basic mode of adaptation and the sense of his own competence. When a teacher is allocated to mainly high stream pupils, this is perceived as a reward to his competence to teach, and because it is easier to teach the higher streams, where the children are more motivated to work hard and not misbehave, the competence will increase. When a teacher is allocated to low streams, this is perceived as a recognition of his limitations as a teacher, and the lack of interest in academic work and tendencies towards misbehaviour evinced by lower stream pupils reinforce the teacher's sense of his own incompetence.

Teachers have a number of basic problems. The class must be under the firm control of the teacher; the children must learn;

the children must show evidence of their learning. The more competent teachers who tend to be assigned to higher streams can solve these problems with comparative ease. The children are not difficult to control. The previous history of A or B stream children has prepared them to behave well in class, to regard themselves as the academic and behavioural elite, to be interested in academic achievement. The teacher thus has little difficulty in persuading the children to work hard and to give evidence of their learning in external examinations in the fourth year. The existence of these examinations encourages the teacher to teach the children and the results confirm his competence to teach.

For teachers of low streams, it is much more difficult to control the class; discipline becomes a much more important problem than in high streams. The pupils are much less motivated to work and thus seek to undermine the efforts exerted by the teacher towards academic achievement. Since these low stream boys do not take external examinations, the ways in which evidence of either the pupils' academic achievement or the teacher's competence can be assessed are restricted. The less competent teachers who tend to be assigned to low streams are faced with much more difficult problems than their colleagues with high streams. At Lumley, low stream teachers adapt to their situation in two basic ways. The first mode of adaptation is that of *withdrawal*. Because this type of teacher is less competent in matters of discipline yet is assigned to forms with the greatest discipline problems, he avoids the problem by ignoring its existence. He does this by sitting in his desk at the front, marking boys' work or some similar activity, whilst the rest of the class continue to enjoy the relative chaos which reigns. The class members are frequently at different stages in each subject so that no check can be made on individual or group progress. Alternatively, withdrawal can take the form of lecturing to the class in a voice sufficiently loud to drown the voices of misbehaving pupils. In this way the teacher appears to be teaching, even though the pupils complete little work. The second mode of adaptation for the less competent teachers with low streams is that of *domination*. This type of teacher imposes a completely rigid discipline, infringements of which incur severe penalties. Because silence reigns in the form, the children appear to be working hard. In reality, they make little effort; they become increasingly bored by the lesson, their interest in the subject declines, and they seek to undermine the authority of the teacher by disturbing the lesson without being apprehended.

In short, the allocation of teachers to upper or lower streams on the basis of teacher competence reinforces the dominant trends of the peer group; the pupils in higher forms increase in achievement and improve their relationships with teachers whom they like, and the pupils in lower streams become increasingly retarded and their relationships with teachers deteriorate to the point of mutual toleration at best and mutual hostility at worst.[3]

Teachers do not approach their pupils without preconceptions; they possess a set of values or expectations concerning the ways in which pupils *ought* to behave. At Lumley 'good' pupils, those who conform to the expectations, generally come from higher streams, and 'bad' pupils, those who deviate from the expectations, come from lower streams.

Whenever two people meet they are forced to make assessments of each other, by taking each other's behaviour, whether verbalized or gestured, into account.[4] The first impressions determine to some degree the form and extent of further interaction. The teacher–pupil relationship in any single case will be a function of many factors, not least of which are the personality and the past experience of the individuals concerned, but every such interaction will have certain common structural similarities. In a secondary school, where teachers usually take large classes for just one or two subjects, the actual interaction between a teacher and any one pupil will be relatively brief. Indeed, it often happens that a teacher does not directly speak to any one pupil for several consecutive lessons. The teacher thus tends to make *indirect* assessments of the pupil, and these will be largely determined by the child's conformity to the teacher's role expectations.[5] For ex-

3. With this hostility shown by low stream boys towards their teachers was mingled a kind of affection. It is perhaps that these boys rejected the teacher's attempt to impose academic standards upon them, not the man himself. They realized that the low stream teachers tolerated or ignored much behaviour for which the boys could justifiably have been punished.

4. This discussion is indebted to the ideas developed by Goffman (1959).

5. Parsons breaks down the characterization of the pupil into two components: the cognitive (i.e. academic achievement) and the moral (i.e. responsible behaviour). Parsons (1959).

ample, the standard of work produced by a pupil will be taken as a basic guide to a more general assessment.

When a teacher takes a new class, he will tend to divide the class into three categories. Firstly, the 'good' pupils who conform to his expectations. Secondly, the 'bad' pupils who deviate. Thirdly, those who are not outstanding in either conformity or deviation. It is the names of the pupils in the first two categories that are learned immediately by the teacher. For those in the residual category, actual names are learned very much more slowly, so that a teacher often has difficulty in connecting the name and the face.

These inferences which the teacher draws in such a highly selective way from the pupils' behaviour, and the 'categorization process' to which it leads, act as a definition of the situation in which teachers and pupils find themselves. This definition provides the plan for all future interaction between the two parties. Because the inferences are selected from limited aspects of the child's behaviour and are interpreted in terms of the teacher's role expectations, there is a constant danger of misinterpretation. The teacher may draw conclusions which are unjustified when we consider the totality of the child's behaviour.

In a streamed school the teacher categorizes the pupils not only in terms of the inferences he makes from the child's classroom behaviour but also from the child's stream level. It is for this reason that the teacher can rebuke an A stream boy for behaving like a D stream boy. The teacher has learned to *expect* certain kinds of behaviour from members of different streams.

In short, the teacher tends to categorize pupils on the basis of stream and the inferences he makes from the child's behaviour and the extent to which it conforms to his role expectations of the pupil. This, of course, is a process of interaction which is entirely 'natural'; it is part of the everyday life of us all. Although the process of categorization may have a real basis, it may also have effects which are deleterious to the self-conception and development of the pupil, and it is these latent effects which we must elucidate. An example of the influence of stream is that the A stream pupils develop a sense of superiority over the others, who, aware of their implied inferiority, come to regard the A stream boys as 'snobs'.

There are, within the teacher's situation, certain factors which tend to exacerbate this process of categorization. One such factor is the informal gossip among the staff. Whenever teachers discuss pupils, they import into the discussion their own interpretations and preconceptions, which provide the 'naïve' teacher, that is one who has no direct contact with the child, with information which categorizes the child in advance of actual interaction and defines the situation in terms of the behaviour the teacher should expect. I do not wish to suggest that teachers always take their colleagues' opinions about pupils as an established fact; to do so would be to distort the situation seriously. On numerous occasions teachers disagree about the behaviour of a pupil with comments such as 'He's not like that in my lesson'. But disagreement can only occur between teachers who both have direct experience of the child. To the naïve teacher, opinions of colleagues will have the effect of acting as a provisional agent of the categorization process. In other words, one of the functions of teachers' gossip about pupils is to add to the preconceptions and expectations by which a pupil is assessed. This may be particularly true for new teachers, or for those who request information about a class prior to taking them for the first time. The form teacher of 3C at Lumley told me how he expected that Clint would be a very difficult boy on the basis of comments from his colleagues, and was very surprised to find that he 'had no trouble with him'.

Perhaps the most important and only partially recognized effect of categorization is the way in which this process sets up counter-expectations in the pupil. Because a teacher has categorized a pupil, however provisionally, he may in his own behaviour toward the pupil emit expectations to which the relatively immature pupil will conform. This by-product of categorization will be most marked at the extremes, that is, with the 'good' and 'bad' pupils. It would hardly be surprising if 'good' pupils thus become 'better' and the 'bad' pupils become 'worse'. It is, in short, an example of a self-fulfilling prophecy.[6] The negative expectations of the teacher reinforce the negative behavioural tendencies. Let us consider some examples.

One day in the Spring Term the Youth Employment Officer visited the school to speak to the boys in the fourth year. As he

6. An excellent study of the self-fulfilling prophecy is given by R. K. Merton as chapter 11 of *Social Theory and Social Structure* (1957).

left the Hall at the end of the speech, someone began to cheer. The Deputy Head teacher, who was standing on the platform, pointed down to the boys and shouted, 'You! Go to my room!' The boy who had cheered was a prefect, but Don of 4D stood up, even though he had not cheered. It was as if he expected to be rebuked even when he had committed no crime.

On another occasion I was observing a lesson in Handicraft. The boys were tidying the workshop in anticipation of the final bell of the school day. As there were several minutes to spare, I asked the teacher if I could send a boy across the road to buy some stamps from the Post Office for me. The teacher agreed, and I asked Derek, the high status boy from 4D. The teacher turned to me and said, 'You don't want to send him if you want to get those stamps today,' and asked another boy to run the errand. Derek, who seemed both surprised and pleased by my request now began to scowl. When I insisted that Derek should go for me, Derek looked at me and said, 'Are you sure?' He felt that it would be more appropriate if I agreed with the teacher's conception of him.

During one Art lesson the teacher picked up a painting done by Derek and took it to the front of the class. When he called the form to attention and said, 'Boys, look what Derek's done,' Derek immediately began to laugh delightedly. But when the teacher continued, 'This is a very good picture,' Derek was overwhelmed with confusion and embarrassment. He had assumed that the teacher was using his picture as an illustration of *bad* work.

It is important to stress that if this effect of categorization is real, it is entirely unintended by the teachers. They do not wish to make low streams more difficult than they are! But it does imply that the teacher needs consciously to adapt away from these effects if he does not wish to reinforce the negative self-conceptions of lower stream boys. To treat 'bad' pupils as 'good' pupils may appear to be unrealistic, but it may be a form of manipulation which is essential to the teacher if he is to change the values and attitudes of those pupils who turn against the system of the school.

References

GOFFMAN, E. (1959), *The Presentation of Self in Everyday Life*, Doubleday.

MERTON, R. K. (1957), *Social Theory and Social Structure*, Free Press.

PARSONS, T. (1959), 'The school class as a social system: some of its functions in American society', *Harvard educ. Rev.*, vol. 29, pp. 297–318. Reprinted in A. H. Halsey, J. Floud and C. A. Anderson, *Education, Economy and Society*, Free Press, pp. 434–55.

PARTRIDGE, J. (1966), *Middle School*, Gollancz, p. 82.

Part Five
Teaching Styles and Management

Some of the most interesting questions about teaching concern the ways in which teachers exercise social control in classrooms and in so doing help to create particular climates and regulate the ongoing behaviour of individual pupils. Answers have been sought at very different levels of measurement of teachers' characteristics. The traditional approach has studied the teacher as a personality, comparing individuals on general, pervasive, dimensions of belief systems or management styles. More recently, work on social control has focused upon discrete aspects of teaching behaviour, sometimes using experimental procedures with teachers trained to exhibit specific behaviours, to tease out those behaviours which bear most closely on the conduct of individuals and groups of pupils.

The study by Harvey, Prather, White and Hoffmeister illustrates the first approach, categorizing teachers in terms of belief systems, and showing how beliefs are associated with teaching behaviour and in turn with the atmosphere of the classroom and the behaviour of pupils. The other two studies, by Kounin, and by Madsen and others, are more behaviouristic and analytic, breaking down management behaviour into such elements as use of praise, use of rules, desist techniques and the handling of activities in the classroom. The Madsen, Becker and Thomas work is an experiment with particular children in classrooms; Kounin, on the other hand, covers a range of studies he has conducted in different settings.

15 O. J. Harvey, M. Prather, B. Jack White and J. Hoffmeister

Teachers' Beliefs, Classroom Atmosphere and
Student Behavior

From O. J. Harvey, M. Prather, B. Jack White and J. Hoffmeister,
'Teachers' beliefs, classroom atmosphere and student behavior',
American Educational Research Journal, vol. 5, 1968, pp. 151-65.

Harvey, White, Prather, Alter and Hoffmeister (1966) found
recently that pre-school teachers of concrete and abstract belief
systems differed markedly in the classroom environments they
created for their students. Teachers representing System 4, the
most abstract belief system treated by Harvey, Hunt and Schroder
(1961) differed from representatives of System 1, the most concrete mode of functioning characterized by Harvey and others
(1961), in what was presumed to be an educationally desirable
direction on all twenty-six dimensions of classroom behavior on
which they were rated.

The difference was statistically significant on fourteen dimensions: System 4 teachers expressed greater warmth toward
children, showed greater perceptiveness of the children's wishes
and needs, were more flexible in meeting the interests and needs of
the children, were more encouraging of individual responsibility,
gave greater encouragement to free expression of feelings, were
more encouraging of creativity, displayed greater ingenuity in
improvising teaching and play materials, invoked unexplained
rules less frequently, were less rule orientated, were less determining of classroom and playground procedure, manifested less
need for structure, were less punitive, and were less anxious about
being observed.

A cluster analysis of these fourteen dimensions (Tryon and
Bailey, 1965, 1966) yielded three factors of resourcefulness,
dictatorialness and punitiveness. System 4 teachers were more
resourceful, less dictatorial and less punitive than System 1
teachers.

While consistent both with our theoretical stance and a wide
range of other differences found between the more concretely and

the more abstractly functioning individuals (Adams, Harvey and Heslin, 1966; Harvey, 1963, 1966; Harvey and Ware, 1967; Ware and Harvey, 1967; White and Harvey, 1965), the finding that teachers' belief systems affect their overt behavior in the classroom does not bear directly upon the more educationally significant question of the influence of teachers' beliefs and behavior upon the learning and performance of their students. It is with this latter question that the present study is concerned.

More specifically, the main aim of this study was to assess the relationship between students' performance and teachers' resourcefulness, dictatorialness and punitiveness. In addition, the study provided a test of the replicability of the earlier findings that concrete and abstract teachers differ in the kinds of classroom behavior they manifest.

The general expectancies were that teachers of more concrete belief systems would display less resourcefulness, more dictatorialness and more punitiveness in the classroom than the more abstract teachers, as found in the previous study (Harvey and others, 1966); and that greater abstractness, greater resourcefulness, less dictatorialness and less punitiveness on the part of the teacher would be associated with more educationally preferable performances of the children.

Method

Concrete and abstract teachers of kindergarten and first grade were rated on the fourteen dimensions found by Harvey, and others (1966) to discriminate significantly between concrete and abstract teachers. Their students were rated, as a class, on a specially constructed thirty-one-item rating scale.

Teacher rating scale

This instrument, while providing the necessary information for a test of the replicability of the earlier results (Harvey and others, 1966), was intended primarily as a measure of teachers' overt resourcefulness, dictatorialness and punitiveness. It consisted of the fourteen items from which these three factors were derived: (1) warmth toward the children, (2) perceptiveness of the children's needs and wishes, (3) flexibility in meeting the needs and interests of the children, (4) maintenance of relaxed relationships with the children, (5) encouragement of individual responsibility, (6) encouragement of free expression of feelings, (7) encouragement of creativity, (8) ingenuity in improvising teaching and play materials, (9) use of unexplained rules, (10) rule orientation, (11) determination of classroom procedures, (12) need for structure, (13) punitiveness, and (14) anxiety induced by the observers' presence.

Student rating scale

This measure of student behavior, which provided the major dependent variables of this study, consisted of the following items: (1) overall adherence to the teacher's rules, (2) immediacy of response to the rules, (3) adherence to the spirit (*v.* the letter) of the rules, (4) information seeking, (5) independence, (6) cooperativeness with the teacher, (7) task attentiveness, (8) enthusiasm, (9) voice in classroom activities, (10) voluntary participation in classroom activities, (11) free expression of feelings, (12) diversity of goal relevant activities, (13) student-initiated activity, (14) amount of activity, (15) considerateness toward classmates, (16) reciprocal affection between classmates, (17) cooperation with classmates, (18) taking turns with classmates, (19) amount of interaction with classmates, (20) novelty of response to problem or teacher's question, (21) appropriateness of response, (22) accuracy of facts, (23) integration of facts, (24) orientation toward specificity of facts (vs. more general principles), (25) roteness of answers or solutions, (26) active hostility toward the teacher, (27) passive hostility toward the teacher, (28) fear attentiveness (anxiety), (29) aggression toward classmates, (30) guidance seeking, and (31) approval seeking.

Each of the dimensions in both the teacher and student rating scale was rated on a six-point scale: 3, 2, and 1 for 'far', 'considerably' and 'slightly' above average respectively; and –1, –2, and –3 for 'slightly', 'considerably' and 'far' below average respectively. The 'average' category was omitted with the aim (by creating a forced choice condition) of avoiding the common tendency of observers (*O*s) to assign a wide variety of discriminably different behaviors to this category. Through a training program described later, an attempt was made to establish equivalent 'averages' for all *O*s.

Subjects

Since the present study was part of a large investigation concerned with the effects of prior participation in Head Start, classrooms were selected for observation if they contained at least one kindergarten or first grade student who had gone to Head Start nine months earlier (i.e. during the summer of 1965) and who was attending public school for the first time. These criteria yielded 118 classes, 92 kindergarten and 26 first grade, in 18 rural and urban Colorado school districts. The 92 kindergarten classes were taught by 64 teachers while the 26 first grade classes were taught by 26 teachers. Each of the 118 classes, with an average of 26 students, was observed and rated *as a class*, not as individual students, on the student rating scale.

Of the 90 teachers, 67 completed the 'This I Believe' (TIB) Test and 66 completed the Conceptual Systems Test (CST). Both the TIB and CST are tests of concreteness-abstractness of belief systems, the former being based upon sentence completions and the latter upon response to objective items.

The 'This I Believe' (TIB) Test

This test, developed specifically as a measure of concreteness-abstractness of conceptual or belief systems (e.g. Harvey, 1964, 1966; Harvey and others, 1966; Ware and Harvey, 1967; White and Harvey, 1965), requires S to indicate his beliefs about a number of socially and personally relevant concept referents by completing in two or three sentences the phrase 'This I believe about —', the blank being replaced successively by one of the referents. The referents employed in the present study were 'religion', 'friendship', 'the American way of life', 'sin', 'education', 'the family', 'people on welfare', 'punishment', 'teaching', and 'sex.'

From the relativism, tautologicalness, novelty and connotative implications or richness of the completions, together with criteria implied below, respondents may be classified into one of the four principal systems posited by Harvey and others (1961) or into some mixture of two or more systems.

More specifically, Ss are classified as representing predominantly System 1, the most concrete mode of dimensionalizing and construing the world, if their completions denote such characteristics as high absolutism, high tautologicalness, high frequency of platitudes and normative statements, high ethnocentrism, high religiosity, assertion of the superiority of American morality and expression of highly positive attitudes toward institutional referents.

Subjects are categorized as representing System 2, the next to the lowest level of abstractness, if, in addition to being highly evaluative and absolute, they express strong negative attitudes toward such referents as marriage, religion, the American way of life – the same referents toward which System 1 representatives manifest highly positive attitudes.

Responses to the TIB are scored as representing System 3 functioning, the next to the highest level of abstractness posited by Harvey, Hunt and Schroder (1961), if they indicate more relativism and less evaluativeness than Systems 1 and 2 and at the same time express strongly positive beliefs about friendship, people and interpersonal relations.

System 4 functioning, the highest of the four levels of abstractness, is indicated by TIB responses that imply a high degree of novelty and appropriateness, independence without negativism, high relativism and contingency of thought, and the general usage of multidimensional rather than unidimensional interpretative schemata.

Of the 67 teachers who completed the TIB, 50 were classified as System 1, none was categorized as System 2, four were scored as System 3, eight were classified as weak instances of System 4, and five were scored as admixtures of Systems 1 and 3. In the analysis involving the TIB the admixtures were omitted; Systems 3 and 4 were combined into the *more abstract group*; and System 1 teachers were treated as the *more concrete group*. Of the 50 concrete teachers, 30 taught 44 classes of kindergartners and 20 taught 20 classes of first-graders. Seven of the 12 abstract teachers taught 11 kindergarten classes while the other five abstract teachers taught five first-grade classes. Thus it should be noted that while both concrete and abstract first grade teachers each taught only one class, kindergarten teachers, both concrete and abstract, each taught an approximate average of $1\frac{1}{2}$ classes.

O. J. Harvey, M. Prather, B. Jack White and J. Hoffmeister 219

The Conceptual Systems Test (CST)

All but one of the 67 teachers who completed the TIB Test also completed the objective measure of belief systems, the CST. From a pool of several hundred items and numerous runs through Tryon's program of cluster analysis (Tryon and Bailey, 1965, 1966) seven factors have been extracted and replicated which are theoretically consistent with the major characteristics of the four principal belief systems posited by Harvey and others (1961). These factors as we have tentatively labeled them (Harvey, 1967) are:

1. Divine fate control.
2. Need for simplicity–certainty.
3. Need for structure–order.
4. Distrust of social authority.
5. Friendship absolutism.
6. Moral absolutism.
7. General pessimism.

While the CST was administered in its entirety, for purposes of this study scores were derived for only the three clusters of Divine fate control, Need for simplicity–certainty and Need for structure–order. The combined scores from these three factors were treated as our second measure of a teacher's concreteness–abstractness. Representative items comprising each of the three of these component factors include:

1. Divine fate control (DFC) is assessed by such items as 'There are some things which God will never permit man to know,' 'In the final analysis, events in the world will be in line with the master plan of God,' and 'I believe that to attain my goals it is only necessary for me to live as God would have me live.'

2. Need for simplicity–certainty (NS–C) is inferred from response to such statements as 'I dislike having to change my plans in the middle of a task,' 'It is annoying to listen to a lecturer who cannot seem to make up his mind as to what he really believes,' and 'A group which tolerates extreme differences of opinion among its own members cannot exist for long.'

3. Need for structure-order (NS–O) is derived from such items

as 'I don't like to work on a problem unless there is a possibility of coming out with a clear-cut, definite answer,' 'I don't like for things to be uncertain and unpredictable,' and 'I like to have a place for everything and everything in its place.'

Training of observers and assessment of inter-observer reliability

Each of the nine *O*s, all females, participated in six training sessions during which six teachers and their classes were observed and independently rated. Each observation session was followed by a lengthy group discussion among the *O*s and other staff members aimed at increasing the reliability of the ratings through improving observation techniques and clarifying and standardizing meaning and usage of the rating categories.

Inter-judge reliability for the nine *O*s was assessed for both the teacher and student rating scales at three points: immediately following the last training session, one week after field observations began, and immediately preceding completion of the experimental observations, 2 weeks later. The mean correlation between every pair of judges for the teacher scale was 0·78, 0·76 and 0·70 for the three periods respectively; the corresponding reliability values for the student scale were 0·84, 0·75 and 0·77.

Procedure

Each teacher and her students were observed in the classroom on a single occasion by a single *O* for approximately two hours. All teachers had been advised earlier by their principals of the dates on which they were to be observed.

Observation occurred during normal classroom activities on a day free of special events in order to render the conditions of observation as comparable as possible across classrooms. The *O* arrived before class, introduced herself, explained (with the aim of allaying the teacher's apprehension and fostering her cooperation) that the purpose of the visit was to gather examples of good teaching procedure that could be utilized as bases for future teacher training programs, and requested that she be allowed to observe while remaining as inconspicuous as possible in order to minimize the effects of her presence upon the children. To further *O*'s unobtrusiveness and simultaneously to increase the likelihood of both the teacher and her students behaving in their usual fashion, each teacher was asked not to converse with O during the observation period.

The teacher and her class were rated by the same O, the students being observed and rated first as independently as possible of the teacher's behavior. This procedure was aimed at minimizing the contamination between the dependent and independent variables likely to result from the students and teacher being rated by the same O. Extensive pretesting indicated that this procedure, of having the O first concentrate on and rate the behavior of the students as a class before focusing on the teacher, yielded a relationship between student and teacher ratings that was no higher than that between separate ratings of the teacher and her students by different judges. In fact, the evidence indicated clearly that, while the use of a single O for both the teacher and her students may have produced contamination, at the same time it produced seemingly more valid ratings than those yielded by the practice of one judge observing only the teacher while the other O noted only the responses of the children. Thus the degree of contamination inherent in the method of observation we employed appears to be preferable to the loss of validity that results from attempts of Os to rate the behavior of the teacher and her students without the use of the other as a referent.

In rating the children, care was exercised to rate the class as a whole and not to give inordinate weight to a small minority by concentrating on the behavior of a single child or a few children.

Results

Tests of assumptions

Before analysing the effects of teachers' overt behavior upon students' performance, it was first necessary to test two basic assumptions: firstly that the fourteen items of the teacher rating scale would yield the three factors of resourcefulness, dictatorialness and punitiveness, as they had in the earlier study (Harvey and others, 1966); and secondly that variations in the concreteness–abstractness of the teachers' beliefs would lead them to score differently on these three behavioral factors.

The validity of the first assumption was demonstrated by the results of a factor analysis of the teacher rating scale by Tryon's method of cluster analysis (Tryon and Bailey, 1965, 1966) which yielded the three anticipated clusters.

Resourcefulness was comprised of four behavioral items. They, together with their factor loadings (represented by the values in the parentheses) were: utilization of physical resources (0·77), diversity of simultaneous activities (0·77), encouragement of creativity (0·72) and ingenuity in improvising teaching and play materials (0·71).

Dictatorialness contained seven items: need for structure (0·90), flexibility (−0·90), rule orientation (0·86), encouragement of free expression of feelings (−0·84), teacher determination of classroom procedures (0·81) and the use of unexplained rules (0·70).

Punitiveness was based on three items: warmth toward the children (−0·86), perceptiveness of the children's needs and wishes (−0·85) and punitiveness (0·77).

The second assumption also proved to be warranted. Teachers classified on the basis of the TIB as being concrete were significantly less resourceful ($t = 4·03$, $p < 0·001$), significantly more dictatorial ($t = 1·67$, $p < 0·05$), and were more punitive, although not significantly more, ($t = 1·05$, $p < 0·10$) than teachers classified as abstract. Moreover, the abstractness measure from the CST correlated significantly positively with teacher resourcefulness ($r = 0·37$, $p < 0·005$), and significantly negatively with both teacher dictatorialness ($r = −0·19$, $p < 0·05$) and punitiveness ($r = −0·19$, $p < 0·05$). These results, through replicating the more essential findings of our earlier study (Harvey and others, 1966), make it clear that variation in the concreteness–abstractness of teachers' beliefs generates theoretically consistent and predictable parallels in the overt behavior of these individuals. Thus an examination of the effects of teachers' beliefs and behavior upon their students, the major concern of this study, becomes appropriate.

Concreteness–abstractness of teachers' beliefs and student performance

Factor analysis of the student rating scale. In order to extricate the more generic dimensions encompassed within the thirty-one-item student rating scale and thus enhance the coherency of the presentation of results, the student rating scale was factorized by

Tryon's method of cluster analysis (Tryon and Bailey, 1965, 1966) and the resulting factors related to variation in teachers' beliefs and overt behavior.

Seven factors were derived from the student rating scale. The first cluster, termed *cooperation*, was comprised of five items, which with their factor loadings were: immediacy of response to rules (0·91), overall adherence to teachers' rules (0·86), child-sustained activity (0·68), cooperativeness with teacher (0·57) and adherence to the spirit of the rules (0·55). The second factor, which centered around *student involvement*, consisted of eight items: enthusiasm (0·89), voluntary participation in classroom activity (0·82), free expression of feelings (0·78), voice of students in class-room activity (0·78), independence (0·76), information seeking (0·72), insecurity (−0·66) and task attentiveness (0·63). The third factor, labeled *activity level*, was derived from two items: amount of activity (0·81) and diversity of goal-relevant activity (0·81). The fourth factor, *nurturance seeking*, contained two items: guidance seeking (0·68) and approval seeking (0·59). The fifth factor, termed *achievement level*, included three items: accuracy of facts (0·81), appropriateness of solution (0·80) and integration of facts (0·71). The sixth factor, *helpfulness*, was comprised of four items: considerateness toward classmates (0·79), cooperativeness with class-mates (0·71), taking turns (0·56) and aggression (−0·49). The seventh cluster, referred to as *concreteness of response*, contained three items: roteness of answers or solutions (0·88), orientation toward specificity of facts (0·71) and novelty of answer or solution (−0·56). Factor scores were obtained by computing the mean score on the items constituting the factor.

Four of the items from the student rating scale were not included in any of the seven clusters: amount of interaction, reciprocal affection, passive and active hostility. Results relating to these four items will not be reported.

TIB classification and student performance. Comparisons were made between the 64 classes taught by the 50 teachers classified by the TIB as being concrete and the 16 classes taught by the 12 abstract teachers on each of the seven factors derived from the student rating scale.

As indicated in Table 1, students of more abstract teachers, in comparison to their counterparts, were significantly more involved in classroom activities, more active, higher in achievement and

Table 1 **Performances of students of concrete and abstract teachers** (as classified by the TIB)

Student rating scale factors	Concrete teachers		Abstract teachers		
	Mean	SD	Mean	SD	t
Cooperation	4·05	0·82	4·34	0·75	1·26
Involvement	3·60	0·87	4·09	0·90	1·96*
Activity	3·29	1·01	4·22	1·02	3·29†
Nurturance seeking	2·91	0·99	2·56	0·95	−1·27
Achievement	3·90	0·71	4·25	0·56	1·81*
Helpfulness	4·03	0·65	4·20	0·63	0·97
Concreteness	3·78	0·88	3·27	0·80	−2·12*

Note: df for all tests = 78.
* one-tailed $p < 0.05$.
† one-tailed $p < 0.01$.

less concrete in their responses. They were also less nurturant seeking, more cooperative and more helpful, but not significantly so, than students of concrete teachers.

Conceptual Systems Test

CST factors and student performance. Teachers' scores on the abstractness measure from the CST and on each of the three factors going into this measure were correlated with each of the seven factors from the student rating scale. These relationships are presented in Table 2.

The CST measure of abstractness related significantly to every one of the student performance factors. Greater abstractness of the teacher was accompanied by greater involvement, greater cooperation, more activity, less nurturance seeking, higher achievement, greater helpfulness and less concreteness on the part of the students.

While all three of the factors constituting the measure of teacher abstractness correlated in the predicted direction with performance of the children, the teachers' need for structure–order correlated the highest and most consistently. In fact, the teachers' need for structure–order had greater influence on the performance of the children than her belief in divine fate control, need for simplicity–consistency and overall abstractness.

Table 2 Correlations between clusters from the conceptual systems test and the student rating scale

Student rating scale factors	Teacher variables: CST clusters			
	1. Divine fate control	2. Simplicity consistency	3. Structure-order	4. Abstract-ness (ϵ 1-2-3)
Cooperation	−0·14	−0·21*	−0·22*	0·21*
Involvement	−0·10	−0·18*	−0·21*	0·18*
Activity	−0·12	−0·13	−0·34†	0·19*
Nurturance seeking	0·14	0·12	0·24*	−0·18*
Achievement	−0·22*	−0·21*	−0·30†	0·27†
Helpfulness	−0·17	−0·17	−0·15	0·19*
Concreteness	0·06	0·23*	0·29*	−0·19*

Note: *df* for all significance tests = 84.
* one-tailed $p < 0.05$.
† one-tailed $p < 0.01$.

Teachers' overt behavior and student performance. Teachers' scores on the behavioral factors of resourcefulness, dictatorialness and punitiveness were correlated with the seven student performance clusters. These results are included in Table 3.

The resourcefulness of the teacher correlated significantly

Table 3 Correlations of teacher dictatorialness, punitiveness and resourcefulness with student performance factors

Student behavior	Teacher behavior		
	Resourcefulness	Dictatorialness	Punitiveness
Cooperativeness	0·23†	−0·18*	−0·34†
Involvement	0·69†	−0·84†	−0·73†
Activity	0·76†	−0·33†	−0·29†
Nurturance seeking	−0·12	−0·05	−0·01
Achievement	0·28†	−0·28†	−0·32†
Helpfulness	0·02	−0·23†	−0·32†
Concreteness	−0·60†	0·67†	0·56†

Note: *df* for all tests of significance = 116.
* one-tailed $p < 0.05$.
† one-tailed $p < 0.01$.

positively with student cooperation, involvement, activity and achievement and significantly negatively with the concreteness of students' responses.

The teachers' dictatorialness correlated significantly negatively with the students' cooperation, involvement, activity, achievement and helpfulness and significantly positively with students' concreteness of responses.

Teachers' punitiveness correlated significantly negatively with student cooperation, involvement, activity, achievement and helpfulness and significantly positively with the concreteness of the students' responses.

Nurturance seeking was the only one of the seven student performance clusters that did not relate significantly to any one of the teacher behaviors.

Discussion

By replicating the findings of our earlier study (Harvey and others, 1966), these results make it clear that the concreteness–abstractness of teachers' belief systems affect their overt resourcefulness, dictatorialness and punitiveness in the classroom. In addition, the results show that the classroom behavior of the teacher and the behavior of the students are significantly related. Clearly, this relationship does not tell us the nature of the causality. Theoretically, the teacher's behavior could determine the children's behavior, the reverse could be true, both could be determined by a third factor, such as the organizational climate, or the effects could be produced by the interaction among all of these factors. The possibility that the relationship between teachers' and students' behavior is a result of organizational climate is minimized by the fact that the concrete and abstract teachers, while selected from the same organizational climates, nevertheless differed markedly in their classroom behaviors, as did their students. Further, while students no doubt affect the behavior of their teachers, it appears more likely that, because of her socially prescribed power, her influence is greater and more direct than theirs.

The obtained differences between concrete and abstract teachers probably would have been accentuated had the group of more abstract teachers been comprised only of clear instances of System 4. Instead unclear instances, together with cases of System 3, were combined with clear instances of System 4 to constitute the abstract group in this study. Yet, if our experiences from the earlier (Harvey and others, 1966) and the present study are typical, a large sample of teachers would be necessary to yield an adequate number of clear cases of System 4. Of the 292 teachers to whom we have administered the TIB, only 18, or six per cent, have been classified as System 4, not all of which were ideal cases. While strongly suggesting that in terms of absolute numbers few teachers operate at the System 4 level, it should be noted that this percentage is almost identical to the seven per cent of System 4 individuals we have found from among approximately 3000 undergraduates administered the TIB. In fact, this percentage appears to be so constant across a large sample of subjects that some special factor(s) may be necessary to account for it.

Indeed the whole question of the determinants of the different belief systems is far from being answered, having been resolved only partially at the theoretical level and even less empirically. One of the more theoretically viable determinants seems to be the freedom the individual had as a child to explore the world of values and to evolve and internalize rules on the basis of direct experience and pragmatic outcomes (Adams and others, 1966; Harvey, 1967). Although this freedom and the differential evolution of systems should be expected to relate to a host of sociological factors, the only significant demographic variable we have found, from the study of two large samples of subjects made up of college students and school teachers, centers around religion. Thus while representatives of the belief systems did not differ in such background factors as socio-economic status, educational level of themselves or their parents, or even in intelligence, they did differ in such religion related behavior as frequency of church attendance. This kind of evidence, together with background information on the present teachers, which showed the representatives of the different systems did not differ in level of education, kind of degrees, years of teaching, indicate that the results obtained in this study can more parsimoniously and directly be attributed to differences in teachers' belief systems than to possible sociological correlates.

References

ADAMS, D. K., HARVEY, O. J., and HESLIN, R. E. (1966), 'Variations in flexibility and creativity as a function of hypnotically induced past histories', in O. J. Harvey (ed.), *Experience, Structure and Adaptability*, Springer, pp. 217–34.

HARVEY, O. J., HUNT, D. E., and SCHRODER, H. M. (1961), *Conceptual Systems and Personality Organization*, Wiley.

HARVEY, O. J. (1963), 'Cognitive determinants of role playing', Technical Report no. 3, Contract No. 1147 (07), University of Colorado.

HARVEY, O. J. (1964), 'Some cognitive determinants of influencibility', *Sociometry*, vol. 27, pp. 201–21.

HARVEY, O. J. (1966), 'System structure, flexibility and creativity', in O. J. Harvey (ed.), *Experience, Structure and Adaptability*, Springer, pp. 242–62.

HARVEY, O. J., and WARE, R. (1967), 'Personality differences in dissonance resolution', *J. Person. social Psychol.*, vol. 7, pp. 227–30.

HARVEY, O. J., WHITE, B. J., PRATHER, M., ALTER, R. D., and HOFFMEISTER, J. K. (1966), 'Teachers' belief systems and preschool atmospheres', *J. educ. Psychol.*, vol. 57, pp. 373–81.

HARVEY, O. J. (1967), 'Conceptual system and attitude change', in C. W. Sherif and M. Sherif (eds.), *Attitude, Ego-Involvement and Attitude Change*, Wiley.

TRYON, R. C., and BAILEY, D. E. (1965), *Try Users Manual*, University of Colorado Computer Centre.

TRYON, R. C., and BAILEY, D. E. (1966), *The B.C. Try System of Cluster Analysis*, University of Colorado Computing Centre, pp. 3–35.

WARE, R., and HARVEY, O. J. (1967), 'A cognitive determinant of impression formation', *J. Person. social Psychol.*, vol. 5, pp. 38–44.

WHITE, B. J., and HARVEY, O. J. (1965), 'Effects of personality and own stand on judgement and production of statements about a central issue', *J. exp. social Psychol.*, vol. 1, pp. 334–47.

16 J. S. Kounin

An Analysis of Teachers' Managerial Techniques

From J. S. Kounin, 'An analysis of teachers' managerial techniques',
Psychology in the Schools, vol. 4, 1967, pp. 221-7.

This paper will summarize some findings relevant to classroom
management. It will also be a brief case study of a research project
that will point out investigative errors made due to asking irrelevant questions with corresponding misguided methodology; will
contrast findings obtained by classical controlled methods with
those obtained by less controlled naturalistic methods; will show
how significant results (chi-square-wise) may be quite insignificant
in their power to answer the original questions raised; will give
an example of how instructions given to subjects ostensibly to
disguise the real purpose of an experiment fooled the investigators
more than the subjects; and sacrilegious though the thought may
be, will cite an example of how the termination of grant monies
actually benefited a particular research.

This series of researches started with an accident. I was teaching
a course in mental hygiene devoted to understanding the dynamics
of human behavior and the development of a diagnostic, 'understanding' attitude, when I glanced around and noticed a student
reading a newspaper. Contrary to what I advocated, I failed to give
the student psychological tests, to invite him to a counseling
session, or even to interview his parents or to study his community.
Rather, I angrily reprimanded him. I succeeded in getting him to
put away his newspaper, or at least to not hold it completely un-
folded in midair. But, the major observable impact seemed to be
upon the other members of the class. Side glances to others ceased,
whispers stopped, eyes went from windows to desks, and the silence
was heavy. I believe that if I had belched they would have copied
the sound in their notes.

This led to a series of studies by Dr Gump and myself (Kounin
and Gump, 1958), in which we were later joined by Dr Ryan

(Kounin, Gump and Ryan, 1961) and supported by a grant from the National Institute of Mental Health. We started to study what we later called the 'ripple effect'; how a teacher's method of handling the misbehavior of one child influences *other* children who are audiences to the event but not themselves targets.

We started with a classical experiment using classical subjects: captive college students. In order to disguise the real purpose of the experiment we told the subjects that we were studying first impressions of people and asked students to rate various qualities of their instructors during the first meeting of the class. At a following class meeting a student-stooge came in late. In two classes he was dealt with supportively and in two threateningly. Following this the original rating scales were readministered for 'reliability'.

The two methods of handling the classroom misbehavior produced statistically significant differences in students' ratings of the instructor's helpfulness, likeability, authoritarianism, fairness, felt tension, and, in the case of the younger of the two instructors, in students' ratings of their felt freedom to communicate and in the instructor's competence.

However, although 97 per cent of the students reported that they did *not* perceive that the event was contrived, they did report that they were surprised that a college instructor would take time out to correct a student for coming late, even though they rated coming late as a serious misbehavior. Comments on a post-incident questionnaire were in the nature of: 'He must have had an argument with his wife,' or 'He probably got caught in a traffic jam.' Since we were not sure whether we were measuring the ripple effect of desist-techniques or the impact of surprise, or the effects of perceived arguments with wives, we decided to study the problem in schools (and later camps) where desist-techniques are within expectations and have some ecological prevalence.

So we next went to kindergartens and obtained Barker-Wright types of specimen records of audience children's behavior immediately before, during and for two minutes after a teacher did something to stop the misbehavior of another child. The desist-techniques were scored for 'clarity', 'firmness', and 'punitiveness'. The audience children's behaviors were categorized as showing increased conformity (or decreased deviancy), overt signs of negative emotionality, and no overt reaction. We found that the 'clarity' of a teacher's desist-technique resulted in more conformity on the part of all audience children; firmness decreased deviancy but only for audience children who were themselves involved or interested in deviancy at the time; and punitiveness increased restlessness and signs of anxiety but had no effect upon conformity.

Armed with the increased success-expectation provided by significant chi-squares, and having no classrooms to observe in summer, we then proceeded to study the same phenomenon in a boys' camp. We found that the predominant effect of a counselor's desist efforts upon an audience-camper was 'no observable effect'. Variations in clarity, firmness, and punitiveness produced no observable differences. The only desist-technique that made any difference was one that contained high attraction novelty (i.e. talk about a watermelon party) and this produced attention above the minimum required for awareness, but had no impact upon conformity or deviancy.

As a result of interviews with the campers, we also found that they had different conceptions of what constituted misbehavior in camp from what constituted misbehavior in school. The reasons given for why their discussed misbehaviors were bad also differed as between camp and school milieus. Moreover, the salient dimensions around which they described teachers and camp counselors also differed. We used this finding to partly 'explain away' the apparent discrepancy between the kindergarten and camp studies.

So we resumed our investigations in schools. We interviewed beginning high school students between the fourth and tenth day of their attendance at the school and again three months later. The interviews centered around students' descriptions and reactions to a most recent incident when another student engaged in a misbehavior which the teacher did something about. Hypothesizing that motivation to learn is a variable determining a student's reaction to a deviancy-desist event, we obtained reports of two such incidents from each student. One was from the academic class with the highest motivation to learn and one was from the class with the lowest motivation to learn.

The findings showed *no* relationship between the qualities of a desist-technique and the effects upon audience students. Neither described nor rated anger, punitiveness, firmness, or clarity made any difference upon effects obtained from open-ended or forced-choiced items in the interview.

An analysis of the interviews by Ofchus (1960) showed that the prevailing variable of motivation to learn did make a difference in how students evaluated and reacted to a deviancy-desist event.

This supported our motivation to learn theory except that the results were made complicated by our happening to have asked students to rate their liking for the teachers. There was a significant relationship between liking for the teacher and motivation to learn the subject. An analysis of the results by Ryan showed that both liking and motivation to learn related to reports of paying more attention to the task and of being inclined to behave better after the deviancy-desist event. Liking for the teacher alone related to various judgments about the event such as: fairness, seriousness of the deviancy, and whether teachers overreacted or not to the event. The relative impacts of the related liking and motivation to learn were made even more complicated by Osborne's (1962) coding of the students' descriptions of the teachers. High-liked teachers were described predominantly around task-dimensions: amount of homework, nature of explanations, making task interesting. These are dimensions quite different from those used by our campers when describing camp counselors ('brings us watermelons') and, I suspect, would be different from those used by persons when describing liked boy friends or girl friends.

Ryan, Gump and I attempted to replicate the findings of the interview in a series of experiments with students from the same grade used in the interviews. We varied both motivation to learn and a teacher's desist-technique with paid subjects brought to the university campus ostensibly to help us evaluate methods of teaching. We found that the desist-techniques did make a difference in how the students reacted to an unknown stooge who misbehaved. Three desist-techniques were used:

1. Intense-punitive
2. Mild reprimand
3. Shown-awareness but ignored

These differed in their effects. The prevailing variable of motivation to learn did *not* make a difference in how students reacted to the deviancy-desist event.

Alden (1959) simultaneously conducted another experiment with students using an unknown teacher. She varied teacher-expertness and liking for children as prevailing independent variables and the teachers' use of learning-focus versus approval-focus of her desist-techniques. The desist-techniques *did* make a difference. The prevailing variables of teacher-expertness versus teacher-liking did *not*.

At this point, we were left with many significant chi-squares. *All* our desist-technique studies in first-time experiments or in the first day of kindergarten produced significant findings showing that desist-techniques did make a difference in audience-children's reactions. We could have continued with an indefinite number of further experiments and might eventually have even evolved a miniature theoretical system that would work. However, the desist-techniques did not make a difference in the camp milieu when the observations extended beyond the first few days of contact with the counselor. Nor did the desist-techniques make a difference in the interview study conducted mostly during the second week of school and again three months later. In these, certain prevailing attitudes (motivation to learn and liking for the teacher) *did* make a difference. But these prevailing variables did not make a difference in the experiments. Which findings correspond to reality?

By this time our grant expired. Our next step was to obtain another United States Public Health Grant for studying the management of emotionally disturbed children in regular class-rooms (Kounin, Friesen and Morton, 1966). We had hoped to secure data for desist-techniques as well as for other possible variables influencing their management.

Months of observing emotionally disturbed children in regular classrooms by Dr Morton and myself left us with many questions and impressions. We felt that the behavior of these children varied between different subsettings in a school, with different teachers (even when the same child was observed with different teachers), and seemed to correlate with the behavior of the other children in a classroom. We were also convinced of our limitations as observers: tendencies to see perceptually impressive events to the exclusion of others; tendencies to 'label' teachers and children; inclinations to arrive at premature interpretations about the control of children's behavior that were not supported by events in classrooms observed later; and the inability to record with adequate completeness all the events going on in a classroom. We concluded that the questions we raised required a data-gathering medium that would provide a nonselective, complete, and objective record of events in a classroom. The method should not only provide a means of measuring pre-selected events (i.e. desist-techniques), or of checking existing hypotheses and ideas, but should also provide data on variables not thought of at the time of data gathering. This meant that the data gathering medium must allow for repeated viewings of the same events, thus precluding checklists, rating scales, and secondary data.

We decided to use television. Two TV cameras were mounted in boxes and placed on stands in a classroom. One camera was placed in a position to record the largest possible area of the classroom continuously and without editing. The second camera, equipped with a remote-controlled pan-tilt mechanism, enabled the engineer to record various positions in the classroom and to superimpose this picture on some part of the major picture. Priority was given to videotaping the teacher or the emotionally disturbed child when they were 'lost' from the main picture. Two microphones were used to record sound – the main source being a wireless radio transmitting microphone worn by the teacher that made possible the recording of everything she said. All recording was done by remote-control using equipment in a truck parked outside the school building.

The data that are already analysed are based upon thirty elementary school classrooms recorded for one-half day each. Additional data not yet completely analysed are based upon fifty first and second grade classrooms recorded for a full day each.

We were concerned with teachers' management of overt behavior. Consequently, children's behaviors were scored for deviancy and for work involvement in academic subsettings.

As to some findings. Emotionally disturbed children manifested less school-appropriate behavior than other children and there was less school-appropriate behavior in seatwork subsettings than in teacher conducted recitation subsettings. However, in all subsettings there was a high and significant correlation between the behavior of disturbed children and the others. And all correlations between a teacher-style variable and children's behavior were in the same direction and approximate magnitude for both disturbed and nondisturbed children. We are therefore justified in talking about classroom management techniques that apply to a classroom as a whole.

What, then, are some of the variables related to managerial success: producing work involvement and reducing behavioral deviancy?

Our first look was at desist-techniques – at direct behavior management efforts. The dimensions of desist-techniques scored were: clarity, firmness, punitiveness, intensity, length, and focus. For only one of thirty teachers was there any correlation between any aspect of her desist-technique and the immediate success of the effort in getting the target child to stop his deviancy or to take up the prescribed task. Teachers were also ranked by their mean desist-style scores for the above dimensions. These rankings did *not* correlate with the rankings on deviancy, work involvement or deviancy contagion, for any subsetting, or for either the disturbed or nondisturbed children.

These findings disagree with the findings of the experiments and with the findings from the kindergarten study. They agree with the findings obtained from the high school interview study. In some respect, they also agree with the findings from the kindergarten study where we found significantly more 'no observable effects' during the second through fourth day than on the first day.

Looking back at the negative findings from the field studies and the positive findings from the experiments we are inclined now to feel that the experimenters were deceived more than the subjects by the reasons we gave them for conducting the studies. Our disguise that we were studying first impressions is probably nearer to the truth than our hidden purpose of studying control techniques. As a matter of fact, we might conjecture that we were actually studying opinions rather than first impressions of teachers. When our high school subjects rated the experimental teacher that used rough techniques as being able to better 'control a bunch of tough students' but *not* as being able to better 'control students like myself' we may have been studying that *opinion*.

What then, are some managerial techniques that do make a difference?

One is *withitness*. The demonstration by the teacher that she knows what is going on (selects correct deviancy targets on time, rather than reprimanding a child for whispering when two others are chasing each other) does correlate with deviancy rate and work involvement scores. Correlated with withitness but not directly with deviancy or work involvement was an *enabling* variable of *overlappingness* – of handling two issues simultaneously and not becoming immersed in one issue to the exclusion of the other.

Another managerial dimension relates to techniques of initiating activities and of handling movement. A smoothness-jerkiness dimension correlates highly with managerial success. This score is based upon the percentage of a teacher's transitions from one activity to another that contain:

1. *Dangles* – initiating an activity without immediate follow through;

2. *Flip-flops* – stopping an old activity and initiating a new one and then engaging in an action such as a question about the old one; and

3. *Thrusts* – busting in with the initiation of a new activity without engaging in any action to ascertain the target group's readiness to receive the induction.

Still another dimension of teacher style has to do with techniques of inducing activity-flow and movement. Movement slow-downs and drags consist of such teacher initiated actions as:

1. *Target fragmentation* – having individual members of a group move when the group as a whole is to move;

2. *Prop and actone over-emphasis* – stressing papers, pencils, books, or sitting straight when 'doing arithmetic problems' is the molar task; and

3. *Sheer overtalk*.

These techniques may be said to produce friction in the activity flow and correlate negatively with managerial success.

Another dimension correlating with managerial success pertains to methods of handling satiation. Mr Wallace Friesen has worked out a method for scoring the amount of variety that the teacher schedules in her day's program. This includes not merely changes in content (reading, arithmetic, social studies) but also changes in the type of cognitive challenge, overt behavior pattern, geographical location, social configuration, and responsibility for pacing. The amount of learning-related variety programmed by the teacher is a highly significant variable predictive of managerial success. It should be pointed out that nonlearning related variety (recess, nonacademic games) is *not* significant in producing work involvement and reducing deviancy in academic settings.

We are currently working on attempts to measure techniques of maintaining progress and avoiding repetitiousness as well as some other dimensions. For example, in our new group of fifty classrooms we already found a significant correlation (but lower than the ones already mentioned) on a group-alerting dimension. Teachers, for example, who become immersed in an individual child at times when the group is the movement-target have lower work involvement and higher deviancy scores than teachers whose actions are target-appropriate.

In general, the management of behavior in classrooms is not a function of the techniques of directly controlling behavior – that is, desist-style. Rather, it is a function of the techniques of creating an effective classroom ecology containing such variables as having a nonsatiating learning program, initiating and maintaining movement flow, and aiming teacher actions at appropriate targets. And no doubt, still others yet to be measured.

In this connection, allow me to mention a finding relating to sex differences. We divided the fifty classrooms into those in which girls had better work involvement scores than boys and those in which boys were either as good or better than girls. We then dichotomized the teachers into those who had high or low scores in transition smoothness and also into those having high or low rates of slowdowns. Significantly, it is only in the group of poor movement managers that girls had better scores than boys. Boys were either better or as good as girls in the classrooms of the smooth and non-draggy teachers. (We chose transition techniques for this comparison because it is the only independent variable for the new group of fifty teachers we have completed scoring.)

In conclusion, I would like to point out the value of naturalistic, ecological researches in which many coexisting events are studied in real settings. And this for purely empirical reasons and not from any Gestalt, organismic, existential, or whatever principles. Rather, and more simple-mindedly, to make sure that important prevailing variables are not overlooked for less important ones, no matter how testable and statistically significant the latter might be. In the current stage of behavioral sciences, there is room for researches conducted in the spirit of inquiry to see what can be learned rather than in the spirit of debate to see what hypothesis or theory can be tested.

References

ALDEN, E. (1959), 'The effects on non-target classmates of the teacher's use of expert power and liking power in controlling deviant students', unpublished doctoral dissertation, Wayne State University.

KOUNIN, J., and GUMP, P. (1958), 'The ripple effect in discipline', *Elementary Sch. J.*, vol. 59, pp. 158–62.

KOUNIN, J., GUMP, P., and RYAN, J. (1961), 'Explorations in classroom management', *J. teacher Educ.*, vol. 12, pp. 235–46.

KOUNIN, J., FRIESEN, W. V., and MORTON, A. E. (1966), 'Managing emotionally disturbed children in regular classrooms', *J. educ. Psychol.*, vol. 57, pp. 1–13.

OFCHUS, L. T. (1960), 'The effects on non-target classmates of teacher's efforts to control deviant behavior', unpublished doctoral dissertation, Wayne State University.

OSBORNE, K. (1962), 'Saliencies in students' perceptions of teachers', unpublished doctoral dissertation, Wayne State University.

17 C. H. Madsen Jr, W. C. Becker and D. R. Thomas

Rules, Praise and Ignoring: Elements of Elementary Classroom Control

From C. H. Madsen, W. C. Becker and D. R. Thomas, 'Rules, praise and ignoring: elements of elementary classroom control', *Journal of Applied Behavioral Analysis*, vol. 1, 1968, pp. 139-50.

Modern learning theory is slowly but surely increasing its potential for impact upon social problems. As problems in social development and interaction are more closely examined through the methods of experimental analysis, the importance of learning principles in everyday life becomes clearer. The potential contribution of these developments to childrearing and education appears to be especially significant. This report is a part of a series of studies aimed at demonstrating what the teacher can do to achieve a 'happier', more effective classroom through the systematic use of learning principles. The study grows out of a body of laboratory and field research demonstrating the importance of social reinforcers (smiles, praise, contact, nearness, attention) in establishing and maintaining effective behaviors in children. Extensive field studies in experimental nursery schools by Wolf, Bijou, Baer and their students (e.g. Hart, Reynolds, Baer, Brawley and Harris, 1968; Allen, Hart, Buell, Harris and Wolf, 1965, pp. 307–12; Bijou and Baer, 1963) provided a background for the extension of their work by the present authors to special and typical elementary classrooms. In general, we have found to date that teachers with various 'personalities' and backgrounds can be trained systematically to control their own behavior in ways which will improve the behavior of the children they are teaching (Becker, Madsen, Arnold and Thomas, 1967). We have also found that teachers can 'create' problem behaviors in the classroom by controlling the ways in which they respond to their pupils (Thomas, Becker and Armstrong, 1968; Madsen, Becker, Thomas, Koser and Plager, 1968). It is hoped that field studies of this sort will contribute to more effective teacher training.

The present study is a refinement of an earlier study of Becker,

Madsen, Arnold and Thomas (1967), in which the behavior of two children in each of five classrooms was recorded and related to experimentally controlled changes in teacher behaviors. The teachers were instructed and guided to follow a program which involved making classroom rules explicit, ignoring disruptive behaviors unless someone was getting hurt, and praising appropriate classroom behaviors. Under this program, most of the severe problem children under study showed remarkable improvements in classroom behavior. However, that study lacked certain controls which the present study sought to correct. First, the teachers in the earlier study were in a seminar on behavior theory and practice during baseline conditions. Some target children improved during baseline, apparently because some teachers were beginning to apply what they were learning even though they had been requested not to do so. Second, public relations and time considerations did not make it possible to introduce the components of the experimental program one at a time (rules, ignoring, and praise) to better study their individual contributions. Third, a reversal of teacher behavior was not attempted. Such a reversal would more conclusively show the importance of teacher's behavior in producing the obtained changes. Fourth, extensive recordings of teacher behavior under all experimental conditions were not undertaken in the earlier study. The present study attempted to deal with each of these problems.

Method
Procedures

Teachers in a public elementary school volunteered to participate in the study. After consultation with teachers and observation of the children in the classroom, two children with a high frequency of problem behavior were selected for study in each class. Previously developed behavioral categories (Becker, Madsen, Arnold and Thomas, 1967) were modified for use with these particular children and baseline recordings were made to determine the frequency of problem behaviors. At the end of the baseline period the teachers entered a workshop on applications of behavioral principles in the classroom which provided them with the rationale and principles behind the procedures being introduced in their classes. Various experimental procedures were then introduced, one at a time, and the effects on the target children's behaviors observed. The experiments were begun in late November and continued to the end of the school year.

Subjects

Classroom A. There were twenty-nine children in Mrs A's middle-primary (second grade) room who ranged in school progress from mid-first-grade level to early-third-grade level. Cliff and Frank were chosen as the target children.

Cliff was chosen because he displayed no interest in school. In Mrs A's words, 'he would sit through entire work periods fiddling with objects in his desk, talking, doing nothing, or misbehaving by bothering others and walking around the room. Lately he has started hitting others for no apparent reason. When Cliff was required to stay in at recess to do his work, he would complete the work in a short time and it was usually completely accurate. I was unable to motivate him into working on any task during the regular work periods.' Cliff is the son of a university professor who was born in Europe and immigrated when Cliff was five years old. Cliff scored 91 on an early (CA 5–3) intelligence test. This score was discounted by the examiner because of language problems. His group IQ scores rose steadily (CA 5–9, IQ 103; CA 6–2, IQ 119; CA 7–1, IQ 123). His achievement scores indicated a low-second-grade level at the beginning of the present study. Cliff was seen by the school social worker throughout the entire first grade and throughout this entire study.

Cliff was observed early in the year and it was noted that he did not respond once to teacher's questions. He played with his fingers, scratched himself repeatedly, played in his desk, paid no attention to the assignment and had to stay in at recess to finish his work. Almost continually he made blowing sounds and talked to himself. On occasions he was out of his seat making noises and talking. He would leave the room without permission. Before the study began the observers made the following notes: 'What a silly kid, writing on the bottom of his shoes, writing on his arms, blowing kisses at the girls. He was vying for the attention of the girl behind him, but she ignored him. . . . Poor Cliff! he acts so silly for his age. He tried to talk to the other kids, but none of them would pay attention to him. . . . Cliff seems concerned with the little girl beside him (girl behind him last week). He has a sign on his desk which reads, "Do you love me?". . . .'

Frank was described by his teacher as a likable child. He had a record of misbehavior in the classroom and intense fighting on the playground. He was often out of his seat talking to other children and did not respond to 'discipline'. If someone was reprimanded for doing something, Frank would often do the same thing. Test scores indicated an IQ of 106 (Stanford-Binet) and achievement level just under beginning second grade at the start of school (average California Achievement Test scores 1·6 grades). The school psychologist noted that Frank's mother was a person 'who willingly permitted others to make decisions for her and did not seem able to discipline Frank'. Father was absent from the home during the entire year in the Air Force.

Classroom B. Twenty children were assigned to Mrs B's kindergarten room. Two children were observed initially; one moved from the community shortly after baseline was taken, leaving only Stan for the study.

Stan was described as coming from a truly pathetic home environment. The mother was not married and the family of four children subsisted on state aid. One older brother was enrolled in a special class for the educable retarded. At the beginning of the year, Stan's behavior was characterized by the teacher as 'wild'. She reported that, 'Stan would push and hit and grab at objects and at children. He had no respect for authority and apparently didn't even hear directions. He knew how to swear profusely, and I would have to check his pockets so I would know he wasn't taking home school equipment. He would wander around the room and it was difficult to get him to engage in constructive work. He would frequently destroy any work he did rather than take it home.'

The difficult home situation was made manifest during the month of March. Stan had been absent for two weeks and it was reported that his mother was taking her children out of public school and placing them in a local parochial school. Investigation by school personnel indicated that Stan's mother had moved the children into a relative's home and had gone to the hospital to have another illegitimate baby. A truancy notice was filed for all four children including Stan. Following legal notice the children were returned to school.

Rating of child behavior

The same rating schedule was used in both classrooms except that Isolate Play was added to the list of Inappropriate Behaviors for the kindergarten. Since the children were expected to be involved in structured group activities during observation periods, going off by oneself to play with the many toys or materials in the room was considered inappropriate by the kindergarten teacher. Inappropriate Behavior was defined as the occurrence of one or more of the behaviors listed under Inappropriate Behavior in Table 1 during any observation interval.

Observers were trained in the reliable use of the rating schedule before baseline recordings began. Training consisted of practice in use of the rating schedule in the classroom. Two observers would each rate the same child for twenty minutes and then return to the research office to compare their ratings and discuss their differences with their supervisors. Training was continued until reliability was above 80 per cent on each behavior code. Training lasted approximately two weeks. Reliability was determined periodically throughout the study by dividing the number of agreements by the number of agreements plus disagreements. An agreement was defined as a rating of the same behavior class in the same observation interval. Average reliability over children, behavior classes, and days for the 69 occasions (out of 238) on which it was checked was 81 per cent. Single day reliabilities ranged from 68 per cent to 96 per cent. Reliabilities were checked in each phase of the study.

Instructions to observers followed those used by Becker, Madsen, Arnold and Thomas (1967). In essence, the observers were not to respond to the children, but to fade into the background as much as possible. Teachers, as well as children, quickly learned not to respond to the observers, although early in the study one observer was attacked by a kindergarten child. The observer did not respond to the behavior and it quickly disappeared. Experimental changes were initiated without informing observers in an attempt to control any observer bias. However, the changes were often dramatic enough that observer comments clearly reflected programmed changes in teacher's behavior.

The target children were observed for twenty minutes per day, three days a week. In the middle primary class, observations were taken when the children were engaged in seat work or group instruction. In the kindergarten class, observations were made when structured activities, rather than free play, were expected. Each observer had a clipboard, stopwatch, and rating sheet. The observer would watch for ten seconds and use symbols to record the occurrence of behaviors. In each minute, ratings would be made in five consecutive ten-second intervals and the final ten seconds would be used for recording comments. Each behavior category could be rated only once in a ten-second interval.

Table 1 Behavioral coding categories for children

1. Inappropriate behaviors

Gross motor. Getting out of seat, standing up, running, hopping, skipping, jumping, walking around, moving chair, etc.

Object noise. Tapping pencil or other objects, clapping, tapping feet, rattling or tearing paper, throwing book on desk, slamming desk. Be conservative, only rate if you can hear the noise when eyes are closed. Do *not* include accidental dropping of objects.

Disturbance of other's property. Grabbing objects or work, knocking neighbor's books off desk, destroying another's property, pushing with desk (only rate if someone is there). Throwing objects at another person without hitting them.

Contact (high and low intensity). Hitting, kicking, shoving, pinching, slapping, striking with object, throwing object which hits another person, poking with object, biting, pulling hair, touching, patting, etc. Any physical contact is rated.

Verbalization. Carrying on conversations with other children when it is not permitted. Answers teacher without raising hand or without being called on; making comments or calling out remarks when no questions have been asked; calling teacher's name to get her attention; crying, screaming, singing, whistling, laughing, coughing, or blowing loudly. These responses may be directed to teacher or children.

Turning around. Turning head or head and body to look at another person, showing objects to another child, attending to another child. Must be of four-second duration, or more than 90 degrees using desk as a reference. Not rated unless seated. If this response overlaps two time intervals and cannot be rated in the first because it is less than four-second duration, then rate in the interval in which the end of the response occurs.

Other inappropriate behavior. Ignores teacher's question or command. Does something different from that directed to do, including minor motor behavior such as playing with pencil or eraser when supposed to be writing, coloring while the record is on, doing spelling during the arithmetic lesson, playing with objects. *The child involves himself in a task that is not appropriate.* Not rated when other Inappropriate Behaviors are rated. Must be time off task.

Mouthing objects. Bringing thumb, fingers, pencils, or any object in contact with the mouth.

Isolate play. Limited to kindergarten free-play period. Child must be farther than three feet from any person, neither initiates nor responds to verbalizations with other people, engages in no interaction of a non-verbal nature with other children for the entire ten-second period.

2. Appropriate behaviors.
Time on task: e.g., answers question, listens, raises hand, works on assignment. Must include whole ten-second interval except for Turning Around responses of less than four-seconds' duration.

The primary dependent variable was percentage of intervals in which an Inappropriate Behavior occurred. Since the varieties of Inappropriate Behavior permitted a more detailed analysis with the schedule used, the presentation of results is focused on them, even though functionally their converse (Appropriate Behavior) was the main behavior being manipulated.

Ratings of teacher behavior

Ratings of teacher behavior were obtained to clarify relationships between changes in teacher behavior and changes in child behavior. Recordings of teacher behavior were also used by the experimenters to help the teachers learn the contingent use of Approval and Disapproval Behaviors. The teacher rating schedule is presented in Table 2. Teacher behaviors were recorded by subclasses in relation to child behaviors. That is, the record would show whether a teacher response followed Appropriate child classroom behavior or whether it followed one of the categories of Inappropriate Behavior. Responses to all children were rated. Teacher behavior was scored as the frequency of occurrence of a specified class of behavior during a twenty-minute interval. Teacher ratings were either recorded during one of the periods when a target child was being rated by another observer, or immediately thereafter when only one observer made both ratings. Teacher behavior was rated on the average of once a week, except during experimental transitions, when more frequent ratings were made. The number of days teacher behavior was rated under each condition is given in Table 3. Most recorded teacher behavior (about 85 per cent) fell in the *verbal* Approval or Disapproval categories. For this reason we have used the term *praise* interchangeably with Approval Behaviors and *criticism* interchangeably with Disapproval Behaviors.

Table 2 Coding definitions for teacher behaviors

Appropriate child behavior is defined by the child rating categories. The teacher's rules for classroom behavior must be considered when judging whether the child's behavior is Appropriate or Inappropriate.

1. Teacher Approval following Appropriate Child Behavior.
Contact. Positive physical contact such as embracing, kissing, patting, holding arm or hand, sitting on lap.
Praise. Verbal comments indicating approval, commendation or achievement. Examples: that's good, you are doing right, you are studying well, I like you, thank you, you make me happy.
Facial attention. Smiling at child.

2. Teacher Approval following Inappropriate Child Behavior.
Same codes as under 1.

3. Teacher Disapproval following Appropriate Child Behavior.
Holding the child. Forcibly holding the child, putting child out in the hall, grabbing, hitting, spanking, slapping, shaking the child.
Criticism. Critical comments of high or low intensity, yelling, scolding, raising voice. Examples: that's wrong, don't do that, stop talking, did I call on you, you are wasting your time, don't laugh, you know what you are supposed to do.
Threats. Consequences mentioned by the teacher to be used at a later time. If — then — comments.
Facial attention. Frowning or grimacing at a child.

4. Teacher Disapproval following Inappropriate Child Behavior. Same codes as under 3.

5. 'Time-out' Procedures.*
The teacher turns out the lights and says nothing.
The teacher turns her back and waits for silence.
The teacher stops talking and waits for quiet.
Keeping in for recess.
Sending child to office.
Depriving child in the classroom of some privilege.

6. Academic Recognition.
Calling on a child for an answer. Giving 'feedback' for academic correctness.

Reliability of measures of teacher behavior were checked approximately every other rating day (21 of 42 occasions for the two teachers) by dividing the agreements as to time interval and behavior codes by the agreements plus disagreements. Average reliability over behavior classes, teachers, and days was 84 per cent with a range from 70 per cent to 96 per cent for individual day measures.

Experimental conditions

In the middle-primary class (Class A) the experimental conditions may be summarized consisting of *Baseline*; introduction of *Rules*; *Rules* plus *Ignoring* deviant behavior; *Rules* plus *Ignoring* plus *Praise* for appropriate behavior; return to Baseline; and finally reinstatement of *Rules*, *Ignoring*, and *Praise*. In the kindergarten class (Class B) the experimental conditions consisted of *Baseline*; introduction of *Rules*; *Ignoring* Inappropriate Behavior (without continuing to emphasize rules); and the combination of *Rules*, *Ignoring*, and *Praise*.

The various experimental procedures were to be used by the teachers for the classroom as a whole throughout the day, not just for the children whose behavior was being recorded, and not just when observers were present.

Baseline. During the Baseline period the teachers conducted

* These are procedural definitions of teacher behaviors possibly involving the withdrawal of reinforcers as a consequence of disruptive behaviors which teacher could not ignore.

their classes in their typical way. No attempt was made to influence their behavior.

Rules. Many people would argue that just telling children what is expected should have considerable effect on their behavior. We wished to explore this question empirically. Teachers were instructed individually and given written instructions as follows:

The first phase of your participation in the use of behavioral principles to modify classroom behaviors is to specify explicit rules of classroom conduct. When this is done, there is no doubt as to what is expected of the children in your classroom. However, do not expect a dramatic shift in classroom control, as we all know that knowing the prohibitions does not always keep people from 'sin'. This is the first phase in the program and inappropriate behavior should be reduced, but perhaps not eliminated. The rules should be formulated with the class and posted in a conspicuous location (a chart in front of the room or a special place on the chalkboard where they will not be erased). Go over the rules three or four times asking the class to repeat them back to you when they are initially formulated and use the following guidelines:

1. Make the rules short and to the point so they can be easily memorized.

2. Five or six rules are adequate. Special instructions for specific occasions are best given when the occasion arises. Children will not remember long lists of rules.

3. Where possible phrase the rules in a positive not a negative manner (for example, 'Sit quietly while working,' rather than, 'Don't talk to your neighbors'). We want to emphasize positive actions.

4. Keep a sheet on your desk and record the number of times you review the rules with the class (strive for at least four to six repetitions per day). Remember that young children do not have the retention span of an adult and frequent reminders are necessary. Let the children recite the rules as you ask them, rather than always enumerating them yourself.

5. Remind the class of the rules at times other than when someone has misbehaved.

6. Try to change no other aspects of your classroom conduct except for the presentation of the rules at appropriate times.

Teacher tally sheets indicated that these instructions were followed quite explicitly. The average number of presentations of rules was 5·2 per day.

Ignoring inappropriate behavior. The second experimental phase involved Ignoring Inappropriate Behavior. In Class A, repetition of rules was also continued. Individual conferences to explain written instructions were given both teachers. Both teachers were given the following instructions:

The first aspect of the study was to make expectations explicit. This you have been doing over the past few weeks. During the next phase of the study you should learn to *ignore* (do not attend to) behaviors which interfere with learning or teaching, unless of course, a child is being hurt by another, in which case use a punishment which seems appropriate, preferably withdrawal of some positive reinforcement. Learning to ignore is rather difficult. Most of us pay attention to the violations. For example, instead of ignoring we often say such things as the following: 'Johnny, you know you are supposed to be working'; 'Sue, will you stop bothering your neighbors'; 'Henrietta, you have been at that window for a long time'; 'Jack, can you keep your hands off Bill'; 'Susie, will you please sit down'; 'Alex, stop running around and do your work'; 'Jane, will you please stop rocking on your chair.'

Behaviors which are to be ignored include motor behaviors such as getting out of seat, standing up, running, walking around the room, moving chairs, or sitting in a contorted manner. Any verbal comment or noise not connected with the assignments should also be ignored, such as: carrying on conversations with other children when it is not permitted, answering questions without raising hands or being called on, making remarks when no questions have been asked, calling your name to get attention and extraneous noises such as crying, whistling, laughing loudly, blowing noise, or coughing. An additional important group of behaviors to be ignored are those which the student engages in when he is supposed to be doing other things, e.g. when the child ignores your instructions you are to ignore him. Any noises made with objects, playing with pencils, or other materials should be ignored, as well as, taking things from or disturbing another student by turning around and touching or grabbing him.

The reason for this phase of the experiment is to test the possibility that attention to Inappropriate Behavior may serve to strengthen the very behavior that the attention is intended to diminish. Inappropriate Behavior may be strengthened by paying attention to it even though you may think that you are punishing the behavior.

Praise for appropriate behavior. The third phase of the experiment included individual contacts with teachers to encourage and train

Praising of Appropriate Behavior. The Praise instructions to the teachers were as follows:

The first phase included specifying explicit rules, writing them on the board and reviewing them four to six times per day. The second phase was designed to reduce the amount of attention paid to behaviors which were unwanted by ignoring them. This third phase is primarily directed toward *increasing* Appropriate Behaviors through praise and other forms of approval. Teachers are inclined to take good behavior for granted and pay attention only when a child acts up or misbehaves. We are now asking you to try something different. This procedure is characterized as 'catching the child being good' and making a comment designed to reward the child for good behavior. Give praise, attention, or smile when the child is doing what is expected during the particular class period in question. Inappropriate Behavior would not be a problem if all children were engaging in a great deal of study and school behavior, therefore, it is necessary to apply what you have learned in the workshop. Shape by successive approximations the behavior desired by using praise and attention. Start 'small' by giving praise and attention at the first signs of Appropriate Behavior and work toward greater goals. Pay close attention to those children who normally engage in a great deal of misbehavior. Watch carefully and when the child begins to behave appropriately, make a comment such as, 'You're doing a fine job, (name).' It is very important during the first few days to catch as many good behaviors as possible. Even though a child has just thrown an eraser at the teacher (one minute ago) and is now studying, you should praise the study behavior. (It might also decrease the rate of eraser throwing.) We are assuming that your commendation and praise are important to the child. This is generally the case, but sometimes it takes a while for praise to become effective. Persistence in catching children being good and delivering praise and attention should eventually pay off in a better behaved classroom.

Some examples of praise comments are as follows:

I like the way you're doing your work quietly, (name).

That's the way I like to see you work —.

That's a very good job —.

You're doing fine —.

You got two right —, that's very good (if he generally gets no answers right).

In general, give praise for achievement, prosocial behavior, and following the group rules. Specifically, you can praise for concentrating on individual work, raising hand when appropriate, responding to questions, paying attention to directions and following through, sitting in desk and studying, sitting quietly if noise has been a problem. Try to use variety and expression in your comments. Stay away from sarcasm. Attempt to become spontaneous in your praise and smile when delivering praise. At first you will probably get the feeling that you are praising a great deal and it sounds a little phony to your ears. This is a typical reaction and it becomes more natural with the passage of time. Spread your praise and attention around. If comments sometimes might interfere with the ongoing class activities then use facial attention and smiles. Walk around the room during study time and pat or place your hand on the back of a child who is doing a good job. Praise quietly spoken to the children has been found effective in combination with some physical sign of approval.

General Rule: Give *praise* and *attention* to behaviors which facilitate learning. Tell the child what he is being praised for. Try to reinforce behaviors incompatible with those you wish to decrease.

The teachers were also instructed to continue to ignore deviant behavior and to repeat the rules several times a day.

Additional training given teachers consisted of: (*a*) discussion of problems with suggested solutions during weekly seminars on behavior analysis, and (*b*) specific suggestions from the experimenter on possible alternative responses in specific situations based on the experimenter's observations of the teachers during experimental transitions, or based on observer data and notes at other times when the data showed that the teachers were not on program.

Additional cues were provided to implement the program. Cards were placed on the teachers' desks containing the instructions for the experimental phase in which they were engaged.

Reversal. In Class A the final experimental conditions involved an attempt to return to Baseline, followed by a reinstatement of the *Rules, Praise*, and *Ignore* condition. On the basis of the earlier observations of Teacher A, we were able to specify to her how frequently she made disapproving and approving comments. The success of this procedure can be judged from the data.

Results

Percentage of observation intervals in which Inappropriate Behaviors occurred as a function of conditions is graphed in Figures 1 and 2. Major changes in Inappropriate Behaviors occurred only

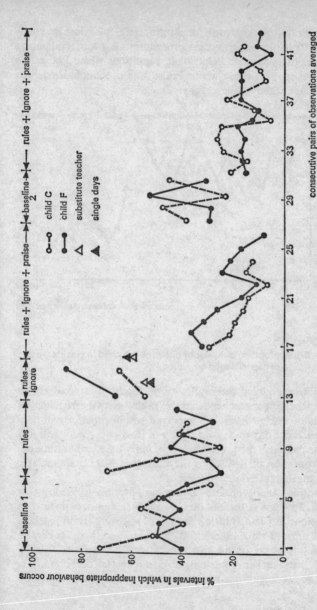

Figure 1 Inappropriate behavior of two problem children in classroom A as a function of experimental conditions

when Praise or Approval for Appropriate Behaviors was emphasized in the experimental procedures. A *t*-test, comparing average Inappropriate Behavior in conditions where Praise was emphasized with those where Praise was not emphasized, was significant at the 0·05 level ($df = 2$).

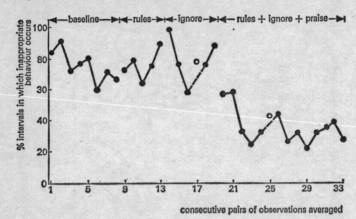

o substitute teacher

Figure 2 Inappropriate behavior of one problem child in classroom B as a function of experimental conditions

Before examining the results more closely, it is necessary to inspect the data on teacher behavior. Table 3 gives the frequency of classes of teacher behaviors averaged within experimental conditions. Since day-to-day variability of teacher behavior was low for the measures used, these averages fairly reflect what went on.

Introduction of Rules into the classroom had no appreciable effect on Inappropriate Behavior.

Ignoring Inappropriate Behaviors produced inconsistent results. In Class A the children clearly became worse under this condition; in Class B little change was apparent. Both teachers had a difficult time adhering to this condition, and Teacher A found this phase of the experiment very unpleasant. Table 3 shows that Teacher A was only able to reduce critical comments from an average of one per 1 minute to an average of three in 4 minutes. Teacher B cut her critical comments in half. In view of these difficulties, the present results cannot be taken as a clear test of the effects of responding with Disapproval to Inappropriate Behaviors.

The failure to eliminate Disapproval Reactions to Inappropriate Behaviors in Phase Three of the experiment, adds some ambiguities to the interpretation of the Phase Four data for Teacher A. The Rules, Ignore, and Praise condition for Teacher A involved both a reduction in critical comments (Ignoring) as well as a marked increase in Praise. As demonstrated previously (Becker, Madsen, Arnold and Thomas, 1967), this combination of procedures is very effective in reducing inappropriate classroom behaviors, but we still lack a clear isolation of effects. The data for Teacher B are not confounded with a simultaneous shift in frequency of Disapproval and Approval Reactions, but they are made less interpretable by a marked shift in Academic Recognition (defined in Table 2) which occurred when the shift in Praise was made. Since Academic Recognition does not show any systematic relations to level of Appropriate Behaviors elsewhere in the study, we are not inclined to interpret this change as showing a causal effect. A best guess is that the effective use of Praise gave the teacher more time to focus on academic skills.

The reversal operation for Teacher A quite clearly shows that the combination of Praising and Ignoring exerts a strong control over Appropriate Behaviors.

As with Academic Recognition, no attempt was made to control how frequently the teacher used procedures labelled 'Time-out' (defined in Table 2). The frequency data reported in Table 4 indicates that during Baseline, Teacher A, especially, used 'Time-out' procedures to try to establish control (usually turning off the lights until the children were quiet). The changes in the frequency of use of 'Time-out' procedures are not systematically related to the behavior changes graphed in Figures 1 and 2.

In summary, the main results indicate: (a) that Rules alone had little effect in improving classroom behavior, (b) the functional status of Ignoring Inappropriate Behavior needs further clarification, (c) the combination of Ignoring and Praising was very effective in achieving better classroom behavior, and (d) Praise for Appropriate Behaviors was probably the key

Table 3 Teacher behavior – averages for experimental conditions (frequency per 20-minute observation)

	Experimental conditions					
Teacher A *Behavior classes*	*Baseline 1*	*Rules*	*Rules + ignore*	*Rules + ignore + praise 1*	*Baseline 2*	*Rules + ignore + praise 2*
Approval to appropriate	1·2	2·0	0·0	18·2	2·5	12·5
Approval to inappropriate	8·7	0·8	2·0	1·2	4·0	5·1
Disapproval to inappropriate	18·5	20·5	15·7	4·1	9·8	3·5
Disapproval to appropriate	0·9	0·7	1·0	0·3	0·9	0·0
Time-out	3·3	1·4	1·7	0·4	0·0	0·1
Academic recognition	26·5	23·6	46·3	52·4	45·4	45·6
Days observed	15	8	3	11	4	9

Teacher B *Behavior classes*	*Baseline*	*Rules*	*Rules + Ignore*	*Rules + ignore + praise*
Approval to appropriate	19·2	14·1	19·3	35·2
Approval to inappropriate	1·9	0·9	0·3	0·0
Disapproval to inappropriate	16·9	22·1	10·6	10·8
Disapproval to appropriate	0·0	0·0	0·0	0·0
Time-out	1·5	1·5	0·3	0·4
Academic recognition	14·5	5·1	6·5	35·6
Days observed	8	6	6	10

teacher behavior in achieving effective classroom management.

The effects of the experimental procedures on individual classes of behavior for the two children in Class A are presented in Table 4. The data in Table 4 illustrate that with a few exceptions the effects on individual classes of behavior are similar to those for Inappropriate Behavior as a whole.

Discussion
Technical considerations

The problems of gaining good data and maintaining adequate experimental control in an ongoing classroom in a public school have not all been recognized as yet, much less solved. The greatest difficulty encountered was that of maintaining stable control over some important variables while others were being changed. When these variables involve aspects of teacher behavior, the problem becomes one of helping the teacher maintain discriminative control over her own behavior. Daily feedback from the experimenter, based on the observer ratings, can help in this task (i.e. show the teacher the up-to-date graph of her behavior). Also, providing the teacher with a small counter to help monitor her own behavior can be helpful (Thomas, Becker and Armstrong, 1968; Madsen, Becker, Thomas, Koger and Plager, 1968). Most difficult to control in the present study was teacher's Disapproving Reactions to Inappropriate Behaviors during the Ignore Phase of the experiment. Teacher A became very 'upset' as her classroom became worse. One solution to this problem might be a pre-study in which the teacher is trained in effective management techniques, and then taken through a series of short periods where both Approval and Disapproval are eliminated and one or the other reinstated. The teacher would then have confidence that she can effectively handle her class and be better able to tolerate short periods of chaos (if such periods did occur). She would also have had sufficient training in monitoring her own behavior to permit more effective control.

No attempt was made to program the frequency of various classes of Academic Recognition behaviors. Since such behavior may be important in interpreting results, and was found to vary with some experimental conditions, future work should strive to hold this behavior constant also.

Table 4 Percentage of intervals in which behaviors occur: averages for two children in classroom A by experimental conditions

	Experimental conditions					
Behavior classes*	Baseline 1	Rules	Rules + ignore	Rules + ignore + praise 1	Baseline 2	Rules + ignore + praise 2
Inappropriate behavior†	46·8	39·8	68·5	20·5	37·6	15·1
Gross motor	13·9	11·3	32·7	5·9	15·5	4·1
Object noise	3·5	1·4	1·3	0·5	1·9	0·8
Disturbing other's property	3·3	1·8	1·9	0·7	0·7	0·3
Turning around	21·6	9·9	11·4	9·1	12·8	7·6
Verbalizations	12·0	16·8	21·8	6·5	8·0	3·5
Other inappropriate behavior	10·9	7·8	16·5	3·9	7·8	2·6
Mouthing objects	5·5	2·9	3·5	0·7	0·2	0·1

* Note: *Contact* occurred less than 1 per cent of the time and is not tabulated here.

† The sum of the separate problem behaviors will exceed that for Inappropriate Behavior, since the latter measure does not reflect the possibility that more than one class of problem behaviors may occur in an interval.

The present study emphasized the importance of contingencies between student and teacher behaviors, but did not measure them directly. While producing similar effects on two children in the same classroom and one child in another classroom, and showing correlated changes in teacher behaviors (including a reversal operation), more powerful data are potentially obtainable with a different technology. Videotape recordings could enable the use of present coding techniques to obtain contingency data on all classroom members over longer observation periods. Just as the children adapted to the presence of observers, a class could be adapted to the presence of a TV camera man. Costs could be trimmed by saving only some sample tapes and re-using others after reliability ratings are obtained. The current observation procedures (short of having an observer for each child) cannot readily be extended to include simultaneous coding of teacher and child behavior without over-taxing the observers. The present findings, and related studies in this series, are sufficiently promising to warrant an investment in more powerful recording equipment.

Teacher reactions

Teacher A. Initially, Mrs A generally maintained control through scolding and loud critical comments. There were frequent periods of chaos, which she handled by various threats.

When praise was finally added to the program, Mrs A had these reactions: 'I was amazed at the difference the procedure made in the atmosphere of the classroom and even my own personal feelings. I realized that in praising the well-behaved children and ignoring the bad, I was finding myself looking for the good in the children. It was indeed rewarding to see the good rather than always criticizing. . . . I became convinced that a positive approach to discipline was the answer.'

Teacher B. During Baseline Mrs B was dispensing a great deal of praise and approval to her classroom, but it was not always contingent on Appropriate Behavior. Her timing was wrong and inconsistencies were apparent. For example, on one occasion two children were fighting with scissors. The instigator was placed under a table away from the rest of the class and left there for 3 minutes. After 3 minutes Mrs B took the child in her arms and brought her back to the group even though she was still emitting occasional loud screams. Mrs B would also ignore behavior for a period of time and then would revert to responding to Inappropriate Behavior with a negative comment; she occasionally gave Approval for Inappropriate Behavior. The training given in seminar and discussions with the experimenter led to an effective use of contingencies. Teacher B was also able to use this training to provide instructions and training for her aide to eliminate problems which arose in the final phase of study when the aide was continuing to respond to Disruptive Behaviors.

Changes in the children

Cliff showed little change until Mrs A started praising Appropriate Behavior, except to get worse during the Ignore phase. He was often doing no academic work, talking to peers, and just fiddling away his time. It took considerable effort by Mrs A to catch Cliff showing praiseworthy behavior. As the use of praise continued, Cliff worked harder on his assigned tasks, learned to ignore other children who were misbehaving, and would raise his hand to get teacher's attention. He participated more in class discussions. He was moved up to the fastest arithmetic group.

Frank showed little change in his 'hyperactive' and 'inattentive' behaviors until praise was introduced. Frank responded rapidly to praise. After just two days in the 'praise' phase, Frank was observed to clean his desk quietly and quickly after completing a handwriting assignment. He was able to finish a task and study on his own until the teacher initiated a new activity. He began to ask for extra assignments and volunteered to do things to help his teacher. He had learned to sit quietly (when appropriate), to listen, and to raise his hand to participate in class discussion, the latter occurring quiet frequently.

Stan slowly improved after contingent praise was instituted, but some of the gains made by Mrs B were in part undone by the teacher aide. The aide was described as playing policeman and it took special efforts by the teacher to get her to follow the program. Mrs B summarized the changes in Stan as follows: 'Stan has changed from a sullen, morose, muttering, angry individual into a boy whose smile seems to cover his whole face.' He became very responsive to teacher praise and learned to follow classroom rules, to pay attention to teacher-directed activities for long periods of time, and to interact with his peers in a more friendly way.

Implications

This replication and refinement of an earlier study by Becker, Madsen, Arnold and Thomas (1967) adds further confidence to the assertion that teachers can be taught systematic procedures and can use them to gain more effective behaviors from their students. Unless teachers are effective in getting children 'ready to learn', their technical teaching skills are likely to be wasted. Knowledge of differential social reinforcement procedures, as well as other behavioral principles, can greatly enhance teachers' enjoyment of the profession and their contribution to effective development of the students.

The reader should note that while we formally recorded the behavior of a few target children, teacher and observer comments indicated dramatic changes in the whole 'atmosphere' of the classroom and in the teachers' enjoyment of their classes.

References

ALLEN, K. E., HART, B. M., BUELL, J. S., HARRIS, F. R., and WOLF, M. M. (1965), 'Effects of social reinforcement on isolate behavior of a nursery school child', in L. P. Ullmann and L. Krasner (eds.), *Case Studies in Behavior Modification*, Holt, Rinehart & Winston.

BECKER, W. C., MADSEN, C. H. Jr, ARNOLD, C. R., and THOMAS, D. R. (1967), 'The contingent use of teacher attention and praise in reducing classroom behavior problems', *Special Educ.*, vol. 1, pp. 287–307.

BIJOU, S. W., and BAER, D. M. (1963), 'Some methodological contributions from a functional analysis of child development', in L. P. Lipsitt and C. S. Spiker (eds.), *Advances in Child Development and Behavior*, Academic Press, pp. 197–231.

HART, B. M., REYNOLDS, N. J., BAER, D. M., BRAWLEY, E. R., and HARRIS, F. R. (1968), 'Effect of contingent and non-contingent social reinforcement on the cooperative play of a preschool child', *J. Applied Behav. Anal.*, vol. 1, pp. 73–6.

MADSEN, C. H. Jr, BECKER, W. C., THOMAS, D. R., KOSER, L., and PLAGER, E. (1968), 'An analysis of the reinforcing function of "Sit Down" Commands', in R. K. Parker (ed.), *Readings in Educational Psychology*, Allyn and Bacon.

THOMAS, D. R., BECKER, W. C., and ARMSTRONG, M. (1968), 'Production and elimination of disruptive classroom behavior by systematically varying teacher's behavior', *J. appl. Behav. Anal.* vol. 1, pp. 35–45.

Part Six
Communication in Classrooms

Communication between teachers and pupils can be represented in many ways: as networks between individuals, as analyses of content, or as distinctive patterns of verbal or nonverbal behaviours. Whichever way we look at it, however, it is complicated in its expression, and of exceptional importance, although it is only in recent years that observation and recording techniques have provided the means for systematic accounts of what is said, how it is said, and to whom and how often teachers speak.

The article by Jackson and Lahaderne shows how a fairly simple observational procedure can be used to bring out the differences in types and frequencies of communication acts within and across classrooms.

The other two articles are both concerned with factors influencing the effectiveness of teacher–pupil communication. Rosenshine reviews available evidence about the effects of teacher enthusiasm and of various more precisely defined behaviours which may be reflected in observers' ratings on a scale of 'enthusiasm'. Wright and Nuthall describe an investigation which is interesting not only because of its findings but also because it exemplifies one current approach to research on the effects of teachers' behaviour upon pupils' learning.

18 P. W. Jackson and H. M. Lahaderne

Inequalities of Teacher–Pupil Contacts

From P. W. Jackson and H. M. Lahaderne, 'Inequalities of teacher–pupil contacts', *Psychology in the Schools*, vol. 4, 1967, pp. 204-11.

Elementary school classrooms are busy places, as every teacher who works in one knows. Activities stop and start, conversations wax and wane, minor crises come and go. The teacher moves about the room, from blackboard to desk, to supply closet, now talking to a group in front of the map, now pausing to quell a disturbance at the science table, now examining the work of a girl in the corner, now shaking his head at a boy on his way to the pencil sharpener. Bells ring, chalk breaks, books drop, and a small boy enters with an announcement that today there will be an indoor recess. Anyone witnessing such events for a considerable length of time is inevitably impressed, if not overwhelmed, by the variety of things going on in these densely populated hives of educational activity.

The purpose of this report is to describe and discuss one aspect of this busyness as it was observed in four sixth-grade classrooms. The observations focused on the flow of communication between the teacher and individual students. Certain features of that flow are evident to even the most casual observer. For example, the teacher's communicative energies are spread about and, sooner or later, they touch all of his students. For a time he talks to Billy, then he turns to Sam, then to Sarah, then back to Billy, then on to Elaine, and so forth. Only slightly less obvious is the uneven distribution of these energies throughout the class. Over a long period of time Billy may get more than his share of personal attention from the teacher, and Sarah less than her share. Another salient feature of these communications is that either the teacher or the student may initiate them. Moreover, some students speak to the teacher only when called on; others are incessant hand-wavers. Finally the careful observer may note that students differ not only in the total amount of attention, or communicative 'bits', they receive from their teacher but also in the overall content of these interchanges. Some students talk about instructional matters more than do others; some receive more disciplinary messages than do most of their classmates. The aim of this study was to describe these apparent inequalities with greater precision than is possible through casual observation.

Method

The data were collected in four sixth-grade classrooms located in a predominantly white, working-class suburb. Two of the classrooms, each containing thirty-four pupils, were in one school; the other two, each containing twenty-nine pupils, were in another school. Two of the four teachers were men and two were women. Pupil placement in the two schools was based solely on the student's place of residence. So far as could be determined by test results and observation, the pupil composition of each room was heterogeneous.

Visits to the classrooms began in late September and continued for two months. The length of the visits ranged from a half hour to a full day. During each visit periodic tallies of teacher-pupil communications were made along with other observations whose content is not relevant to this paper. When the visit lasted for an hour or longer, the communication tallies were spaced throughout that time in units of approximately twenty minutes each.

Cumulatively, the periods during which communication counts were taken averaged about nine-and-a-half hours in each room. The exact totals for the four classrooms were 9·0, 9·4, 9·7, and 10·2 hours. These totals comprised approximately thirty-six periods of tallying in each room. The observations were distributed over the entire school week and sampled all the activities of each room.

The observation schedule required an entry to be made on a tally sheet each time there was an intentional transmission of information between the teacher and an individual student. Messages directed to more than one student were ignored. The tally sheet was designed so that each entry designated (a) which student was involved in the communication; (b) whether the initiator of the message was the teacher or the student; and (c) whether the content of the message was primarily instructional, managerial, or prohibitory. Instructional messages were defined as those in which some reference was made to curriculum content or to the attainment of educational objectives. Managerial messages dealt with the interpretation of classroom rules and the definition of permissible behavior. Prohibitory messages dealt with keeping order and punishing misbehavior.

A major advantage of the observational technique, from the standpoint of the person using it, is its simplicity. The number of content categories are relatively few and fairly clear-cut. A second advantage is that it can be employed even when the precise content of the teacher's or student's remarks cannot be heard or when the communication is non-verbal. When a student approaches the teacher with an open workbook in his hand or when the teacher leans over the desk of a student to examine his seatwork, the observer is usually safe in classifying the interchange as instructional, even though the remarks are inaudible. Similarly, when a teacher snaps his fingers and points to a student across the room, the observer can be fairly certain that he is witnessing a prohibitory message even though no words are spoken. The ability to categorize messages that are only partially overheard or that do not entail words is particularly important in elementary classrooms where teachers and students are very mobile and where the occasion for certain messages recurs so frequently that their transmission becomes highly stylized and abbreviated.

Although the simplicity of the observational scheme is one of its chief advantages, it is also its major weakness. When the buzz of classroom talk is reduced to a set of hash marks clustered under three broad headings, the resultant picture reveals only the palest outline of the complex reality from which it was extracted. Instructional talk can be clear or confused, managerial messages can be consistent or inconsistent, disciplinary commands can be shouted or whispered. Under the present scheme all of this richness, which includes much of the information on which teacher evaluations are commonly based, is lost. It is true that all observational procedures succeed in capturing only a small fraction of the events to which they are applied, but the device employed here is perhaps a more ruthless filter than most.

Results

The choice of four classrooms at the same grade level and in the same community was designed to reduce the effect of grade level and social class variation. An eleven-year-old child in this community might have been assigned, by chance, to any one of the four rooms. What difference would the assignment make to the individual teacher-pupil contacts he would witness and participate in? A partial answer to that question is provided by the data in Table 1.

Table 1 **Hourly rates of teacher-pupil interaction**

Content of interaction	*Classroom*			
	A	B	C	D
Instructional	73	76	82	88
Managerial	24	9	8	12
Prohibitory	24	8	13	10
Total	121	93	103	110

The most obvious conclusion to be derived from Table 1 is that no matter in which room a student found himself he would discover his teacher to be busy talking to individual students. The number of hourly interchanges described in that table becomes even more impressive when it is recalled that communications with groups of students or with the entire class are not included in this summary. Here, incidentally, is one more scrap of evidence, if any more is needed, to explain why teachers are fatigued at the end of a working day.

Only slightly less obvious than the rapid rate of interaction is the fact that most of the four teachers' time is taken up in instructional interchanges. In other words, the teachers spend much energy communicating with individual students and most of that energy is spent talking about or listening to academic matters. Moreover, so far as the sheer frequency of instructional interchanges is concerned, it still does not seem to matter too much in which of the four classrooms an eleven-year-old lands. No matter where he goes he is apt to see his teacher talking with an individual student about an instructional matter slightly more often than once a minute.

The four rooms, however, no longer look alike when compared on hourly rates of managerial and prohibitory interchanges. Classroom A is noticeably different from the other three. Presumably a student in that room would witness or be involved in almost three times as many managerial interchanges as would, say, a student in Classroom C. He might also perceive three times as many disciplinary commands as might a student in Classroom B – the room directly across the hall.

Although they usually can be clearly differentiated by the observer, managerial and prohibitory messages have something in common. They both deal with the institutional workings of the classroom. They entail the expectations defining the rights and privileges of students and governing the flow of people and material in the room. In these terms, the teacher in Classroom A seemed to be much more involved in institutional matters than were his colleagues. This is not to say that such a difference in involvement is good or bad, only that it exists and seems pronounced enough to be noticed by a student moving from Classroom A to one of the other rooms.

Finally, in order to appreciate the size of the differences revealed in Table 1 it is necessary to recall that the numbers depicted there are hourly rates based on observations spanning a period of two months. If each of those rates were multiplied by the number of hours in a school year (approximately 1000), the absolute differences among the four classrooms would become quite striking. Thus, over the year a student in Classroom A might witness as many as 16,000 more disciplinary messages than might a student in Classroom B. In Room A, when the teacher turns to a misbehaving student and says, 'If I've told you once, I've told you a thousand times . . .' he probably means it. Admittedly, this kind of comparison is questionable because it assumes that the hourly rates hold throughout the year. None the less, the projected yearly totals call attention to the cumulative significance of events that otherwise might pass unnoticed during a brief observation.

The data in Table 2 reveal who initiates the interchanges. The line showing the totals reveals that the flow of communication in these four classrooms is much more under the control of the teacher than of the students. Moreover, the hourly rate of initiated messages is fairly uniform for the four teachers. In each room the teacher sets into motion about 80 individual interchanges every hour.

Although the initiation rates are roughly equal for the four teachers, the rates for the students are not. In two of the classrooms, A and D, students are much more active in initiating messages than

Table 2 Hourly interactions initiated by teachers and pupils

Content of interaction	Classroom							
	A		B		C		D	
	Teacher	Pupil	Teacher	Pupil	Teacher	Pupil	Teacher	Pupil
Instructional	49·0	24·0	67·0	8·0	67·0	15·0	56·0	32·0
Managerial	9·0	15·0	3·0	6·0	6·0	2·0	6·0	6·0
Prohibitory	23·7	0·3*	7·9	0·1	13·0	0·0	9·5	0·5
Total	81·7	39·3	77·9	14·1	86·0	17·0	71·5	38·5

* A pupil occasionally requested a teacher to discipline one of his classmates. This was the only way in which a pupil could initiate a prohibitory message.

they are in the other two. Also, in Classrooms A and D the students directed unsolicited communications to their teacher two or three times as often as they did in Classrooms B and C. One gets the feeling that the teachers in rooms with high student initiation are kept more on the go, in the sense of being called on to respond to students' queries.

The subdivision of the interactions into the three categories – instructional, managerial, and prohibitory – reveals further differences in the patterns of initiating messages. The rooms having high student initiation rates differ in the way students divide their energies between instructional and managerial matters. When students initiate contacts with the teacher in Classroom D they are more likely to deal with instructional affairs than is true in Classroom A. In the latter classroom, student queries more frequently have an institutional focus. Thus, although the teachers in both rooms seemingly deal with about the same number of students' requests every hour, the professional demands represented by those requests are noticeably different in the two settings.

The classroom differences revealed by this crude analysis are blurry, to be sure, but they are sufficiently clear to confirm what every schoolboy knows: the quality of school life depends partially on the particular room in which fate deposits him. In addition, the differences call attention to the institutional character of school life, a feature so pervasive that it is often overlooked. Classrooms may be designed for instructional ends, but much that goes on there has little to do with instruction *per se*. Furthermore, there seem to be real differences from room to room in the extent to which the institutional aspects of school are salient. In some rooms, if our data are to be believed, students seem to bang against the bars more than in others.

So far as total classroom experience is concerned it matters not only in which room a pupil is but also whether the pupil is a boy or a girl. Even with observational categories as broad as those employed in this study, there emerges a marked sex difference in teacher-pupil interaction. This difference is summarized in Table 3.

The percentages in Table 3 almost speak for themselves. They show, first, that though sex makes a difference in every classroom it does not always make the same difference. Second, they dramatically confirm the popular notion that boys are the major source of classroom misbehavior. Each of these findings deserves comment.

Table 3 Percentages of teacher–pupil interactions involving boys

Classroom	Percentage of male pupils	Percentage of interactions		
		Instructional	Managerial	Prohibitory
A	50·0	60·9†	61·6†	89·6†
B	58·8	61·2	75·0*	85·5†
C	44·8	36·4†	42·0	69·6†
D	44·8	61·0†	58·9†	90·1†

* $p < 0.01$.
† $p < 0.02$.

The least clear pattern of sex differences is seen in the findings on instructional messages. In Classrooms A and D, boys receive more than their share of such messages and in Classroom C, they receive less than their share. The boys in Classroom B participate in a proportion of instructional interchanges commensurate with the size of their sub-group. Thus, at least with respect to this observational category there seems to be no sex difference that holds across all four classes. Yet the fact that three of the four percentages differ significantly from what might be expected by chance suggests that the sex of students is an important variable even though it may function differently from room to room.

The percentages of managerial interchanges involving boys are somewhat more consistent than are those dealing with instructional matters. In three of the four classrooms boys are involved in noticeably more than their share of these interactions. Even in Classroom C, where they received proportionately fewer instructional interchanges than did girls, boys seem to hold their own when it comes to talking with the teacher about managerial affairs. Remembering what was said earlier about the institutional character of managerial communications, we might consider these percentages to mean that boys, more often than girls, are actively engaged in coping with the network of rules, regulations, and routines in which they are embedded as students.

The final set of differences in Table 3, involving the percentages of prohibitory messages, is clearest of all and leaves no doubt about this one aspect of classroom life. When these four teachers responded to instances of classroom misbehavior they were almost always reacting to a boy. This fact comes as no surprise but although the direction of the difference might have been easily predicted, the actual percentages are impressively large. The psychological significance of these differences becomes more evident when the percentages are transformed into the absolute number of prohibitory messages observed in the various rooms. In Classroom A, for example, the teacher delivers approximately 24 prohibitory messages every hour, or roughly 120 messages each day. About 108 of those daily messages are received by one or another of the 17 boys in that room.

Another aspect of the sex differences in teacher-pupil interaction is revealed in relationships observed among the three different message categories. These relationships are summarized in the form of correlation coefficients in Table 4. The correlations in that table show the communicative behavior of boys to be more of a piece, as it were, than is true for girls. Boys who are active in instructional interchanges tend also to be active in managerial interchanges and those same boys, it would seem, tend to have more than their share of disciplinary messages from the teacher. A similar phenomenon is not apparent for girls, and though it does seem to appear in the relationship between managerial and control messages, it is much less pronounced than is true for boys.

Table 4 Intercorrelations among three types of teacher–pupil interactions

	Instructional	*Managerial*	*Prohibitory*
Instructional		0·41†	0·43†
Managerial	0·20		0·66†
Prohibitory	0·18	0·29*	

† $p < 0.01$. * $p < 0.05$.	Correlations for girls below the diagonal	Correlations for boys above the diagonal

The greater cohesiveness of the three types of interaction for boys was not predicted and, therefore, the reaction to it can only be speculative. If boys have as many brushes with teachers as the data indicate, the teachers may find it advantageous to sidestep as many open clashes as possible. Thus, they sometimes might use instructional or managerial messages as preventive measures for averting harsher and more disruptive interchanges. When a teacher calls on a boy whom he suspects of daydreaming or when he refuses to give a pupil permission to go to the pencil sharpener because of what he believes will happen on the way, he is using nonprohibitory messages for control purposes. Anyone who has ever watched teachers at work can doubtlessly offer many more examples of these somewhat devious strategies. If these techniques were used frequently enough they would result in heightened correlations among the three interaction categories such as those appearing for the boys in Table 4.

In the final analysis, the quality of school life is determined not only by a pupil's sex or by what room he is in but also by what he is like as a person. Within each room and within each sex group there remain wide differences in the pattern of teacher-pupil interactions. Such differences only become discernible when the descriptive unit is the individual student and his experience.

In each of the four classrooms one or two students have fewer than one interchange per hour with their teacher. At the other extreme a few students in each room have so many communications that, if the interactions were distributed equally throughout the day, these students would be in contact with their teacher every five or ten minutes. Unexpectedly, the totals for the least active students are strikingly similar for the four classrooms, whereas the totals for the most active students are markedly different from room to room. A plausible explanation for the differences between these two extremes is that some minimal level of interaction with the teacher is demanded by the mere fact of membership in the class whereas the maximal number possible is more a function of the idiosyncratic matching of teachers and students.

The educational significance of these differences emerges when we imagine a classroom composed exclusively of either low-interacting or high-interacting students. If it were necessary for a teacher to interact with each student only once an hour, and if he maintained a 'moderate' rate of interaction, that is, engaging in a hundred or so individual interactions each hour, he possibly could manage a class of a hundred or so students. Conversely, if a teacher had to interact with each student ten or twelve times an hour and he maintained the same rate of interaction, he could barely accommodate a dozen students in his class.

These extreme situations are no more than fanciful speculations, but they do lead to further thoughts about what life must be like in a regular classroom. For at least a few students, individual contact with the teacher is as rare as if they were seated in a class of a hundred or more pupils, even though there are actually only 30 or so classmates present. For others, the teacher's presence is the same as it might be if there were but a handful of classmates in the room. What does it mean, therefore, when we describe a child as being in a classroom of thirty pupils? Such a description does tell us how many people are present, but it tells very little about the social density of the child's psychological world and the relative saliency of his teacher in that world.

Discussion

The view of classroom activity provided by the observations is exceedingly narrow, but it was sufficient to direct attention to several important educational issues. These issues have been discussed partly in the presentation of results and now are briefly reviewed to bring them into sharper focus.

First, the data have shown how classrooms can be very different from one another even when described in ways that were not meant to underscore the differences. Moreover, the differences revealed by the findings are not easily placed on a continuum whose poles represent pedagogical vice and virtue. It is difficult to say, for example, whether a great number of managerial interchanges is a good or a bad thing, or whether it is better to have students or teachers initiate instructional interchanges. This ambiguity is tolerable so long as the differences described hold the promise of being related to the total quality of the student's experience in school – so long, in other words, as the differences cannot be brushed aside as psychologically trivial.

Second, the data have called attention to the institutional character of classroom life. Schools are places where large groups of people congregate and work together. Inevitably, a significant portion of the total energy required to operate a classroom is spent in the mundane business of managing the movement of social traffic and of responding to violations of institutional expectations. Perhaps these matters are incidental to the main business of teaching and learning, but psychologists in particular need no reminder that school has a greater impact on a student's total personality than an examination of textbooks and curriculum guides would have us believe. In addition to learning their ABCs children must learn to make their way in the social labyrinth of the school. The high frequency of managerial and control messages in the observations suggests how important, and possibly how tough, that learning can be.

Third, the findings support the commonly held belief that boys have a more difficult time in school than do girls. If control messages are treated as crude measures of that difficulty, these sixth-grade boys, as a group, have eight or ten times more trouble than do their female classmates. Although it is wrong to leap to the conclusion that the boys are miserable in school and girls wild about it, the experience of going to school is clearly very different for boys than for girls. Perhaps this fact is too well known to require further scrutiny, but the frequency with which sex is ignored in educational research would lead one to suspect otherwise.

Fourth, and finally, the findings reveal a range of individual differences in each classroom broad enough to weaken any hopes of making facile generalizations about what goes on there. In each classroom there are a few students who are almost out of the teacher's range of vision, so to speak, and a few others who are almost always underfoot. What this difference means and how it comes about is anybody's guess, but it is fair to conclude that by the end of the year some students likely will be more familiar to the teacher than will others, even though they have all lived together in the same room for about the same number of days. This observation calls into question the conventional view of looking upon each classroom as a unit whose participants have shared a common educational experience. In a sense, each classroom contains as many environments as it does pairs of eyes through which to view them.

19 B. Rosenshine

Enthusiastic Teaching: A Research Review

B. Rosenshine, 'Enthusiastic teaching: A research review', *School Review*, vol. 78, no. 4, 1970, pp. 499–514.

In the folklore of education, the teaching behaviors considered desirable include enthusiasm, energy, and surgency. Even educational psychologists have endorsed teacher enthusiasm. For example, Ausubel wrote, 'It is . . . important that teachers be able to communicate a sense of excitement about the subjects they teach' (Ausubel, 1964). But this idea was one of the few for which Ausubel did not cite evidence. After pages of documentation on the ineffectiveness of structural innovations in education, Stephens hypothesized that effective teaching depends upon the 'lively interests of teachers' (Stephens, 1967).

This paper is a review of the attempts to assess the relationship of enthusiasm to pupil achievement and to specify the behavioral components of enthusiasm. Correlational and experimental studies in classrooms ranging from elementary school to college will be examined. I shall discuss the results of the studies, estimate the relevance of the results to teacher training programs, and suggest directions for future research. An important element of this paper is the discussion of how high-inference and low-inference measures can be used together in the study of teaching.

High- versus low-inference measures

The correlational and experimental studies to be cited here are divided into studies of high-inference and low-inference measures, following conventions described by Ackerman (1954) and Gage (1969). 'Inference' here refers to the process intervening between the objective data seen or heard and the judgment concerning a higher-order construct of cognitive or social interaction. It is similar to 'extrapolation' as used by Gage and Cronbach (Gage and Cronbach, 1955). High-inference measures are those which require considerable inferring from what is seen or heard in the classroom to the labeling of the behavior, such as ratings of the teacher on such scales as 'partial-fair', 'autocratic-democratic', or 'dull-stimulating'. Low-inference measures are those which require the observer to classify teaching behaviors according to relatively objective categories. Examples of these measures are words per minute, movements per minute, and the behaviors in relatively objective category systems, such as Interaction Analysis (Flanders, 1965).

Ratings on high-inference variables are particularly useful in exploring new ideas, and they have generally yielded higher correlations with teacher effects than more specific, or low-inference behavioral measures (Rosenshine, 1968), probably because such measures allow a rater to consider more evidence before making a decision. But the results of studies using low-inference measures are easier to use in teacher training programs because the variables are easier to translate into specific behaviors (Gage, 1969).

High-inference studies

Six studies were located which contained high-inference variables and measures of adjusted pupil achievement: some significant results were obtained in each of the six studies. Solomon, Bezdek, and Rosenberg[1] studied the behaviors of twenty-four teachers of evening college courses in introductory American government. Two criterion measures were used: scores on a test on the American constitution (factual gain); and scores on a passage on political philosophy (comprehension gain). (Both residual gain scores and raw gain scores were computed, but because these correlated 0·90 or above, for simplicity the investigators used the raw gain scores as the criteria.) In all, 169 independent variables were investigated: 61 frequency measures developed from an analysis of the tape recordings of two class sessions for each teacher; 38 observer ratings of the same two sessions; mean student ratings on 52 items, and the teachers' responses to 18 items on a questionnaire. Scores on these 169 variables were factor analysed by the principal

1. The major results of the study are more readily available in Solomon, Bezdek and Rosenberg (1964a and 1964b).

components method with varimax rotation and yielded eight factors accounting for 66 per cent of the variance.[2]

The factor labeled Clarity had a significant[3] relationship with factual gain ($r = 0.58$), and the factor Energy had a significant relationship with comprehension gain ($r = 0.44$).[4] The factors 'energy' and 'clarity' appear to describe a stimulating or enthusiastic teacher. Energy contained high loadings for observer ratings on 'energy', 'enthusiasm', 'relaxation', and 'mobility'. Clarity contained loadings for student ratings on 'expressiveness' and 'enthusiasm', as well as a loading for observer ratings on 'enthusiasm' (Table 1). The low-inference variables listed on Table 1 will be discussed below.

Additional evidence for the validity of the student ratings of 'expressiveness' and 'enthusiasm' may be seen in a subsequent study by Solomon (1966), in which a similar student questionnaire was used to describe the classroom behavior of 229 teachers of a broad range of adult evening courses at five schools throughout the country. The criterion measure was the mean student rating on the question: 'Considering everything, how would you evaluate the instructor in this course?' This criterion measure had been found in the previous study (Solomon, Bezdek and Rosenberg, 1963, 1964a and b), to correlate significantly ($r = 0.46$) with factual gain. Factor analysis of the data in the 1966 study yielded ten factors, two of which were significantly related to the criterion rating. Of these two factors, the one labeled Energy versus Lethargy contained high loadings (0.75 or higher) for student ratings of the teacher's 'enthusiasm', 'energy', and 'expressive-

2. One difficulty with this approach is that the ratio of variables (169) to subjects (24) tends to invalidate the assumptions of the factor analytic method. Because there are so many behaviors to observe, and administrative difficulties preclude the use of 200–300 classrooms, every study in this area contains more variables than classrooms.

3. In this paper, the level of significance is $p < 0.05$ unless otherwise noted.

4. The procedures used to determine factor scores and factor loadings for each teacher appear to be incorrect (Glass and Maguire, 1966). These procedures yielded factor scores which correlated highly with the true factor score (r's $= 0.85$ or above), but the resulting factor scores are not independent of one another.

ness'. This factor contained equally high negative loadings for 'monotony' and 'dullness'.

Fortune (1966) asked student teachers in social studies, mathematics, and English to teach three ten- to fifteen-minute lessons to randomly selected halves of their fourth-, fifth-, and sixth-grade classes. The average class size for each lesson was fourteen pupils. After each lesson, the teacher was rated independently by two supervisors on two scales, a bipolar adjective checklist similar to that used by Ryans (1960) and a modification of the Stanford Teacher Appraisal Guide.

Of the eighteen bipolar adjectives, only one is of interest in this review: dull–stimulating. The simple correlations between ratings

Table 1 Loadings of variables on two factors

Factor	High-inference variables		Low-inference variables	
	Item	Loading	Item	Loading
Energy v. lethargy	Energy	86*	Teacher requests interpretation	76
	Enthusiasm	68	Positive reinforcement	71
	Relaxation	61	Teacher requests opinions	63
	Mobility	60	Teacher requests facts	62
	—	—	Amount of gesturing	53
	—	—	Teacher factual statements	−53
Clarity v. obscurity	Expressiveness	62	—	—
	Enthusiasm (student rating)	46	—	—
	Enthusiasm (observer rating)	40	—	—

Source: Solomon (1964 a, b).
* Decimals omitted.

on this dimension and the adjusted class achievement scores on a twelve-item test were significant ($p < 0.01$): the more stimulating teachers had pupils who achieved higher scores (Table 2). Although none of the items on the Appraisal Guide was similar to animation, it is noteworthy that the ratings of all forty-two teachers on the variable dull–stimulating had significant correlations (r's = 0·30–0·61) with seven of the eight items on the Appraisal Guide.

Wallen (1966) studied the relationship of teaching behaviors to class scores in vocabulary, reading comprehension and arithmetic, as measured by the California Achievement Test. Post-test scores were adjusted for initial reading ability. Separate analyses were made for thirty-six first-grade teachers and forty third-grade teachers.

The behaviors of the teachers were measured with rating scales, Q-sort ratings, and counts of the frequencies and proportions of specific behaviors recorded by trained observers in the classroom. No factor analysis was made. Of the twenty-five independent variables measured, three had nearly significant to significant correlations with pupil gain scores on all six dependent variables (Table 3).

Table 2 Correlations between adjusted class achievement and ratings of teachers on dull–stimulating

Subject	Number of teachers	Linear correlations
Social studies	13	63*
Mathematics	14	62*
English	15	52*

Source: Fortune (1966).
* $p < 0·01$; decimals omitted.

These variables were the Q-sort ratings of behaviors labeled 'stimulating', 'intellectual effectiveness', and 'achievement oriented'. The variable relevant to this review – 'stimulating' – had significant correlations with adjusted achievement scores in arithmetic in both grades. The stimulating teacher was defined as one who was 'interesting and/or dynamic in her role as a teacher' (Wallen, 1966, p. 2.18).

This investigation by Wallen (1966) was intended to clarify the results obtained in an earlier study by Wallen and Wodtke (1963). In their investigation, sixty-five teachers of grades 1 through 5 were observed, and separate correlations were reported for each

Table 3 Correlations between class achievement and measures of teacher behavior

| High-inference measure | Achievement measure | | | | | |
| | Reading vocabulary, spring | | Reading comprehension, spring | | Arithmetic, spring | |
	Grade 1	Grade 3	Grade 1	Grade 3	Grade 1	Grade 3
Stimulating	29	28	32*	27	51†	37†
Intellectual effectiveness	34*	38*	37*	37*	38*	30
Achievement oriented	41†	42†	52†	45†	53†	39†

Source: Wallen (1966)

Note: Grade 1, $N = 36$ teachers; grade 3, $N = 40$ teachers. Decimals omitted.

* $p < 0.05$

† $p < 0.01$

grade; the number of teachers of each grade was 'approximately 12'. The highest correlations were those between observer ratings on 'recognition' and adjusted pupil reading achievement scores (r's $= 0.29$–0.65); four of the five correlations were significant. Recognition was defined as the 'degree to which the teacher is the center of attention' (Wallen and Wodtke, 1963, p. 3.02). According to the investigators, the correlations suggested that 'the more stimulating teacher ... obtains a greater growth in reading achievement regardless of grade (Wallen and Wodtke, 1963, p. 4.07). Because the term 'recognition' was ambiguous, Wallen used 'stimulating' as the observational variable in his concluding study (Wallen, 1966).

In a series of independent analyses of the same data Gage *et al.* (1968), Rosenshine (1968), Unruh (1968), and Dell and Hiller (1968), sought correlates of effective 'explaining behavior'. In the basic investigation, forty-five social studies teachers gave two lectures – one on Yugoslavia and one on Thailand – on successive days to their twelfth-grade classes. Immediately after each lecture, the pupils took a ten-item comprehension test. The lectures were ranked according to the residual mean scores of the pupils in each class, after statistical adjustment for (*a*) the relevance of the material in each lecture to the criterion test and (b) the pupils' ability as measured by comprehension scores on a tape-recorded lecture on Israel.

Unruh (1968) assigned thirty high school students to observe and describe the videotapes of the lectures on Yugoslavia and an additional thirty to observe and describe those on Thailand. After viewing each videotape, the raters were asked to write at least six adjectives or phrases describing strengths and weaknesses of the teacher. The frequency of free-response mentions of 'enthusiasm, vitality, energy, etc.' was clearly related to the adjusted class mean achievement score on the Thailand lectures but the corresponding results were not consistent or significant for the Yugoslavia lectures (Unruh, 1968, pp. 26–7).

Unruh then showed six-minute segments of the videotapes to the raters and asked them to rate each teacher on a series of twenty-seven seven-point, bipolar scales consisting of adjectives and phrases selected from the research literature. In this analysis the results were the opposite of those obtained using the free-response data. The ratings on items such as 'enthusiastic-unenthusiastic' and 'energetic-lethargic' correlated significantly with the achievement measure for the Yugoslavia sample (r's = 0·35 and 0·42), but the correlations were significant and negative for the Thailand sample (r's = −0·33 and −0·35). The studies by Unruh thus provide some support for the relevance of animation; but they raise difficult questions about the consistency of results when free-response and fixed-response rating procedures are used.

In an experimental study by Mastin (1963), teacher enthusiasm was manipulated as the independent variable. Twenty teachers of sixth-grade and seventh-grade pupils were asked to give two illustrated lectures to their classes; one lecture dealt with ancient Egypt, and the other, with ancient Rome and Pompeii. Each lecture was accompanied by a set of fifteen mounted photographs and a map of the Mediterranean area. The report of the study did not indicate the length of the lectures, nor whether a control was applied for differences in length. Each teacher was instructed to teach one lesson with enthusiasm, that is, 'in such a manner as to convey to his pupils the impression that he was enthusiastic about the ideas and illustrative materials of the lesson and the subject covered by the lesson' (Mastin, 1963, p. 385). Each teacher was instructed to teach the other lesson with indifference, that is, 'in such a manner as to convey to the group a feeling that he had an indifferent attitude about the ideas, etc.' Every teacher taught one randomly chosen lesson with enthusiasm and the other with indifference. The pupils took a 102-item, multiple-choice test after each lesson. The fact that the two lessons and the tests were of unknown relative difficulty and may not be comparable was presumably taken into account by the random assignment of lessons to treatments (enthusiastic versus indifferent) for each teacher.

The class mean for the lesson which was taught with enthusiasm, whether that lesson was presented first or second, and whether that lesson was the lecture on Rome or on Egypt, was higher for nineteen of the twenty classes than the mean of the lesson presented with indifference. Of the nineteen comparisons, fifteen were significant ($p < 0.01$); in one class, the lesson presented with indifference was significantly superior. Apparently, no observation of the teachers' performances during the lessons was made, and no behavioral definition of enthusiasm and indifference was obtained.

With the possible exception of the study by Unruh (1968), the results of which are not clear, these high-inference studies provide strikingly consistent results. They suggest that one of the patterns of effective teaching behavior identified by Ryans (1960), namely, Pattern Z, described as 'stimulating, imaginative, surgent v. dull, routine teacher behavior' is significantly related to pupil achievement.

The results above are not particularly useful for teacher training programs because they do not tell us how a teacher should behave in order to be stimulating. To determine the specific behaviors, we must review studies that used low-inference measures.

Low-inference studies

The ideal design for low-inference studies to determine the behaviors which comprise stimulating teaching would be one in which both rating scales and objective observation instruments are used in the same study, and the results are examined in a table of intercorrelations. Administrative difficulties and cost factors frequently preclude these arrangements. Nevertheless, Solomon, Bezdek and Rosenberg (1963, 1964a and b), and Wallen (1966) have conducted such studies.

In the study by Solomon and his co-workers the factor Energy versus Lethargy contained loadings for several low-inference variables. There were high loadings for teacher requests interpretation, teacher requests opinions, teacher requests facts and amount of gesturing; positive reinforcement also had a positive loading, and there was a negative loading for teacher factual statements (Table 1). Thus, the teacher who scored high on the Energy factor appears to exhibit three types of related behaviors. First, he is energetic, a rapid speaker, mobile, and enthusiastic, but relaxed. Second, he asks varied questions, emphasizing questions of interpretation and opinion as well as factual questions. Third, he praises frequently.

Wallen (1966) correlated Q-sort ratings with the frequency or percentage of specified teaching behaviors. The behaviors were tabulated by means of a modification of the Flanders (1965) Interaction Analysis (IA) categories. In grade 1, the ratings on the behavior 'stimulating' had significant correlations with four of the low-inference measures: asking questions, praise and encouragement, personal control, and hostility and reprimands (Table 4). In grade 3, the ratings for 'stimulating' were significantly correlated

Table 4 Significant correlations between low-inference measures and ratings of teachers on 'stimulating'

Low-inference measure	Correlation coefficient‡
Grade 1 ($N = 36$):	
Asking questions	32*
Praise and encouragement	39*
Personal control	−44†
Hostility and reprimands	44†
Grade 3 ($N = 40$):	
Praise and encouragement	41†
Personal control	−35*

Source: Wallen (1966)
* $p < 0.05$
† $p < 0.01$
‡ Decimals omitted

with two behaviors: praise and encouragement, and personal control (Table 4). These correlations are not impressive. The lack of clearer evidence on the objective behaviors representing stimulating teaching may be due to the socio-emotional orientation of the I A categories, and the lack of cognitive variables in the I A system.

More studies are needed which contain both high-inference and low-inference measures; it is hazardous to draw conclusions from two studies in which the pupils were of widely different ages. The results are similar in that counts of teacher use of praise or approval were related to ratings of 'stimulating' or 'enthusiastic' in both studies; however, in neither of the two samples studied by Wallen were frequencies of 'praise and encouragement' significantly correlated with any of the three criterion measures. (Frequencies of 'personal control' were significantly related only to growth in vocabulary in grade 1.)

Mobility and animation

In two of the studies, low-inference behaviors representing mobility or animation may have been components of the high-inference behavior, stimulating. In the study by Solomon *et al.*, the factor Energy contained high loadings for student ratings on 'rapidity of speech' and 'mobility', this factor structure was replicated in the subsequent study by Solomon (1966). In the study by Mastin (1963), teachers were limited to the technique of lecturing in both the enthusiastic and indifferent presentations; movement and variation of voice may have been the only behaviors which teachers could use in order to show enthusiasm.

Some additional correlational and experimental studies illustrate the effects of animated behavior. Rosenshine (1968) studied lectures in order to determine the correlates of effective explaining behavior. One variable which discriminated significantly between the high-scoring and low-scoring classes with both lecture topics was the frequency and amount of time the teacher gestured or moved: the teachers of high-scoring classes moved and gestured more.

In an ingenious study, McCoard (1944) investigated the relationships between certain 'speech factors' of the teacher and pupil achievement. Although no details were given concerning the criterion measure, it was described as a 'composite of pupil change scores' in 'measurable attitudes, ideals, and information in the social studies field' (McCoard, 1944, p. 57). These criterion tests were administered to the seventh- and eighth-grade pupils of forty teachers in one-room, rural, Wisconsin schools. Each of the teachers prepared two audio recordings, a three-minute recording reading standard materials (reading), and a three-minute talk on the topic, 'My Preparation for Teaching' (speaking). Twenty-two speech teachers listened to each recording twice and rated each recording on fourteen seven-point speech variables.

The results were remarkably consistent. On the reading tapes, all fourteen rated variables had significant correlations (r's = 0·34–0·46) with the criterion measure. On the speaking tapes, eleven of the fourteen variables were significantly correlated with achievement (r's = 0·32–0·42). Of the fourteen rated variables, ten can be analysed as pairs, the first variable in a pair was a rating of a speech characteristic, the second variable was a rating of variation in that characteristic. Thus both 'pitch' and 'variation of pitch', and 'volume' and 'variation in volume' were rated. Ten comparisons of these pairs of variables can be inspected – five each for the reading tapes and the speaking tapes. In eight of the ten comparisons, the rating of the variation correlated more highly with pupil achievement than did the rating of the characteristic itself. These results suggest that inflection is an important correlate of achievement.

The results of four experimental studies support the importance of animation in enhancing comprehension. Coals and Smithers (1966) had two teachers present two ten-minute lectures in two ways – statically and dynamically. The static speaker 'read the entire speech from a manuscript. He made no gestures, had no direct eye contact, and held vocal inflection to a minimum. However, he did speak with good diction and sufficient volume.' The dynamic speeches were 'delivered from memory, with much vocal inflection, gesturing, eye contact, and animation on the part of the speaker.' The college students took a ten-item multiple-choice test after each lecture; the mean score of the students who heard the dynamic lecture was significantly higher ($p < 0·01$) than that of the students who heard the static lecture.

Similar conclusions on the importance of inflection can be drawn from part of a study by Gauger (1951). Two independent variables were investigated in this study: (a) the high school students only heard, or heard and saw the speaker; and (b) the speaker gestured or did not gesture. No significant differences in achievement were reported between hearing and seeing compared with only hearing the speaker, but those students who heard and saw or only heard a speaker who gestured achieved significantly higher adjusted post-test scores than those who heard and saw or only heard a speaker who did not gesture.[5] In addition, when the results in the hearing-only condition were analysed separately, there was a nearly significant ($p < 0.10$) effect for gesture, even when the audience could not see the speaker.

In two studies, the use of gestures was experimentally manipulated. Both Jersild (1928) and Ehrensberg (1945) varied the method of presenting approximately fifty statements. The speakers varied their presentations by speaking in a loud or soft voice, pausing, saying, 'Now get this,' and gesturing, defined as a 'simple gesture with hand, or pointing with the first finger' (p. 97). The criterion was the score on a fill-in test (Jersild) or a multiple-choice test (Ehrensberg) on each of the statements in the presentation. Both experimenters found that statements were remembered significantly more often when accompanied by gesture than when presented in a neutral manner.

Summary and discussion

In summary, the results of high-inference studies provide evidence that ratings given to teachers on such behaviors as 'stimulating', 'energetic', 'mobile', 'enthusiastic', and 'animated' are related to measures of pupil achievement. The results of low-inference studies suggest that the frequencies of such variables as movement, gesture, variation in voice, and eye contact are related to pupil achievement.

These results may occur because animated behavior arouses the attending behavior of pupils. Because it is content free, animated behavior enhances learning instead of distracting the pupils. It is possible, of course, that extreme animation would distract the pupils from the lesson because the pupils might focus upon the ani-

5. No significant main effect for gesture was reported in the original study. However, I reanalysed the data using a 2 × 2 analysis of covariance design in place of the one-way analysis of variance design reported by Gauger. The covariates were IQ and pretest score, and the criterion was the post-test score. The data were obtained from the original dissertation by Gauger.

mation rather than on the content. But apparently, such extremes did not occur in the studies reviewed. Animated behavior may also serve as a secondary reinforcer: hearing and seeing an energetic speaker may positively reinforce certain responses of the pupil during the lesson.

In some of the correlational studies, the animated behavior may have been a by-product of either the teacher's superior organization of the material or his greater task orientation. Although such an explanation is plausible, the experimental studies demonstrate that superior organization is not necesssary, because merely instructing a teacher to increase his enthusiasm (Mastin, 1963) or manipulating the amount of teacher animation (Coaes and Smithers, 1966) without modifying content resulted in superior achievement.

Future research using high-inference and low-inference variables

Although the high-inference variables and the low-inference variables discussed above appear to be similar, we must be cautious in claiming that high frequency of movement, variation in voice, and use of eye contact represent all, or even a significant part, of high-inference dimensions such as 'energetic' and 'stimulating'. The task of validating the connection between the proposed low-inference and high-inference behaviors will be difficult. In addition, there is a need to search for additional low-inference behaviors in this area.

One relevant area for future research on low-inference behaviors which form part of the dimension labeled 'stimulating' might be the study of teacher questions. The study by Wallen (1966) suggests that the frequency of questions might be important, and the research of Solomon and his associates (1963, 1964 a and b) suggests that the types of questions may be related to ratings of 'energetic'. Additional low-inference behaviors may include teacher responses to pupil answers, and teacher use of phrases about the importance or relevance of certain material.

There is a need for future studies similar to those conducted by Wallen and Solomon in which both high-inference and low-inference variables are included in the observation schedules. The correlations between these two sets of variables can then be studied more intensively. For example, in the study by Wallen (1966) very little of the potential of the relatively objective I A was utilized in the analysis, nor was there a classification of questions. More intensive comparison of high-inference and low-inference variables may result in a better understanding of the correlates of teacher effects.

Future research on animated behaviors

The identification of such low-inference teacher behaviors as frequent movement and gesture, variation in voice, and use of eye contact as correlates of pupil achievement suggests that these low-inference behaviors might be employed profitably in teacher education programs. At the same time, three types of studies could be conducted to add evidence about animation to that already gathered. First, replications of the original studies could be made with improved controls; second, correlational and experimental studies could be made to compare animation with other behaviors of teachers that are known to increase the comprehension of pupils; third, experiments could be conducted using the denotable, operationally defined behaviors included in the category, animation.

A note about controls is appropriate. The experimental studies should include teaching in a manner described as 'regular', in contrast to 'enthusiastic' and 'indifferent'. That is, a test should be made of the possibility that the effect of enthusiasm is really the effect of novelty. A test should also be made of the possibility that indifference detracts from learning more than enthusiasm enhances learning.

Can teachers who characteristically teach without animation, whose pupils achieve low comprehension scores, be trained to increase the comprehension of their pupils by teaching with more animation? An experiment to test this question should include measures of retention for both teachers and pupils, to show whether teachers trained to increase their animation maintained this new behavior. Pupils could also be tested periodically to determine whether they maintained their improved comprehension while the teachers continued to use animation.

References

ACKERMANN, W. I. (1954), 'Teacher competence and pupil change', *Harvard Educ. Rev.*, vol. 24, pp. 213–84.

AUSUBEL, D. P. (1964), 'How reversible are the cognitive and motivational effects of cultural deprivation? Implications for teaching the culturally deprived child', *Urban Education* 1, vol. 19.

COAES, W. D., and SMITHERS, U. (1966), 'Audience recall as a function of speaker dynamism', *J. educ. Psychol.*, vol. 57, pp. 189–91.

DELL, D., and HILLER, J. E. (1968), 'Computer analysis of teacher's explanations', in N. L. Gage (1968).

EHRENSBERG, P. (1945), 'An experimental study of the relative effectiveness of certain forms of emphasis in public speaking, *Speech Monogrs.*, vol. 12, pp. 94–111.

FLANDERS, N. A. (1965), 'Teacher influence, pupil attitudes and achievement', *US Office of Education Cooperative Research Monograph*, no. 12, OE–25040, Government Printing Office.

FORTUNE, J. C. (1966), *The Generality of Presenting Behaviors in Teaching Pre-school Children*, Memphis State University.

GAGE, N. L., and CRONBACH, L. V. (1955), 'Conceptual and methodological problems in interpersonal perception', *Psychol. Rev.*, vol. 62, pp. 412.

GAGE, N. L. *et al.* (1968), 'Explorations of the Teacher's Effectiveness in Explaining'. Technical Report no. 4, Center for Research and Development in Teaching, Stanford University.

GAGE, N. L. (1969), 'Teaching methods', in R. L. Ebel (ed.), *Encyclopedia of Educational Research*, 4th ed., Macmillan.

GAUGER, P. L. (1951), 'The effect of gesture and the presence or absence of the speaker on the listening complications of eleventh and twelfth grade high school pupils', University of Wisconsin.

GLASS, G. V., and MAGUIRE, T. O. (1966), 'Abuses of factor scores', *Amer. educ. Res. J.*, vol. 3, pp. 297–304.

JERSILD, A. T. (1928), 'Modes of emphasis in public speaking', *J. appl. Psychol.*, vol. 12, pp. 611–20.

MASTIN, V. E. (1963), 'Teacher enthusiasm', *J. educ. Res.*, vol. 56, pp. 385–6.

McCOARD, W. B. (1944), 'Speech factors as related to teaching efficiency', *Speech Monogrs*, no. 11, pp. 53–64.

ROSENSHINE, B. (1968), 'Objectively measured behavioral predictors of effectiveness in explaining', in N. L. Gage, 'Explorations of the Teacher's Effectiveness in Explaining', Center for Research and Development in Teaching, Stanford University.

RYANS, D. G. (1960), *Characteristics of Teachers*, American Council on Education.

SOLOMON, D., BEZDEK, W. E., and ROSENBERG, L. (1963), *Teaching Styles and Learning*, Center for the Study of Liberal Education for Adults, Chicago.

SOLOMON, D., BEZDEK, W. E., and ROSENBERG, L. (1964a), 'Dimensions of teacher behavior', *J. exp. Educ.*, vol. 33, pp. 23–40.

SOLOMON, D., BEZDEK, W. E., and ROSENBERG, L. (1964b), 'Teacher behavior and student learning', *J. educ. Psychol.*, vol. 55, pp. 23–30.

Solomon, D. (1966), 'Teacher behavior dimensions, course characteristics and student evaluation of teachers', *Amer. educ. Res. J.*, no. 3, pp. 35–47.

Stephens, J. M. (1967), *The Process of Schooling: A Psychological Examination*, Holt, Rinehart & Winston.

Unruh, W. R. (1968), 'The modality and validity of cues to lecture effectiveness', in N. L. Gage, *et al.* (1968), Explorations of the Teacher's Effectiveness in Explaining', Technical Report no. 4, Centre for Research and Development in Teaching, Stanford University.

Wallen, N. E., and Wodtke, K. H. (1963), *Relationships Between Teacher Characteristics and Student Behavior: Part I*, US Office of Education Contract no. 2–10–113, Department of Educational Psychology, University of Utah.

Wallen, N. E. (1966), *Relationships Between Teacher Characteristics and Student Behavior: Part 3*, US Office of Education Cooperative Research Project no. SAE OE5–10–181, University of Utah.

20 C. J. Wright and G. Nuthall

The Relationships between Teacher Behaviors and
Pupil Achievement in Three Experimental Elementary
Science Lessons

From C. J. Wright and G. Nuthall, 'The relationships between teacher
behaviors and pupil achievement in three experimental elementary
science lessons', *American Educational Research Journal*,
vol. 7, 1970, pp. 477-91.

Despite considerable growth in the number of observational
studies of teaching in the last five years, there have been relatively
few investigations of the relationships between what teachers do in
the classroom and pupil achievement (Nuthall, 1968; Meux, 1967).
As Gage has noted (1966), observational data-gathering in classrooms has an obvious attraction to educational researchers, but
there is little if any empirical evidence which makes it clear just
what aspects of teacher behavior are most relevant to the major
concerns of schools.

Further than this, it is difficult to find evidence on the related
question of how much effect differences in teacher behaviors are
likely to have on the amount which pupils learn in school. Do
teachers using different techniques make much difference to how
pupils learn? Or is it a matter of little consequence how teachers
perform, so long as they cover the same curriculum content in
approximately the same time?

In a review of studies which have included measures of pupil
achievement, Rosenshine (1969) found evidence for the importance
of teacher use of approval and criticism (e.g. Spaulding, 1965;
Soar, 1966), teacher use of pupil ideas (e.g. Fortune, 1967; Morrison, 1966), and frequency of teacher questions (Conners and
Eisenberg, 1966; Wallen, 1966). However, most of these studies
were concerned with the long term effects of major characteristics
of teacher behaviors. They were not designed to identify relationships between teacher behaviors and pupil learning of subject-
matter content *at the time of observation*.

Studies reported by Furst (1967) and Rosenshine (1968) did
include specific control of the subject-matter taught by teachers,
which made it possible to relate teacher behavior measures directly

to measures of pupil achievement. Both of these studies produced provocative and interesting results which pointed up the need for more controlled studies of this kind.

The investigation which is reported here was an attempt to identify the short-term effects of teacher behaviors in a set of three subject-matter controlled lessons of the discussion or recitation type common in most elementary school classrooms. It was primarily an exploratory study, designed to identify the most significant relationships between pupil performance on an achievement test and those teacher behaviors which have been studied by Bellack *et al.* (1966), Smith, Meux, *et al.* (1962), Taba, Levine and Elzey (1964), and Nuthall and Lawrence (1965). In addition, an attempt was made to relate the effects of teacher behavior differences to the effects of individual pupil differences in intelligence and prior knowledge.

It is important to note that, because of the practical impossibility of true randomization in the selection of pupils, teachers, or subject-matter content in an experiment of this kind, the results obtained cannot be credited with a wide degree of generalizability. The best that can be hoped for is that, with a relatively high degree of internal validity, the results suggest what is likely to be found in further replications of the same experiment.

Method
Subjects

In order to provide for a maximum of variation in teaching behaviors, the following groups of teachers were selected:

1. Six highly experienced teachers (four men and two women).

2. Five student teachers completing a two year teacher training course which had included a pilot micro-teaching experience program.

3. Six student teachers in the first year of a three year teacher training course.

For the latter group this was their first practice teaching experience.

The pupils involved were all from Standard Two classes.[1] The

1. The Standard Two class in New Zealand is approximately equivalent to US Grade Three or British Primary Fourth Year (modal age 8 years).

experienced teachers worked with their own classes, seven of the student teachers were assigned to four week practice teaching sections with selected classes, while the remaining four student teachers were especially assigned to appropriate classes for the duration of the experiment. The sample thus included 17 of the 49 Standard Two classes available in the city of Christchurch, and was representative of major variations in type and locality of school.

Because of the difficulties expected with the group administration of standardized tests with eight-year-old children, and problems associated with obtaining clear tape-records of the verbal behavior of children at this age, it was decided that the teacher should teach a group of approximately twenty children, selected at random, from within each class. Only these selected pupils (Total $N = 296$) were the experimental subjects in each class.

Content of lessons

A pilot study with three experienced teachers instructing pupils on the life and habits of the 'black-backed seagull' was used to determine the content and sequence of topics within three lessons of approximately ten minutes each.

The experimental teachers were supplied with:

1. Two stuffed and mounted specimens of 'black-backed gulls' (one mature, one immature).

2. Reproductions of material extracted from two standard texts on New Zealand birds.

3. An outline of content from the three lessons.

The first lesson was to deal with characteristics of the birds; the second with habitat, food and nesting; the third with adaptation and ecological relations.

Instrumentation

Three tests were used in obtaining the results. Intelligence of the pupils was measured with the Revised Tomlinson Junior School Test, a recently standardized, multi-facet group test of intellectual ability.

A test of the pupils' general knowledge of concepts and terms in elementary science (the Nature/Science Concepts Test) was developed especially for this study. Content was selected from available textbooks and from official curriculum prescriptions. The results obtained from trial forms were discussed with Christchurch Teachers' College Science Department faculty and fifteen multiple-choice items selected with optimal indices of discrimination and difficulty. The content of these items covered basic principles and concepts related to adaptation, classification and characteristics of plant and animal life.

The achievement test was developed on the basis of the lesson content outline supplied to the teachers. Items were written for each of the points contained in the lesson outline. A preliminary version of the test was used in a pilot experimental teaching trial and items modified accordingly. The final version of the test contained twenty-nine multiple-choice items of which four were included to make the test more attractive to pupils, but were not scored.

Procedures

The selected teachers were each given thirty minute briefing sessions in which the nature of the experiment and the content of lessons was discussed. Specific instructions were given to ensure that treatment of lesson content was confined to the experimental sessions.

Teaching and test administration were carried out in each class during the span of one week. The timetable of events was as follows:

Monday	Specimens of black-backed gulls put on display in class.
Tuesday	First lesson (9.00 a.m.)
Wednesday	Second lesson (9.00 a.m.)
Thursday	Third lesson (9.00 a.m.)
Friday	Black-backed Gull Achievement Test
	Nature/Science Concepts Test
Monday	Revised Tomlinson Junior School Test

All tests were administered by the senior author. Each lesson was tape recorded with the senior author present to supervise recording operations and to record names of participating pupils (Wright, 1968).

Teacher behavior variables

The selection of teacher behavior variables took place in two stages. In the first stage, sixty-two variables were selected or modified from those described in the observational studies of teaching cited above. Procedures for identifying these variables in the tape-scripts of the three lessons for each of the seventeen teachers were developed from the reports of these observational studies. Modifications were made to the procedures where the special conditions and content of the lessons required them.

In the second stage, the frequencies of occurrence of these sixty-two variables were intercorrelated with each other and subjected to a detailed analysis. Variables were eliminated which had a very low frequency of occurrence, or did not show an approximately normal and continuous distribution across the seventeen teachers. Several variables were combined to form a new composite variable where there was a high correlation between the original variables and they appeared to be logically very similar.

The result of these procedures was a set of twenty-eight teacher and pupil behavior variables which were relatively distinct from each other, and showed a reasonably normal distribution across the seventeen teachers. These variables are listed in Table 1.

The variables are separated into five major categories. Teacher 'structuring' refers to the teacher supplying information either before or after a question-answer sequence. Teacher 'solicitation' refers to verbal moves which are intended to elicit a verbal or physical response from a pupil. Within this category 'reciprocation' refers to the teacher asking the pupil who made the previous response to extend or lift (to a higher thought level) what he has just said. Teacher 'reaction to pupil response' includes the kinds of comments that teachers make to a pupil response which are not in the form of a further solicitation.

Results

In order to avoid the probable effects of pre-testing on the pupils included in this experiment, no tests were administered prior to the three experimental lessons. This presented the problem of finding the most effective method of correcting pupil achievement scores for initial differences between classes in pupil intelligence and prior knowledge. This problem was overcome in the following manner.

Multiple regression analysis was used to determine the relationship of intelligence and knowledge of nature/science concepts to achievement test scores for individual pupils. The multiple regression formula was used to determine for each pupil a 'predicted' achievement test score, and a 'residual' (actual minus predicted) achievement test score. The residual achievement test scores were assumed to represent the effects on achievement of factors other than intelligence and prior knowledge.

Table 1 Means and standard deviations of frequencies of occurrence of teacher behavior variables identified in tapescripts

Teacher behavior variable	Mean	S.D.
Category 1: teacher and pupil talk		
1. Teacher talk (lines of tapescript)	399·8	43·6
2. Pupil talk (lines of tapescript)	185·7	34·6
3. Pupil extended talk (utterances with more than two lines of tapescript)	6·8	6·7
4. Teacher utterances	149·8	27·4
Category 2: teacher structuring		
5. Structuring (lines of tapescript)	69·3	16·5
6. Teacher gives information immediately following own question	9·8	8·1
7. Terminal structuring (information following pupil responses)	19·8	6·0
Category 3: teacher solicitations		
8. Utterances containing one question	100·0	24·2
9. Utterances containing two questions	20·8	13·1
10. Utterances containing more than two questions	6·4	5·2
11. Closed questions	115·2	26·2
12. Open questions	18·0	8·9
13. Alternative subsequent questions	62·5	40·9
14. Names child to answer question	31·8	14·3
15. Redirects question to another pupil	24·4	15·0
16. Reciprocates response (extending)	2·3	1·6
17. Reciprocates response (lifting)	6·4	4·2
Category 4: teacher reaction to pupil response		
18. Simple affirmative and negative comment	42·7	18·3
19. Indefinite and complex comment	12·3	5·6
20. Reflecting comment	3·1	2·7

Teacher behavior variable	Mean	S.D.
21. Thanks and praise	26·4	23·1
22. Managerial comment	2·8	1·5
23. Challenging comment	7·8	8·8
24. Repetition of pupil response	50·4	36·3
Category 5: monologues and review		
25. Monologues	3·6	2·9
26. Recapitulation beginning 2nd lesson (lines of tapescript)	12·1	13·6
27. Recapitulation beginning 3rd lesson (lines of tapescript)	17·6	20·3
28. Revisions ending lessons (lines of tapescript)	34·7	42·9

Pupils' residual achievement test scores were averaged for classes, and these class averages were used as the criterion test scores reflecting the effects of variations between teacher behaviors in each class. This procedure was based on the assumption that the common (systematic) variation between classes in pupil residual achievement scores could be attributed largely to differences in teaching.

The assumptions involved in these procedures are obviously relatively crude,[2] but they are probably the best available if the contaminating effects of pretesting are to be avoided within the limits of a practicable experimental design.

The data relevant to the calculation of the residual achievement scores are reported in Table 2.

Differences between teachers

Analyses of variance were performed on the regression analysis data, in order to determine the amount of variance in achievement scores being removed by the predicted achievement scores, and the proportion of the residual achievement variance attributable to differences between classes. The results of these analyses are reported in Table 3.

The data in Tables 2 and 3 suggest that about 30 per cent of the variance in achievement test scores is attributable to the intelligence and the nature/science concepts test scores. Of the remaining

2. They assume the additivity of the effects of intelligence, prior knowledge, and teacher behaviors, and ignore the possibility of interactions.

Table 2 **Data from intelligence, science-knowledge and achievement tests used in the calculation of residual achievement scores (296 pupils from 17 classes)**

Tests	All pupils Mean	s.d.	Range of class means	Correlation with achievement
Tomlinson Junior IQ	104·21	15·60	88·80 to 117·37	+0·5302
Nature/Science concepts test	8·15	2·34	6·13 to 9·87	+0·4311
Achievement test	17·40	3·30	14·05 to 20·89	
Residual achievement scores	0·000	2·75	+3·12 to −1·66	

Multiple linear correlation of IQ and Nature/Science Concept score on Achievement Test Score: +0·5546.

variance, about 14 per cent can be attributed to differences between classes.

A further analysis of variance was carried out to determine the relationship between pupil achievement and the experience of the teachers. No significant differences or trends were identified.

Table 3 **Analyses of variance of achievement test and residual achievement test scores**

Source of variance	Sums of squares	df	Mean squares	F ratio	Est.* ω^2
Total achievement test scores	3218·75	295			
Regression of IQ+ Nature/Science scores	990·02	2	495·01	65·076	0·302
Deviation from regression	2228·74	293	7·61		
Total residual achievement scores	2228·74	295			
Between classes	407·38	16	25·46	3·900	0·136
Within classes	1821·36	279	6·53		

* An estimate of ω^2, calculated from formula reported in Schutz (1966).

Relationship of teacher variables to pupil achievement

The 28 teacher behavior variables were intercorrelated with each other and with class mean scores on intelligence, knowledge of nature/science concepts, and residual achievement. These intercorrelations are reported in Table 4.

While the results reported in Table 4 show a number of significant relationships, it was decided to explore the data further to see if general kinds of significant teacher behaviors could be identified. Variables which showed some reliable relationship with pupil achievement ($p \leq 0.10$) were examined in detail, and different

Table 5 **Relationship of additional teacher variables to pupil achievement**

Teacher behavior variable	Correlation with mean class residual achievement score
1. Per cent of questions leading to pupil response	+0·452
2. Per cent of questions: closed	+0·456
3. Per cent of questions: open	—0·207
4. Pre-question structuring as per cent of total structuring	+0·066
5. Post-question structuring as per cent of total structuring	—0·488
6. Terminal structuring as per cent of total structuring	+0·550
7. Total lines of recapitulation as per cent of total lines	+0·042
8. Total lines of revision as per cent of total lines	+0·663
9. Total lines of recapitulation plus revision as per cent of total lines	+0·587

ways of representing and quantifying them were explored. This *post-hoc* analysis suggested a set of further teacher behavior variables which were correlated with pupil achievement (see Table 5). These additional variables should not be treated as additional significant findings, but rather as additional information about the findings reported in Table 4.

The results of the examination of the data suggested that there were six major kinds of teacher behaviors related to pupil achieve-

Teacher behavior variables	1	2	3	4	5	6	7	8	9	10	11	12	13	14
1. Teacher talk		-0·17	-0·32	0·05	0·32	0·34	0·12	-0·10	0·28	0·32	-0·06	0·33	0·32	-0·12
2. Pupil talk			0·62	0·64	-0·32	0·06	-0·18	0·51	0·09	0·00	0·52	0·20	0·05	0·34
3. Pupil ext. talk				-0·14	-0·12	-0·01	0·14	-0·16	-0·15	0·07	-0·20	0·01	-0·09	-0·06
4. Teacher utterances					-0·24	-0·02	-0·10	0·83	0·14	-0·13	0·85	0·18	0·05	0·53
5. Structuring (total)						0·00	-0·10	-0·16	-0·05	0·07	-0·09	-0·18	0·00	-0·45
6. Teacher infr. foll. q.							-0·39	-0·38	0·89	0·85	0·14	0·23	0·89	0·11
7. Terminal structuring								-0·10	-0·40	-0·28	-0·22	-0·33	-0·37	0·00
8. Utterances with one q.									-0·21	-0·51	0·75	0·21	-0·32	0·38
9. Utterances with two qs.										0·84	0·39	0·20	0·97	0·36
10. Utterances with more qs.											0·05	0·18	0·94	0·17
11. Closed questions												0·01	-0·28	0·61
12. Open questions													0·23	0·03
13. Alternative subsequent q.														0·32
14. Names child														
15. Redirects question														
16. Reciprocates to extend														
17. Reciprocates to lift														
18. Affirmative & negative														
19. Indefinite & complex														
20. Reflecting comment														
21. Thanks and praise														
22. Managerial comment														
23. Challenging comment														
24. Repetition of response														
25. Monologues														
26. Recapitulation (2nd less)														
27. Recapitulation (3rd less)														
28. Revisions														
29. Nature/Science concepts														
30. Tomlinson IQ														
31. Residual achievement														

Table 4 Intercorrelations between teacher behavior variables and intelligence, science concept knowledge, and achievement of pupils

16	17	18	19	20	21	22	23	24	25	26	27	28	29	30	31	
-0·02	0·24	-0·15	0·15	0·30	0·08	-0·04	0·33	0·44	0·07	0·01	0·17	0·17	0·40	0·14	-0·09	1.
-0·25	0·36	0·47	-0·40	0·56	-0·20	0·08	-0·33	0·14	-0·28	0·05	0·07	0·12	0·06	0·18	0·02	2.
-0·60	0·43	-0·04	-0·03	0·46	-0·31	0·33	-0·22	-0·46	0·08	-0·08	-0·19	-0·39	-0·06	0·07	-0·23	3.
0·42	-0·01	0·57	-0·33	0·22	0·10	-0·04	-0·36	0·52	-0·29	0·06	0·04	0·61	0·18	0·27	0·35	4.
-0·08	0·18	-0·72	0·08	0·05	0·36	-0·18	0·17	0·05	0·09	0·02	-0·10	0·14	-0·02	-0·04	-0·13	5.
0·16	-0·10	0·11	-0·30	0·06	-0·14	-0·20	0·38	0·31	-0·49	0·03	-0·20	-0·38	0·32	0·14	-0·52	6.
-0·35	0·08	-0·17	0·17	-0·32	0·03	0·06	-0·05	0·29	0·39	0·05	0·32	0·23	-0·25	-0·28	0·41	7.
0·30	-0·09	0·43	-0·16	0·18	0·35	0·01	-0·41	0·22	-0·15	0·03	0·16	0·71	0·12	0·23	0·54	8.
0·26	-0·18	0·25	-0·27	-0·02	-0·11	-0·22	0·54	0·40	-0·62	-0·06	-0·14	-0·19	0·17	0·02	-0·42	9.
0·07	-0·18	-0·11	-0·04	-0·04	-0·13	-0·27	0·57	0·17	-0·43	0·02	-0·20	-0·32	0·19	0·09	-0·43	10.
0·47	-0·19	0·43	-0·37	0·22	0·29	-0·13	-0·11	0·51	-0·49	0·00	-0·02	0·62	0·11	0·19	0·31	11.
-0·05	-0·13	0·30	0·23	-0·10	0·02	-0·06	0·21	-0·17	-0·11	-0·08	0·00	-0·12	0·21	0·11	-0·08	12.
0·21	-0·22	0·10	-0·14	-0·03	-0·08	-0·28	0·59	0·31	-0·57	-0·01	0·17	-0·23	0·18	0·04	-0·40	13.
0·29	-0·33	0·44	0·19	-0·01	0·18	0·04	0·04	0·19	-0·38	0·12	-0·03	0·14	-0·11	-0·24	0·24	14.
0·24	-0·19	0·51	0·11	0·19	0·35	-0·05	0·36	0·19	-0·15	0·25	-0·08	0·44	-0·04	-0·05	0·54	15.
	-0·53	0·22	0·07	-0·13	0·20	-0·02	-0·13	0·21	-0·18	-0·10	-0·40	0·37	0·31	0·36	0·20	16.
		0·02	-0·25	0·40	-0·48	0·18	-0·25	0·21	0·11	-0·04	0·05	-0·15	0·18	0·06	-0·20	17.
			-0·39	-0·07	-0·36	0·26	-0·17	0·20	-0·13	-0·13	0·14	0·03	-0·02	0·02	-0·14	18.
				-0·31	0·41	0·05	0·12	-0·48	0·30	0·12	-0·25	-0·08	-0·06	-0·23	0·35	19.
					-0·10	-0·32	-0·41	0·05	-0·36	0·30	-0·27	-0·18	0·14	0·08	0·06	20.
						-0·27	-0·13	-0·11	0·11	0·44	-0·08	0·44	0·02	-0·03	0·49	21.
							-0·15	-0·32	0·53	-0·67	-0·20	-0·03	0·05	0·19	-0·22	22.
								0·07	-0·32	-0·32	-0·29	-0·19	-0·28	-0·36	-0·38	23.
									-0·43	0·07	0·25	0·42	0·21	0·07	0·17	24.
										-0·07	-0·08	0·03	-0·14	0·00	-0·01	25.
											0·17	-0·09	-0·07	-0·26	0·18	26.
												0·15	-0·36	-0·34	-0·08	27.
													0·18	0·38	0·67	28.
														0·84	0·18	29.
															0·18	30.
																31.

ment in this experiment. These six kinds of teacher behaviors are described below.

1. *Patterns of solicitation.* Some teachers tend to ask only one question at a time while others will frequently ask two or more questions in rapid succession in a single utterance. The data indicated a clear relationship between these patterns of questioning and pupil achievement. The tendency to ask one question is positively related to achievement, while the tendency to ask several questions is negatively correlated (Table 4, variables 8, 9, 10, 13). Those teachers whose skill at questioning was such that they expected and got the response they required without having to repeat the question or supply their own answers produced higher pupil achievement. This interpretation was supported by the finding that the percentage of teacher questions which were answered by pupils was positively correlated with achievement, and the frequency with which a teacher provided information immediately following his own question was negatively correlated (Table 5, variable 1; Table 4, variable 6).

2. *Type of solicitation.* Teacher questions were classified into those which were *closed* (required single statements of fact, description, definition, naming) and those which were *open* (required statement of opinion, evaluation, explanation, inference). The *frequencies* of these two types of questions were not significantly related to achievement, but when the frequencies were converted to *percentages*, a significant relationship was indicated. Thus, the greater the percentage of a teacher's questions which were closed, the higher the achievement of the pupils (Table 5, variable 2). Since the percentage of closed questions was closely related to the percentage of teacher questions which were answered by pupils ($r = +0.90$), this finding is clearly related to the results obtained for patterns of solicitation discussed above.

3. *Teachers' reactions to pupil responses: reciprocation and redirection.* Following a pupil response, and his own comment on that response, a teacher may *redirect* the question to another pupil, or he may ask further questions of the same pupil, requiring the pupil to elaborate, expand, or explain what he has just said (*reciprocation*). The frequency of redirection was significantly related to achievement, while the frequency of reciprocation was not

(Table 4, variables 15, 16, 17). Further analysis of percentages did not alter these results.

4. *Teachers' reactions to pupil responses: comments.* The comments and remarks which teachers made to pupil responses were categorized into: simple affirmative and negative comments; indefinite and complex comments; comments consisting of repetition of pupil response; thanks and praise; and so on (Table 4, variables 18, 19, 20, 21, 22, 23, 24). The only one of these variables which showed a relationship with achievement was the teachers' use of thanks and praise. Detailed analysis of this variable indicated that saying 'good' and thanking the pupil were most clearly related to achievement.

5. *Structuring.* When teachers provide content-relevant information during the course of discussion, this frequently occurs either before or after a significant question and serves to set the stage for, or structure, the ensuing discussion. Further structuring also occurs at the completion of an episode initiated by a question.[3] The results reported in Table 4 indicated that structuring prior to a question was not related to achievement; structuring following a question was negatively related to achievement, while structuring at the end of an episode was positively related to achievement (Table 4, variables 5, 6, 7). These relationships were thrown into sharper contrast when pre-question, post-question and terminal structuring were considered as percentages of the total number of structuring moves employed by a teacher (Table 5, variables 4, 5, 6). Thus while there was no general relationship between the total amount of structuring and achievement, the teacher who introduced information at the end of an episode initiated by a question, rather than at the beginning, was more likely to produce higher achievement in pupils.

6. *Recapitulation and revision.* The teacher's review of the content of discussion may occur at the beginning or end of a lesson. Review of previous lessons at the beginning of the next lesson is referred to as *recapitulation* and summary review at the end of a lesson as *revision*. The data in Table 4 indicated a clear relationship between

3. An 'episode' is a section of the discussion initiated by a teacher solicitation and ended by the next different solicitation. See Smith, Meux *et al.* (1962).

revision and achievement, but not between recapitulation and achievement (Table 4, variables 26, 27, 28). Further analysis indicated that even when recapitulation is summed and added to revision, it does nothing to increase the relationship with achievement (Table 5, variables 7, 8, 9). Apparently review at the end of a lesson was significant, but review at the beginning had no discernible effect.

Variance related to teacher behavior variables

An attempt was made to determine the percentage of the variance in mean class residual achievement scores which could be associated with significant teacher behavior variables. One significant variable from each of the six categories of variables discussed above was selected and entered into a multiple regression analysis. The variables selected were: per cent of solicitations which were closed; terminal structuring as a per cent of total structuring; lines of revision as per cent of total lines (Table 5, variables 2, 6, 8); number of utterances containing only one solicitation; number of questions redirected to another pupil; and frequency of thanks and praise (Table 1, variables 8, 15, 21). The multiple correlation obtained with these six variables was $+0.891$, suggesting that about 79 per cent of the variance in residual achievement (class means) was associated with the selected teacher behavior variables.

Discussion

The results reported above may be summarized by suggesting that greater pupil knowledge of subject-matter objectives will be produced by the teacher who:

1. asks relatively direct (closed rather than open) questions which can be and are answered by pupils without the need for additional information or rephrasing of the question;

2. tends to provide an informative summary (structuring) at the end of an episode of discussion rather than at the beginning;

3. involves more pupils by redirecting each question to several pupils;

4. makes frequent use of thanks to pupil responses; and

5. provides comprehensive revision at the end of lessons.

It would, however, be a mistake to interpret these results as a general prescription about how teachers *should* teach. The findings are limited to a particular set of educational objectives (knowledge of an elementary science topic) which do less than justice to the full range of educational objectives in which most teachers are interested. It was interesting to note in the data obtained that the experienced teachers made more use of 'open' questions and more use of 'reciprocation' (asking pupils to explain, expand, etc. their responses) than the inexperienced student teachers. While these behaviors did not show a positive relationship with achievement they may well have been positively related to other long-term cognitive objectives. Thus it would be inappropriate to exclude variables which have not been identified as having a significant relationship with achievement from further consideration in future studies.

It is also important to note that the nature of the variables identified as having a significant relationship with achievement depends on the nature of the variation which occurred between teachers. A replication of this study with another group of teachers might not produce the same results if the teachers did not differ from each other in the same way. The inclusion in this study of experienced teachers alongside student teachers had the effect of highlighting those behaviors which change with teacher experience. This was deliberate and appropriate to the concern of the investigators with teacher training programs. Studies concerned with the differences between good and poor experienced teachers, which select teachers appropriately, are likely to identify different kinds of teacher behaviors related to pupil achievement.

It is the opinion of the present writers that, while further replications of this kind of study are desirable, the greatest need in this area is for adequate psychological theory which can be used to explain and predict observable teacher behavior–pupil learning relationships. The studies reported by Rosenshine (1968), like this study, suggest a strong relationship between pupil learning and a certain degree of linguistic precision and clarity (lack of vagueness, careful structuring) on the part of teachers. These are not the kinds of concepts that psychologists have traditionally concerned themselves with, nor are they discussed in educational psychology texts. The greatest service which this kind of study can do for educational psychology is to point up behavioral variables which have functional significance in the classroom.

References

BELLACK, A. A., *et al.* (1966), *The Language of the Classroom*, Columbia University Press.

CONNERS, C. K., and EISENBERG, L. (1966), *The Effect of Teacher Behavior on Verbal Intelligence in Operation Headstart Children*, Johns Hopkins University School of Medicine (US Office of Economic Opportunity Headstart Contract No. 510).

FORTUNE, J. C. (1967), *A Study of Generality of Presenting Behaviors in Teaching Preschool Children*, Memphis State University (US Office of Education Project No. 6–8468).

FURST, N. F. (1967), 'The multiple languages of the classroom', paper presented AERA Annual Meeting.

GAGE, N. L. (1966) 'Research on cognitive aspects of teaching', *report of the seminar on teaching: The way teaching is*, National Educational Association, 1966.

MEUX, M. O. (1967), 'Studies of learning in the school setting', *Rev. educ. Res.*, 1967, vol. 37, pp. 539–62.

MORRISON, B. M. (1966), 'The reactions of internal and external children to patterns of teaching behavior', unpublished doctoral thesis, University of Michigan

NUTHALL, G. A. (1968), 'Studies of teaching: II. Types of research on teaching', *New Zealand J. educ. Studies*, vol. 3, pp. 125–47.

NUTHALL, G. A., and LAWRENCE, P. J. (1965), *Thinking in the Classroom*, New Zealand Council for Educational Research.

ROSENSHINE, B. (1968), 'Objectively measured behavioral predictors of effectiveness in explaining', paper presented AERA Annual Meeting.

ROSENSHINE, B. (1969), 'Teaching behaviors related to pupil achievement', in I. Westbury and A. Bellack (eds.), *Research into Classroom Processes*.

SCHUTZ, R. E. (1966), 'The control of "error" in educational experimentation', *The School Review*, vol. 74, pp. 150–58.

SMITH, B. O., MEUX, M. O., *et al.* (1962), *A Study of the Logic of Teaching*, University of Illinois Bureau of Educational Research (Cooperative Research Project No. 258).

SOAR, R. S. (1966), 'Teacher-pupil interaction and pupil growth', paper presented AERA Annual Meeting.

SPAULDING, R. L. (1965), *Achievement, Creativity, and Self-Concept Correlates of Teacher-Pupil Transactions in Elementary Schools*, Hofstra University (Cooperative Research Project No. 1352).

TABA, H., LEVINE, S., and ELZEY, F. F. (1964), *Thinking in Elementary School Children*, San Francisco State College (Cooperative Research Project No. 1574).

WALLEN, N. E. (1966), *Relationships Between Teacher Characteristics and Student Behavior, Part 3*, University of Utah (Cooperative Research Project No. SAE OE5–10–181).

WRIGHT, C. J. (1968), 'An analysis of verbal teaching behavior and its relationship to pupil intelligence, prior knowledge, and achievement in standard two nature study lessons', unpublished master's thesis, University of Canterbury, N. Z.

Part Seven
Teachers' Assessments

Much of the writing on educational assessment has dealt with the objectives and techniques of formal examining. Assessment in classrooms, however, is largely a matter of relatively informal and ongoing procedures in which teachers and pupils seek information on the performances of themselves and one another. Much of it goes on independently of set occasions, and operates in the contexts of impression formation and expectancy processes. Furthermore, it is global in its concerns with scholastic and personality characteristics of individuals, and it relies heavily upon oral and non-verbal modes of communication.

The first article, by Jackson, examines teachers' skills in perceiving the attitudes of their pupils. The following studies by Victor Beez and Anthony and Pickup show how experimental techniques have been applied to examine the effects of teachers' and pupils' expectations upon teaching behaviour and pupils' work.

21 P. W. Jackson

Teachers' Perceptions of Pupils' Attitudes Towards School

Abridged from P. W. Jackson, *Life in Classrooms*, 'Students' Feelings about School', Holt, Rinehart and Winston, 1968, chapter 2.

From the few studies (Tenenbaum, 1940, 1944; Josephina, 1959; Leipold, 1957; Jackson and Getzels, 1959) which have been made of the general attitudes of elementary school students towards school and teachers, the general impression emerges that students are relatively content with their life at school. Although the proportions differ markedly for boys and for girls, it looks as if about 80 per cent of students in upper elementary grades would place themselves in the 'like' category if asked to describe themselves as either liking or disliking school. Closer examination, however, shows that students' attitudes are more complex than is implied by such a generalization. This complexity derives from two related aspects of student opinion. First is the admixture, to be found in some, of strong likes and dislikes and of contradictory attitudes towards specific features of school life. Second, and perhaps partially as a consequence of these contradictory elements, there seems to develop, in some students, a separation between their feelings and the daily business of classroom life. For these students (and no one seems to know how many fit this description) school is just another of life's inevitabilities towards which is adopted an I-can-take-it-or-leave-it attitude.

Yet, despite this complexity, stable differences do exist among students in their overall liking for school. It is evident, for example, that girls react more positively to school than do boys. We know, further, that thousands of students dislike school sufficiently to withdraw from it at the earliest opportunity, while others look forward with regret to the end of their days in school. The purpose of this paper is to ask how visible these differences are to teachers, and what factors affect their visibility.

Certain aspects of the teacher's perception of students' attitudes are almost too obvious to bear comment, and therefore, can be dispensed with rather quickly. It seems clear, for example, that extreme forms of student opinion are often visible to even the most insensitive teacher. When a student openly declares his distaste for school or does it only slightly more subtly by indicating his desire to quit school, the need for guesswork on the part of the teacher is eliminated.

When it comes to the more subtle aspects of student opinion, however, less is known of their visibility to the teacher. It is safe to say that the teacher typically does not know all there is to know about his students' attitudes towards school, but this does not say much. In order to say more some kind of empirical evidence is called for.

One way of considering the visibility of students' attitudes is to ask whether teachers can predict how their students will respond to a school attitude questionnaire. Naturally, no teacher could accurately predict his students' responses to each and every item on such a questionnaire. No one would expect him to be that perceptive. A more reasonable task might be to ask for a categorization of the students into groups representing varying levels of satisfaction. The teacher might be asked, in other words, to identify the most and least satisfied students in his room, allowing several students in each category, and this classification could be matched against a similar one based on the students' actual responses to questions about their school attitudes. This approach was used in a study of sixth graders[1] from which the results, while not highly generalizable, are sufficiently interesting to warrant a detailed discussion.

Two hundred and ninety-three students from eleven classrooms (all of the sixth grade rooms in the public school system of a suburban community) responded to a forty-seven-item questionnaire designed to assess attitudes toward school.[2] The

1. The data were collected by Miss Henriette M. Lahaderne while working under the author's direction.
2. The questionnaire was a revised version of the Student Opinion Poll described by Jackson and Getzels (1959). It consisted of 47 multiple choice questions relating to four aspects of school life: teachers, students, curriculum and classroom practices. For each item one alternative expressed complete satisfaction with that particular feature of school life, and a student choosing that alternative was given one point.

teacher in each classroom was shown sample items from the questionnaire and was given a brief description of its avowed purpose. He was then asked to predict, in a relative way, how each of his students might respond to such a set of questions.[3]

When expressed as a correlation coefficient the overall relationship between the teachers' ratings and the students' responses to the questionnaire yielded a value of 0·35. This single statistic does not provide much information, but it does indicate that the accuracy of the teachers' predictions were decidedly better than chance. The same statistic also indicates, of course, that these teachers were far from perfect in their estimates. Apparently some aspects of students' attitudes are visible to teachers and others are not. To learn more about this partial visibility we must undertake a more refined analysis.

A second way of depicting the gross character of the relationship between the teachers' predictions and the actual responses of the students is by applying the concepts of 'hits' and 'misses' in describing the accuracy of the teachers' judgements. 'Hits', as the term implies, are instances in which the teacher guessed correctly and 'misses' are instances in which he guessed incorrectly. What is meant by a correct or incorrect guess needs definition, of course, because the judgements (teachers' placement of the students into five categories) and the qualities being judged (students' total scores on a school opinionnaire) are not expressed in the same units.

In order to make the definition as unambiguous as possible, and, thus, to increase the ease with which the findings can be discussed, certain of the complexities in the raw data have been ignored or

3. The procedure for obtaining the ratings was as follows: Each teacher was presented with an alphabetized list of students. He was asked, first, to divide the group into thirds by classifying his students into three levels of satisfaction: 'most', 'average', and 'least'. He was then asked to identify from within the groups labelled 'most' and 'least' a smaller number of students (one fourth of each group) who seemed to represent extreme positions ('very satisfied' and 'very dissatisfied'). Thus, each student's attitudes were described by his teacher as falling into one of five categories. In each classroom the approximate proportion of students in the five categories were: $\frac{1}{12}, \frac{1}{4}, \frac{1}{3}, \frac{1}{4}, \frac{1}{12}$. When the ratings were treated quantitatively the values 15, 12, 10, 8, and 5 were assigned to the five groupings, the highest number being used to represent the students whom the teacher described as 'very satisfied'.

eliminated. First, the students who themselves expressed a middling attitude toward school, and whose scores therefore might be the most difficult to interpret, were withdrawn from the sample. Thus, in the analysis that follows we are concerned only with the teachers' judgements of those students who have expressed rather clear-cut opinions, either positive or negative, of what life in school is like. Second, the teachers' judgements have also been simplified by reducing, from five to three, the number of categories into which the predictions were grouped. This reduction was accomplished by ignoring the labels 'most' and 'least' attached to the extreme groups and by treating the entire sample as if the students had been classified into three groups, 'satisfied', 'average', or 'dissatisfied', with approximately one-third of the sample in each.

A teacher's judgement was considered a 'hit' if he classified as 'satisfied' a student whose score on the Student Opinion Poll was at least one-half a standard deviation above the mean of the total sample, or as 'dissatisfied', a student whose score was at least one-half a standard deviation below the mean. A 'miss' was defined as occurring when the teacher judged the student to be in the top or bottom third of the class but his actual score in the questionnaire placed him in the opposite group. The teacher's judgement was considered 'uncertain' when he placed into the 'average' category any of the students whose score on the opinionnaire were more than one-half of a standard deviation away from the mean. Applying these definitions, we would expect the teacher's judgements to be classified, by chance alone, as one-third 'hits', one-third 'misses', and one-third 'uncertain'. Deviations from these chance expectations were tested to see if they were statistically significant and the results, along with the actual numbers and percentages in each category, are presented in Table 1.

The data in Table 1 confirm the information contained in the correlation coefficient for the total group (that is, the teachers can predict student attitudes with a greater-than-chance accuracy). But a refinement can now be added to that general conclusion. Apparently the teachers can identify 'satisfied' students more accurately than they can 'dissatisfied' ones. Also, the reduced accuracy with the 'dissatisfied' group does not arise from a larger proportion of outright 'misses' with these students, rather the

Table 1 Accuracy of teachers' predictions of students' attitudes

Predictions	Students' attitudes 'Satisfied'		'Dissatisfied'	
	N	%	N	%
Hits	53	52·7	30	35·7
Uncertain	25	24·8	36	42·8
Misses	23	22·7	18	21·5
	$X^2 = 16 \cdot 7^a$		$X^2 = 6 \cdot 00^b$	

a Significant at the 0·01 level.
b Significant at the 0·05 level.

teachers are less likely to judge these students as fitting either extreme. In other words, the teachers were no more likely to misjudge one group than the other but the opinions of the satisfied students were somehow more visible than were the opinions of the dissatisfied students.

If the fact that girls seem happier with their school experience than do boys were recognized by teachers, the job of predicting student attitudes should become somewhat easier when both boys and girls are to be judged than when either sex is considered separately. This effect can be observed in that, whereas the correlation coefficient between the teachers' ratings and the actual responses of the total student sample was 0·35, the coefficients for the two sexes considered separately were 0·28 for boys and 0·27 for girls.

Sex differences in the accuracy of the teachers' judgements, expressed in terms of 'hits' and 'misses', are summarized in Table 2. As before, the students under consideration include only those whose expressed attitudes were relatively extreme. Table 2

Table 2 Accuracy of teachers' predictions related to sex of students

Predictions	Boys 'Satisfied'		'Dissatisfied'		Girls 'Satisfied'		'Dissatisfied'	
	N	%	N	%	N	%	N	%
Hits	11	35·4	24	46·1	42	60·0	6	18·7
Uncertain	10	32·3	21	40·4	15	21·4	15	46·9
Misses	10	32·3	7	13·5	13	18·6	11	34·4
	$X^2 = 0 \cdot 06$		$X^2 = 9 \cdot 5^a$		$X^2 = 22 \cdot 48^a$		$X^2 = 3 \cdot 81$	

a Significant at the 0·01 level.

reveals a striking sex difference in the accuracy of the teachers' predictions. This difference, however, is not the simple one of teachers being more accurate in predicting the scores of girls than of boys, or vice versa. It involves the quality of the attitude as well as the sex of the person holding it. The teachers seem to perceive two of the groups – the 'satisfied' girls and the 'dissatisfied' boys – more accurately than they do the other two. In other words, the girls who seem to be the happiest with their school experience and the boys who seem to be the least happy are the ones the teachers have the least difficulty in assessing, whereas the attitudes of the contrasting groups of 'satisfied' boys and 'dissatisfied' girls are not predicted with greater-than-chance accuracy by the teachers.

Naturally, we must be cautious in making inferences from these findings. But it is important to point out that they do make sense in the light of what is already known about sex differences and classroom characteristics. There is some evidence, for example, that dissatisfied boys are more willing to criticize persons in positions of authority than are dissatisfied girls. Jackson and Getzels (1959) found that when students were asked to describe their typical classroom feelings, the dissatisfied boys, more frequently than the dissatisfied girls, used 'extrapunitive' adjectives – words that placed the blame for the students' condition on others (for example, 'misunderstood', 'rejected'). The dissatisfied girls, in contrast, tended to employ more 'intropunitive' adjectives – words that placed the blame for the students' condition on the student herself (for example, 'inadequate', 'ignorant'). If a similar phenomenon were in operation in the sixth grade classrooms under discussion – that is, if dissatisfied boys were more willing to express criticism towards authorities – it would help to explain why such boys might be more visible to the teacher than are dissatisfied girls.

The reasons why the satisfied girls are more visible to the teachers than are the satisfied boys is not so easily apparent. Perhaps girls are just more willing to give direct expression to their satisfactions than are boys. Or perhaps the girls who are particularly pleased with school are more likely than are boys to express their feelings to their teachers indirectly by volunteering to help on classroom chores (most of which are feminine by character) or by preferring to stay with or near the teacher when alternative activities are available (on the playground, before and after school).[4]

Somewhat unexpectedly, another variable, the IQ scores of students, was found to be related to the accuracy of the teachers' predictions. As a group these teachers were noticeably more accurate in estimating the attitudes of students with high IQ than they were in estimating the attitudes of the students with low IQ. For the group of sixth graders whose IQ scores were 120 and above (49 students in all) the correlation between the teachers' predictions and actual scores on the Student Opinion Poll was 0·56; for those whose IQ scores were between 90 and 119 (193 students) the corresponding correlation was 0·30; finally, for those with scores below 90 (46 students) the correlation was 0·11.

To this point the findings from the sixth-grade classes may be summarized as follows. In general, satisfaction seems to be more visible to the teachers than is dissatisfaction, satisfied girls and dissatisfied boys tend to be particularly salient, and students whose IQ scores are average or above manage in some way to communicate their attitudes more clearly to teachers than do students with low IQs. These findings are evident when the total group of students and teachers is considered, but they cannot always be seen clearly in the results from each classroom. Some teachers seem to be plainly better than others in estimating how their students will respond to a school attitude questionnaire. Moreover, differences in the accuracy of individual teachers do not seem to be accounted for by differences in the composition of their class, at least not with respect to the student's sex, intelligence level, or degree of satisfaction with school. This conclusion is derived from the data presented in Table 3.

The data in Table 3 support two generalizations. First, there is considerable variability from teacher to teacher in the accuracy of their predictions. The estimates from the teacher in Class 4, as an instance, bear no systematic relation to the actual responses of her

4. The possibility that the sex of the teacher may be related to the perception of student attitude was considered, but no evidence was found to support it. Four of the eleven sixth grade teachers were men, and so far as could be determined the correlations between their predictions of student attitudes and the responses of their students did not differ systematically (even when examined separately for boys and girls) from those obtained from the women teachers.

Table 3 Accuracy of individual teacher's prediction of student attitudes

| Class | r* between predicted and actual SOP score | Classroom characteristics | | | | |
		Sex of teacher	Boys	Girls	Average IQ	SOP† score
1	0·10	F	12	19	101·1	28·71
2	0·38	F	18	12	109·0	31·00
3	0·52	F	13	15	105·1	25·43
4	0·00	F	12	10	98·0	28·27
5	0·45	M	20	8	107·4	27·96
6	0·30	F	10	19	112·5	21·44
7	0·56	F	11	13	93·5	24·67
8	0·42	M	18	10	97·0	28·11
9	0·46	M	11	19	99·3	28·33
10	−0·51	F	6	4	109·9	28·90
11	0·26	M	17	16	106·2	28·36

* Pearson correlation coefficient.
† Student Opinion Poll.

students, whereas those from the teacher in Class 7 parallel, at least roughly, her students' scores on the questionnaire.[5] Second, the variability among the teachers does not seem to be related in any systematic way to the variability of the classes on those characteristics that have already been discussed. That is, the teachers who seem to have done relatively well in estimating their students' attitudes do not seem to owe their success to the fact that their classes contained an unequal sex distribution or large numbers of very bright students, or students who were unusually satisfied with school. Why some teachers do seem to do better than others on this task is a question yet to be answered.

Thus far the discussion has focused on the conditions that enhance the visibility of student attitudes. But it is also possible to focus on a consideration of the conditions that cloud the teacher's

5. The correlation obtained with the data from Class 10 would obviously provide an even more dramatic example of the difference among the teachers. However, that coefficient is based on such a small number of students that it seems unwise to emphasize its atypicality.

vision. Instead of asking, as we have been, what student qualities are associated with an unusual proportion of 'hits' for these teachers, we might change the question to: What student qualities are associated with 'misses'?

One answer to this question is indicated by a closer examination of teacher accuracy in relation to the I Q levels of students. There were ten 'misses' in the low I Q group all of which involved students who seemed to be satisfied with school, but whom the teachers perceived as dissatisfied. In contrast, there were six 'misses' in the high I Q group all of which involved students who seemed to be dissatisfied with school but whom the teachers perceived as satisfied. In other words, the teachers tended to overestimate the amount of satisfaction to be found among students with high I Qs and the amount of dissatisfaction to be found among the students with low I Qs. The teachers' 'misses' in the middle I Q group were almost equally divided between 'satisfied' students whom the teachers predicted would be dissatisfied (twelve of the twenty-five 'misses') and 'dissatisfied' students whom the teachers predicted would be satisfied (the remaining thirteen).

This apparent bias in the teachers' judgements raises the question of whether these teachers are basing their estimates of student attitudes largely upon evidence of the student's intellectual prowess or possibly on related evidence of the student's success in mastering academic objectives. Perhaps the teachers' beliefs, if summarized in the form of an adage, would be expressed in something like: 'The student who does well in school thinks well of school'. A hint of this kind of belief is revealed in Table 4 in which are shown the correlations between the teachers' estimates of student attitudes and the students' scores on I Q and achievement tests. The correlations between the teachers' estimates and the student scores on the Student Opinion Poll, which have already been presented, are included in Table 4 for purposes of comparison.

In the judgement of these sixth-grade teachers the brighter students, who are also among the top performers on achievement tests, are the ones who appear to be the most satisfied with school. Indeed, the teachers' estimates of their students' responses to a school opinionnaire turn out to be more closely related to the students' academic standing than to their actual responses to the questionnaire. This effect is more pronounced for boys than for girls, but it is evident for both sexes. According to these teachers, 'good' students are the ones who appear to be satisfied with school and 'poor' students are the ones who appear to be dissatisfied.

Table 4 Correlations between teachers' estimates of students' attitudes and measures of intellectual performance

| | IQ | Achievement tests | | | SOP Scores |
		Reading	Language Arts	Arithmetic	
Boys (148)	0·44	0·49	0·51	0·45	0·28
Girls (144)	0·39	0·36	0·37	0·31	0·27

But are the teachers really in error? After all, there does seem to be something logically compelling about the conjoining of success and satisfaction. Perhaps the better students really are more content with what goes on in the classroom, and the poorer students more discontent. Perhaps the teachers have merely overestimated the extent to which this is so. The weight of evidence (e.g. Tenenbaum, 1944; Jackson and Getzels, 1959), however, is against such a conclusion. With almost complete consistency, research has shown students' liking for school to be negligibly correlated with their scores on achievement tests.

It was acknowledged at the beginning of this paper that certain crude relationships between attitudes and achievement do exist and are visible to most teachers. For example, potential drop-outs probably like school less than do average students and their dislike is coupled with lower-than-average achievement records. Most teachers would take this fact to be incontrovertible. Indeed it is extreme cases, such as the potential drop-out, or the obviously contented valedictorian at the other extreme, that lead to the general expectation that there will be a linkage between attitude and achievement all along the line.

But suppose the gradations of differences revealed by attitude questionnaires do not represent significant differences in the subjective feelings of the students. Suppose, that is, that a small number of students dislike school intensely and an equally small number are correspondingly positive in their opinion, but that most students have either mixed or very neutral feelings about their classroom experience. Perhaps for attitudes to interact with achievement they have to be extreme, and extreme attitudes, positive or negative, may be much rarer than is commonly thought.

References

JACKSON, P. W., and GETZELS, J. W. (1959), 'Psychological health and classroom functioning: a study of dissatisfaction with school among adolescents', *J. educ. Psychol.*, vol. 50, pp. 295–300.

SISTER JOSEPHINA (1959), 'Study of attitudes in the elementary grades', *J. educ. Sociol.*, vol. 33, pp. 56–60.

LEIPOLD, L. E. (1957), 'Children do like school', *Clearing House*, vol. 31, pp. 332–4.

TENENBAUM, S. (1940), 'Uncontrolled expressions of children's attitudes towards school', *Elem. Sch. J.*, vol. 40, pp. 670–78.

TENENBAUM, S. (1944), 'Attitudes of elementary school children to school, teachers and classmates', *J. appl. Psychol.*, vol. 28, pp. 134–41.

22 W. V. Beez

Influence of Biased Psychological Reports on Teacher Behavior and Pupil Performance

Adapted by the author from a paper read at the American Psychological Association Meetings, San Francisco, 1968, published in M. W. Miles and W. W. Charters (eds.), *Learning in Social Settings*, Allyn and Bacon, 1970, pp. 328-34.

Experimental research in the area of effects of expectancies (Rosenthal, 1964a, 1964b, 1966) indicates that the experimenter's orientation and expectation can influence the data. As Rosenthal (1964a) has demonstrated, expectancies of this sort can be communicated in very subtle ways. A variety of cues, so-called *demand characteristics*, unintentionally communicate to the subject something of what the experimenter is after (Orne, 1962). Communication can be subtle, unintentional, and differential depending upon the subjects or the expectations the experimenter holds for them. Even in highly standardized situations, a subject can be influenced by another person's expectations (Rosenthal, 1966).

That expectancies also influence behavior outside the laboratory has in recent years been demonstrated in educational research (Cahen, 1965; Rosenthal and Jacobson, 1966, 1967, 1968). The findings of these investigators raise serious questions as to present practices in our educational system, and make further investigation imperative. It appears that teacher–pupil interaction operates similarly to laboratory interaction between experimenter and subject.

While Rosenthal and Jacobson investigated changes in IQ due to differential information given to teachers, the present study was mainly concerned with changes in teaching behavior and performance by pupils. It also attempted to investigate the question raised by Rosenthal's work as to how a teacher's expectation becomes translated into behavior in such a way as to elicit the expected pupil behavior (Rosenthal and Jacobson, 1966).

Method
Subjects

Sixty children from the summer Head Start program in Bloomington, Indiana participated in this study. They ranged in age from 5 years, 7 months to 6 years, 6 months, and had I Qs on the Peabody Picture Vocabulary Test from 55 to 127, with a mean of 91. I Q assessment was made *after* completion of the experimental study, so that at the time of experimentation the actual I Q was not known. Children were randomly assigned to either a 'low ability' or a 'high ability' group. With the exception of name and age nothing was known about a particular child prior to assignment to one of the groups. The names of the children were taken from the list of children attending the Head Start program and none of the children was discussed with either the principal or the regular teacher. Each of the two groups consisted of fifteen boys and fifteen girls. None of the children in the study had previously attended regular classes.

Sixty 'teachers' served as the actual subjects of this study. Ss were graduate students in the School of Education of Indiana University during the summer of 1967. Ss ranged in age from 19 to 51 years ($M = 28 \cdot 9$) and had from 0 to 22 years teaching experience ($M = 4 \cdot 6$). Ss were assigned at random to one of the two groups.

Experimenters

Two graduate students in English served as experimenters. Although Es were not given details of the study they did guess the general idea. However, throughout the study they did not know what group a particular child was in nor what Ss had been told about the child's intellectual prospects. Instructions were given in writing to Es.

Procedure

Experimentation took place in separate rooms in the elementary school which was used for the Head Start program. Of the school personnel, the principal alone was aware of the purpose of the study. Each S worked individually with one child. S was told that the purpose of the study was to see how well Head Start children would perform on a number of experimental tasks. Prior to seeing the child, *S* was given a folder containing a faked 'psychological evaluation' of the child (see Tables 1 and 2).

All reports were identical for the children belonging to the same groups, with the exception of name and age of child. Reports included 'background information', 'testing behavior and clinical observation', and 'recommendations'. The fake IQ data described all children as falling within the average range of intelligence. The

Table 1 Psychological evaluation

Name: James Carpenter   Date: 27 June 1967
Sex: male
Birthdate 8–3–61   Confidential
Age: 5–11
Examiner: R. L. Simons

Reason for testing
Intelligence Testing for Special Project in Educational Research, summer 1967.

Background
James lives with his parents in Bloomington, Ind. Mr Carpenter is employed at a local department store as a stock clerk and has completed the eighth grade. Mrs Carpenter is a housewife and completed nine years of school. There are two younger siblings in the family.

Test behavior and clinical observation
James was an open and friendly boy who related well to the examiner. He smiled readily and seemed to enjoy adult attention. He frequently initiated conversation and reported at length about things he liked, his home, his play activities, etc.

The boy responded freely to the questions asked him and seemed to be interested in most all the tasks. He responded well to encouragement, was quite attentive and seemed to be well motivated.

Both the Peabody Picture Vocabulary Test, Form A, and the Stanford-Binet, Form L-M, were administered to James. On the PPVT he obtained an IQ of 102, and he received an IQ of 105 on the Stanford-Binet. The two IQ scores are quite similar, and one can classify James as falling within the normal range of intelligence in comparison to children his age.

Recommendations
Although James comes from a culturally disadvantaged home he has, nevertheless, very good potential for school related tasks and

activities. He seems highly motivated and well adjusted to learning situations. It is expected that he will experience little or no difficulty in his school work and should do quite well on the proposed project tasks.

reports for the 'low ability' children, however, (Table 2) called the I Q score 'low average', and interpreted the results negatively, stressing negative aspects of cultural deprivation, and predicted that school adjustment would be difficult. The reports for the 'high ability' group children (Table 1) interpreted the I Q information positively, terming it 'normal', stressed positive aspects in the child's fictional behavior, and suggested that despite cultural deprivation the child should do well in school. These reports were given in closed folders to Ss so that Es would not know what they contained. Ss were also told not to discuss the 'case' with Es.

After S had read the report, the child was brought into the room and given the first task. This task (symbol learning) consisted of a series of twenty signs printed on individual cards (e.g. 'Stop', 'Walk', 'Go', 'Boys', 'Girls', 'Danger', etc.). S was told to teach

Table 2 Psychological evaluation

Name: Richard Walters   Date: 27 June 1967
Sex: male
Birthdate: 10–28–61   Confidential
Age: 5–8
Examiner: R. L. Simons

Reason for testing
Intelligence Testing in connection with Special Project in Educational Research, summer 1967.

Background
Richard is a member of a family of seven, living in a two room house. The owner of the house is currently adding one room which will be used as a bedroom. His father is employed in Martinsville as a truck driver, and his mother is a full time housewife. Both parents were born in Gary, Ind., and moved to Bloomington eight years ago. Both parents have an eighth grade education.

When Richard appeared for testing he was somewhat carelessly dressed. He was sulky, appeared unresponsive, and it was difficult to engage him in any lengthy conversation. It is the feeling of the examiner that the boy disliked the testing situation and, in general, feels uncomfortable in adult company.

Test behavior and clinical observation

Despite the examiner's attempts to establish good rapport with Richard the boy did not appear to feel comfortable. It was often difficult to elicit a response from him, or at times he even remarked that he did not like the test and it was 'dumb'. It was necessary to ask him repeatedly to sit up and to pay attention. He was quite fidgety, asking how much longer it was to last, yawned and put his head on the table. It would appear from this that motivation for school related tasks is lacking in Richard.

Richard was first administered the Peabody Picture Vocabulary Test, Form A, on which he obtained an IQ of 95. On the Stanford-Binet Intelligence Scale, Form L-M, he obtained an IQ of 94. The results of the two tests are quite similar and it is suggested that they can be taken as a fairly good estimate of Richard's intellectual abilities. This would place the boy in the 'low average' range of intelligence in comparison to children his age. Richard, coming from a culturally disadvantaged home, lacks many of the experiences of normal children his age, and shows a lack of motivation toward learning tasks.

Recommendation

Richard's present level of intellectual functioning would suggest that school adjustment will be difficult for him, and there are serious doubts that he will profit from average learning tasks. This might be due in part to a lack of motivation but mainly also because of a lack of previous experience. It is doubtful that he will be able to perform satisfactorily on the proposed learning tasks of the project.

as many signs as he could in a standard order within a ten-minute period, using whatever technique or strategy he wanted to use. *E* unobtrusively recorded the time spent on each sign, the number of signs covered, and tallied *S*'s responses, such as the number of times a word was read to the child, the child was asked to say the word, the child was asked to identify the word from the card, the meaning of the word was explained or demonstrated, etc.

After the ten-minute teaching period, the signs were removed and *S* was asked to present a series of five jigsaw puzzles to the child for a five-minute period, in a standard order. Each puzzle had to be successfully completed before the next could be given. *S* was told to present it any way he wished and that he could interact with the child. *E* again recorded the time spent on each puzzle and number of times *S* gave clues to the child. After this task the child was moved to a different room, where he was retested by *E* for recall of the signs covered in the first task.[1]

Finally, after *E* returned to record *S*s' estimates of their children's intelligence test performance level, *S* was asked to complete a questionnaire, rating the child as to expected achievement level, social competency, and intellectual ability, as compared with children in the regular classroom. *S* also had to indicate on a rating scale how difficult he thought the sign task was for the child.[2]

Results and discussion

1. Teachers who had been given favorable expectations about a pupil tried to teach more symbols than did the teachers given unfavorable expectations ($p < 0.001$). The mean for the 'high ability' group was 10·43 words, the mean for the 'low ability' group was 5·66 words attempted. The difference in teaching effort was dramatic. Eight or more symbols were taught by 87 per cent of the teachers expecting better performance, but only 13 per cent of the teachers expecting poorer performance tried to teach that many words ($p < 0.0000001$).

2. The two groups differed significantly ($p < 0.001$) in the number of symbols learned by the children. While the mean for the 'high ability' group was 5·9, the 'low ability' group had a mean of only 3·1 symbols. Most (77 per cent) of the children alleged to have better intellectual prospects learned five or more symbols but only 13 per cent of the children alleged to have poorer intellectual prospects learned five or more symbols ($p < 0.000002$).

1. During this time *S* made an estimate of the level of performance the child would achieve on the French Pictorial Test of Intelligence (one of four levels of difficulty into which the French cards had been sorted). In the 'low ability' group, only four children were judged by *S*s to be able to master the test above the second level of difficulty; in the 'high ability' group, twenty-two children were judged as performing above the second level.

2. *S*s also indicated whether they liked or disliked working with the child (all reported liking it); rated the helpfulness of the psychological report (all but three subjects felt they were 'very' or 'somewhat' helpful, with no differences across treatments); and rated how comfortable they had felt with the tasks (the majority of the *S*s felt comfortable, with no significant differences across treatments).

3. *S*s' ratings of achievement, social competency, and intellectual ability were made on 5-point scales. On achievement, the 'low ability' group received a mean of 1·93 as compared with 3·50 for the 'high ability' group ($p < 0.001$). The difference for social competency is smaller, but still significant beyond the 0·01 level. The 'low ability' group had a mean of 2·57 and the 'high ability' group a mean of 3·33. Ratings of intellectual ability gave the 'low ability' group a mean of 1·93 and the 'high ability' group a mean of 3·43 ($p < 0.001$).

4. There was also a difference between the groups in the number of times the meanings of the symbols were explained and, of course, the time spent on each symbol. *S*s in the 'low ability' teaching group explained the meaning of a word significantly more often, gave more examples, and spent more time on non-teaching activities than did *S*s in the 'high ability' teaching group ($p < 0.01$).

5. All children, except one, completed the puzzles within the permitted time. No significant difference was found between the groups in the number of clues given by *S*s.

6. Only one *S* evaluated the symbol-learning task as too difficult for the pupil in the 'high ability' group (3·3 per cent) whereas 63 per cent of *S*s felt that it was too difficult for children in the 'low ability' group.

The results strongly support findings by others (e.g. Rosenthal and Jacobson, 1966) that pupils are influenced by their teachers' expectations and have a tendency to behave accordingly. Teachers also act differently depending upon their expectations for the child. When they expect the child to do poorly they attempt to teach less, spend more time on each task, give more examples of meaning, are more likely to engage in non-teaching activities, and repeat the task more often than when they expect better performance from the child. It needs to be pointed out that in this study *S* had practically no time to get acquainted with the child prior to the start of the teaching task and, therefore, relied heavily on the faked 'psychological report'. However, the data of the evaluation and rating of the child by *S* would support the hypothesis that even in the face of successful performance on the puzzle tasks, *S*'s expectation is not changed.

Some anecdotal material is of interest. One child in the 'high ability' group whose actual IQ was 71 (measured *after* the experiment) was taught 14 signs and learned 7; another child in the 'low ability' group with a tested IQ of 127 was taught only 5 signs and learned 3.

After the total experiment was over, the author reported to the groups of *S*s on the actual intent of the experiment. While the 'high ability' teachers were rather pleased, the 'low ability' teachers seemed more inclined to argue ('but my child *really* was retarded'). Two teachers, in fact, believed that the report had given the IQ as falling within the retarded range.

Mismatches between the report and the events of the teaching situation occurred, but did not seem to affect *S* expectations. One child did not speak, though the report had described him as 'frequently initiating conversation'. *S* nevertheless rated the report as 'most helpful'. In another case, a boy was mis-identified as a girl in the report; *S* found the report 'most helpful' and proceeded with 'high ability' expectations.

Conclusions

Results of this sort have serious implications for present practices in educational settings. Even if we consider that this was a somewhat artificial situation and that normally the teacher has a much better knowledge of the child, we are, nevertheless, overwhelmed by the data suggesting drastic effects of expectancies. School children are frequently evaluated throughout their school years in terms of IQ tests, psychological reports, labeling through special classes, etc. For example, a child who is labeled a 'slow learner' or 'mentally retarded' is automatically expected to do less well than a 'normal' child. This expectation might, in fact, retard the performance of the child even more than is necessary. The findings would suggest that one should be very careful as to what information a teacher should receive about a child. On the other hand, the findings may be applied in a constructive way; that is, positive aspects in a child's behavior or ability should be stressed.

References

CAHEN, L. S. (1965), 'An experimental manipulation of the "halo effect": A study of teacher bias', unpublished manuscript, Stanford University.

ORNE, M. T. (1962), 'On the social psychology of the psychological experiment: With particular reference to demand characteristics and their implications', *Amer. Psychol.*, vol. 17, pp. 776–83.

ROSENTHAL, R. (1964a), 'The effect of the experimenter on the results of psychological research', in N. A. Maher (ed.), *Progress in Experimental Personality Research*, vol. 1, Academic Press, pp. 79–114.

ROSENTHAL, R. (1964b), 'Experimenter outcome-orientation and the results of the psychological experiment', *Psychol. Bull.*, vol. 61, pp. 405–12.

ROSENTHAL, R. (1966), *Experimenter Effects in Behavioral Research*, Appleton-Century-Crofts.

ROSENTHAL, R., and JACOBSON, L. (1966), 'Teacher expectancies: determinants of pupils' I.Q. gains', *Psychol. Reports*, vol. 19, pp. 115–18.

ROSENTHAL, R., and JACOBSON, L. (1967), 'Self-fulfilling prophecies in the classroom: teachers' expectations as unintended determinants of pupils' intellectual competence', paper read at the American Psychological Association meetings.

ROSENTHAL, R., and JACOBSON, L. (1968), *Pygmalion in the Classroom: Teacher Expectation and Pupils' Intellectual Development*, Holt, Rinehart and Winston.

23 A. J. Pickup and W. S. Anthony

Teachers' Marks and Pupils' Expectations: The Short-term Effects of Discrepancies upon Classroom Performance in Secondary Schools

From A. J. Pickup and W. S. Anthony, 'Teachers' marks and pupils' expectations: the short-term effects of discrepancies upon classroom performance in secondary schools', *British Journal of Educational Psychology*, vol. 38, 1968, pp. 302-9.

Introduction

When a teacher asks his pupils to perform tasks for which they will be returned marks or grades he is initiating an activity which is one of the most extensively applied methods in use in education. The situation which arises when a mark or grade is returned to a pupil is at first sight a simple application of an essential 'feedback' process; a method by which the teacher can assess the success of his teaching and by which a learner can assess the adequacy of his learning. In the typical educational context however, the process of returning marks to pupils on completion of a task is not merely informational. The situation contains a number of elements which may affect the subsequent motivational state of the pupil. The simplest motivational element is the avoidance of the lack of interest which would result from no knowledge of results, but other elements are also present. A good mark may be considered a reward and a poor mark a punishment. Marks may be accompanied by statements or comments so that together or singly they constitute a situation of praise or of blame. The motivational state of the learner may be influenced by his perception of the likelihood of success or failure and the perceived status of the teacher may influence the reception of marks, grades or comments.

The now notorious unreliability of marks which may be awarded (Vernon, 1962, Britton *et al.*, 1966) may be further complicated by the teacher deliberately distorting marks for motivational purposes (Vernon, 1962, p. 33). The practice of deliberately distorting marks introduces a dangerous assumption. The teacher who does this presumably makes a number of assumptions about the effects which a mark will have upon a pupil's later performance. Is a low mark (whatever that may mean) necessarily discouraging?

It is reasonable to assume that when a pupil has completed a task for which he is to receive a mark or grade, the pupil forms an expectation of some kind regarding this mark or grade. This expectation may be of a crude nature; a 'good' mark or a 'poor' mark. It may be further refined in relation to the pupil's past performance; a 'better mark than usual' or a 'worse mark than usual'. If the teacher asks his pupil to state what he (the pupil) considers his work is worth, this evaluation may be the closest approximation to the pupil's 'true' expectation that can be found. Any vague 'hopes' which may be entertained by the pupil will be modified by some realism, because the recipient of his evaluation is the teacher who will mark his work. This evaluation is therefore described throughout the present report as the pupil's expectation.

The aims of the research here described were to examine, *in typical classroom settings*, the following:

1. The relationship between pupil's expectations and the teacher's mark.

2. The effects upon subsequent performance of a discrepancy between the pupil's expectation and the mark awarded by the teacher.

Previous related work

A search of the literature concerned with educational incentives revealed no previous work directly related to this topic. While a number of analogies may be drawn with research in the area of 'praise or blame', these do not present precise guidelines for the formation of hypotheses. Kennedy and Willcutt (1964) in their review of literature in this area, have shown that the experimental history of praise and blame studies has failed to produce clear-cut conclusions, though recent evidence appears to support the belief that praise is a superior incentive to blame. 'Level of aspiration' studies offer further analogies, limited by the fact that goal-setting is a pre-performance factor while the present research is concerned with the post-performance factor of expected mark. Child and Whiting (1949) illustrate a number of widely accepted generalizations in the area of level of aspiration. Murstein (1965), studying the relationship of grade expectations to grades actually received, found that students did not change their expectations of grades as a result of receiving actual grades. High ability students expected high grades and received them. Low ability students similarly expected high grades and did not modify their optimism as a result of experience.

The authors were impressed with the method of the Page (1958) research, concerned with the effectiveness of teachers' comments. This research has been popular with reviewers (Campbell and Stanley, 1963, Charters and Gage, 1963) because of its avoidance of many pitfalls in a 'generalizable' design. The experimental methods used in the research described below are evolved from the Page (1958) research.

Plan of investigation
Preliminary work

A six-class study, described in full elsewhere (Pickup, 1967, ch. 6), was carried out to examine the relationship between teachers' marks and pupils' expectations which would occur in schools under non-experimental conditions. Measures were taken of pupils' expected marks following classroom tests and of teachers' marks for the tests. Precautions taken to avoid the 'artificiality' of experiment included the use of the usual classroom teacher as a sub-experimenter. The main findings of this study were as follows:

1. Out of a final sample of 123 pupils three had estimated their mark correctly, relative to the teacher's mark.

2. Of those pupils who were not accurate in their estimate 68·3 per cent over-estimated their mark and 31·7 per cent under-estimated their mark on the first occasion of being asked to evaluate their work. (This is a highly significant difference, $p < 0.001$.)

3. Girls who had over-estimated their mark on the first occasion modified this optimism significantly more than over-estimating boys when both were asked to evaluate their work on a second occasion.

4. Low pre-test scorers over-estimated more often than high pre-test scorers. (This was a highly significant difference, $p < 0.001$.)

Result 4 listed above, the correlation between pre-test score and frequency of over-estimation, arose in the following way: The data were examined for indications of a possible effect of discrepancy between expected and teacher's mark upon subsequent test performance. It was recognized that *if* there were a correlation between pre-test score and discrepancy, then the well-known phenomenon of statistical regression (Campbell and Stanley, 1963, p. 181) would produce the false appearance of an effect of discrepancy upon subsequent performance. Therefore result 4 was looked for, and the actual finding of the result meant that this particular study would not yield a true picture of the possible effect of discrepancy. In any case, this was a correlational study and hence less satisfactory than an experimental study in elucidating cause-and-effect relationships. It was therefore decided to carry out an experimental study in which the discrepancy between expectation and testscore would be manipulated as an independent variable, while retaining (as far as possible) the real-life aspects of the situation.

A two-class pilot study was carried out to test a possible experimental design. This study (Pickup, 1967, ch. 7) yielded useful information which led to the improved design described below.

The main study

The major purpose of the main study was to examine by experimental means the effects upon subsequent classroom performance of a discrepancy between a teacher's mark and a pupil's expectation. A secondary purpose was to check the findings of the preliminary work described above.

Six non-selective single-sex secondary schools provided a final sample of 243 pupils from ten classes. The school subjects used in the experiment were English and Mathematics.

The measures used
Performance tests

Participating teachers were requested to set two tests of their normal classwork. The material to be tested was to be as independent of previous learning and experience as possible. The teachers were asked to construct their tests as follows:

1. A section of twenty 'objective' questions which could be scored easily on a right/wrong basis.

2. A 'woolly' question containing a subjective element. The pupil

should not be able to assess easily whether marks are gained or lost on this question. (This question was never marked because its sole purpose was to disguise the fact that marks had been tampered with.)

3. The tests were to be so constructed as to give every pupil an opportunity of gaining some marks, but extreme difficulty in obtaining full marks.

These tests were to be marked by the experimenter, following a marking scheme devised by the participating teacher. Teachers were informed that the marks returned after the first test may differ from the actual performance of the pupil.

Pupils' expected marks

Pupils were asked to enter upon an additional slip of paper the mark (out of twenty) that they believed their test paper to be worth. These assessment slips were to be given to the experimenter together with the test scripts.

Additional information

The Junior Eysenck Personality Inventory (Eysenck, 1965a, b) was administered to the pupils during a testing session separate from the experiment. A measure of the pupils' academic motivation was obtained during the same session by means of a modified nineteen-item test described by Buxton (1965). A measure of the participating teachers' leadership attitude was taken by means of a modified version of the Assumed Similarity of Opposites test described by Fiedler (1958).

Procedure

Participating teachers were supplied with an instructional leaflet concerning their part in the experiment. After the administration of the pre-test and collection of the pupils' assessment slips, the experimenter collected this material and marked the pre-test scripts following the teacher's marking scheme; these marks are referred to as 'actual' marks. All pupils who had indicated that they had been absent for some portion of the work tested in the pre-test were assigned to a 'no treatment' group. Similarly, all pupils who had recorded an expected mark of 0–3 or 17–20 were assigned to the 'no treatment' group. (However, in one class of 26, 10 pupils expected a mark of 17–20, and in this case only those pupils who would have fallen into the 'high treatment' group were excluded, which resulted in a loss of three pupils.)

Pupils remaining after these exclusions were randomly assigned to one of three treatment groups (high, low and matching treatments) within levels of 'actual' score rank. Thus, within any one class-list, actual scores were converted into rank order; the three top ranks (1, 2, 3) were grouped into a triplet, the next three ranks (4, 5, 6) were grouped into a next triplet, and so on. Ties had previously been ranked by the toss of a coin. Two numbers on an ordinary six-sided die were selected to represent each of three treatments, for the purpose of random assignment: within each triplet, the first member was assigned to a treatment by a throw of the die; the second member was similarly assigned to a second treatment; and the third member was assigned to the remaining treatment. This procedure was repeated for each triplet.

The experimenter administered experimental treatments by writing, on a mark list, a mark which was 3 marks above ('High' treatment), 3 marks below ('Low' treatment), or exactly matching ('Matching' treatment) the pupil's expected mark, according to the treatment group in which that pupil fell. This mark list was returned, with the pupils' assessment slips, to the participating teacher. The teacher entered the mark from this list on to each pupil's assessment slip and this was returned to the pupil (i) immediately prior to the work which was to be tested on the post-test or (ii) immediately prior to the post-test where (i) was not possible. (An excuse was made to the pupils that the actual test scripts were not available at that moment; in fact neither pre-test nor post-test scripts were ever returned to the pupils.)

Post-test scripts, marking scheme and assessment slips were collected by the experimenter and a post-test mark list, based upon the teacher's marking scheme, was returned to the teacher with the assessment slips. During this visit to the school, the experimenter administered the personality and academic motivation tests to the pupils while the participating teacher completed the ASO test in another room. All pupils were eventually informed that an experiment had taken place and that the scripts were required for records.

The percentile rank of each raw score in a class test was calculated and converted into a T score (Garrett, 1958, pp. 314–18, Table G). Thus each set of test scores has a normal distribution with a mean of 50 and a standard deviation of 10.

Results

Pupils' expected mark and actual mark

1. When the pre-test data were examined it was found that 72·6 per cent of the pupils over-estimated their mark relative to the actual mark. A considerable number of pupils (almost 10 per cent) were accurate in their estimate. Of those who were not accurate in their estimate, 81·3 per cent over-estimated their mark. This tendency to over-estimate is highly significant ($p < 0.001$) and confirms the finding of the preliminary work.

2. The data were examined for significant direction of change of expectation following experimental treatment. It was found that girls who been exposed to low treatment following the pre-test showed a highly significant tendency ($p < 0.001$) to reduce their expectations for the post-test. No other significant directions of change were found.

3. Pre-test score was correlated with the difference between actual mark and expected mark ($r = 0.33$, $p < 0.001$). That is, low test scorers were especially liable to over-estimate their marks, as had also been found in the preliminary work.

The effects of the experimental treatment

1. The effects of each treatment upon gain scores were examined by means of the analysis of variance by ranks. Each intact triplet in the experiment yielded ranks for a Friedman two-way analysis of variance (Siegel, 1956, pp. 166–72). The ranked data from each triplet were cast into various categories to examine treatment effects. There were no significant effects here. Other analyses, carried out to examine possible subject differences, also proved non-significant.

2. Analyses concerned with the exploration of treatment effects in relation to personality factors, academic motivation and teachers' leadership attitude, proved non-significant except for some minor sex-differences.

3. Examination of the data on 'high' and 'low' treatment and pre-

test position in class showed a correlation between pre-test score and differential effect of treatment. It is to be noted that in this experimental design, treatments are applied with equal frequency within each level of pre-test score, and therefore there is no misleading effect of statistical regression as there was in the earlier correlational study. This correlation was at first tested by relatively crude techniques which failed to yield significant results, and then by the product–moment method, as follows. The variables studied were matched-pairs difference scores and mean pre-test scores. Each randomized triplet in the experiment was examined for losses of individuals; any triplet which had lost a high or low treatment pupil was excluded from analysis. (a) The standardized scores for the high treatment pupil and the low treatment pupil yielded a mean pre-test score for that pair. (b) The gain score for the high treatment pupil was subtracted from the gain score for the low treatment pupil to yield a difference score for that pair. A product–moment correlation between the variables in (a) and (b) yielded $r = 0.275$ ($N = 74$ pairs). The significance of this obtained r was tested (Walker and Lev, 1953, p. 251) yielding $t = 2.43$, df. $= 72$. This correlation is significant beyond the 0.02 level (two-tailed test).

This significant correlation indicated the need to examine all differences between treatments in the same way. No significant differences were found other than between 'high' and 'low' treatment.

A crude indication of treatment effects related to pre-test score is to be found in Figure 1. In this graph three performance groups (pre-test) 'failing' pupils (45 marks and less) 'average' pupils (between 46–54 marks) and 'successful' pupils (55 marks and more) are studied to show average gain scores following experimental treatment. The general downward slope is a reflection of statistical regression, but the significant aspect of the figure is the difference between experimental treatments at the various levels of pre-test score.

Conclusions and discussion

This research aimed to investigate (a) the relationship between pupils' expected marks and actual marks and (b) the effects, upon subsequent performance, of discrepancies between expected marks

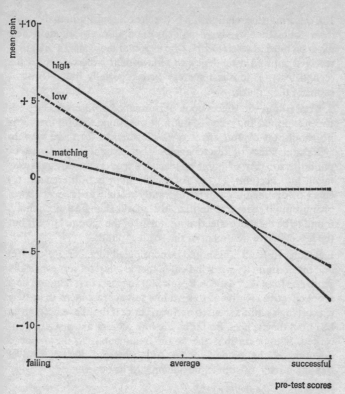

Figure 1 The effects of three experimental treatments at different levels of pre-test score. The gain score is the post-test score minus the pre-test T score

and marks received by the pupil from the teacher. The method of the research was designed for generalizability to the normal school setting; the only divergence from normal classroom procedure was in the collection of pupils' expected marks. It was intended, and it is believed that pupils were unaware that observation or experiment were taking place.

The results naturally fall into two categories corresponding to the two aims of investigation.

A. J. Pickup and W. S. Anthony 341

1. Concerning the relationship between expected and actual marks, it was found that (a) a large majority of pupils over-estimated their mark on the first test; (b) girls who expected more marks than they received showed a tendency to reduce their expectation on the second test; (c) low test scorers were especially liable to over-estimate their mark.

2. Concerning the effects upon performance of discrepancies between expected and received mark, it was found that (a) there was no significant overall effect of discrepancies; (b) there was no significant effect of discrepancies when school subject, sex of pupil, personality of pupil or teacher's leadership attitudes was taken into account, except for some minor sex-differences; (c) effect of discrepancy was significantly related to pre-test score: giving a pupil more (rather than less) marks than he expected was found to be the more effective treatment of the 'poorer' pupils but the less effective treatment of the 'better' pupils.

Results 1(c) and 2(c) should be considered together. Result 1(c) and the preliminary work indicated that low test scorers especially score *less* than they expect. Result 2(c) suggests that it would be a more effective treatment to give low test scorers *more* than they expect; high scorers seem to perform better if they have been given less than they expect. So far as the low scorers at least are concerned, it appears that the better treatment is in the opposite direction to what tends to occur. Any beneficial effect of a novel treatment may, of course, be due only to its novelty.

Implications for further research

From the present study it seems that if there is a single motivational effect of a discrepancy between a pupil's expected mark and the mark received from the teacher, this effect is so small as to be insignificant in the normal classroom setting. Such an effect might, however, appear with the use of more sophisticated performance tests and laboratory-type conditions. Other experiments employing a method similar to that employed in the main study could investigate the effects of repeated discrepancies over a larger period of time. Some participating teachers suggested that the procedure of asking a pupil for a written assessment of his own work was in itself a motivating influence; this is worth investigating.

It seems that the effectiveness of one treatment relative to its opposite, as an incentive, reverses as the opposing treatments are applied at different levels of test-score in the class. This 'reversal effect' could conceal a treatment effect if positive effects of a treatment at top ability levels are 'cancelled-out' at the bottom levels. In no study of educational incentive which has been found has the possibility of this reversal effect been considered. Further investigation of the effect would be desirable.

References

BRITTON, J. N., MARTIN, N. C., and ROSEN, H. (1966), *Multiple Marking of English Compositions*, Examinations Bulletin no. 12 Schools Council, HMSO.

BUXTON, C. E. (1965), 'Evaluation of forced-choice and Likert-type tests of motivation to academic achievement', *Brit. J. educ. Psychol.*, vol. 36, pp. 192–201.

CAMPBELL, D. J., and STANLEY, J. C. (1963), 'Experimental and quasi-experimental designs for research on teaching', in N. L. Gage (ed.), *Handbook of Research on Teaching*, Rand McNally.

CHARTERS, W. W., and GAGE, N. L. (1963), *Readings in the Social Psychology of Education*, Allyn and Bacon.

CHILD, I. L., and WHITING, J. W. M. (1949), 'Determinants of level of aspiration', *J. Abn. Soc. Psychol.*, vol. 44, pp. 303–14.

EYSENCK, S. B. G. (1965a), *Junior Eysenck Personality Inventory*, University of London Press.

EYSENCK, S. B. G. (1965b), *Manual of the Junior Eysenck Personality Inventory*, University of London Press.

FIEDLER, F. (1958), *Leader Attitudes and Group Effectiveness*, University of Illinois Press.

GARRETT, H. E. (1958), *Statistics in Psychology and Education* (5th ed.), Longman.

KENNEDY, W. A., and WILLCUTT, H. C. (1964), 'Praise and blame as incentives', *Psychol. Bull*, vol. 62, pp. 323–32.

MURSTEIN, B. I. (1965), 'The relationship of grade expectations and grades believed to be deserved to actual grades received', *J. Exp. Educ.*, vol. 33, pp. 357–62.

PAGE, E. B. (1958), 'Teachers' comments and student performance', *J. Educ. Psychol.*, vol. 49, pp. 173–81.

PICKUP, A. J. (1967), 'Teachers' marks and pupils' expectations: the short-term effects of discrepancies upon classroom performance', unpub. M.Ed. thesis, University of Leicester.

SIEGEL, S. (1956), *Nonparametric Statistics for the Behavioral Sciences*, McGraw-Hill.

VERNON, P. E. (1962), *The Measurement of Abilities*, University of London Press.

WALKER, H. M., and LEV, J. (1953), *Statistical Inference*, Holt, Rinehart & Winston.

Further Reading

General

R. C. Anderson *et al.* (eds.), *Current Research on Instruction*, Prentice-Hall, 1969.

M. Argyle, *Social Interaction*, Methuen, 1969.

C. Backman and P. Secord, *A Social Psychological View of Education*, Harcourt, Brace and World, 1968.

B. J. Biddle and W. J. Elena (eds.), *Contemporary Research on Teacher Effectiveness*, Holt, Rinehart & Winston, 1964.

W. W. Charters and N. L. Gage (eds.), *Readings in the Social Psychology of Education*, Allyn and Bacon, 1963.

N. L. Gage (ed.), *Handbook of Research on Teaching*, Rand McNally, 1963.

R. T. Hyman (ed.), *Contemporary Thought on Teaching*, Prentice-Hall, 1971.

P. W. Jackson, *Life in Classrooms*, Holt, Rinehart and Winston, 1963.

M. W. Miles and W. W. Charters (eds.), *Learning in Social Settings*, Allyn and Bacon, 1970.

A. Morrison and D. McIntyre, *Teachers and Teaching*, Penguin, 1969.

B. Rosenshine, *Teaching Behaviors and Student Achievement*, NFER, 1971.

B. O. Smith (ed.), *Research in Teacher Education: A Symposium*, Prentice-Hall, 1971.

W. Waller, *The Sociology of Teaching*, Wiley, 1967.

M. C. Wittrock and D. E. Wiley (eds.), *The Evaluation of Instruction: Issues and Problems*, Holt, Rinehart & Winston, 1970.

Theoretical Approaches

M. Banton, *Roles*, Tavistock, 1968.

A. A. Bellack, *The Language of the Classroom*, Columbia University Press, 1966.

B. J. Biddle and E. J. Thomas (eds.), *Role Theory: Concepts and Research*, John Wiley, 1966.

J. S. Bruner, *Towards a Theory of Instruction*, Harvard University Press, 1966.

N. L. Gage, 'Paradigms for research on teaching', in N. L. Gage (ed.), *Handbook of Research on Teaching*, Rand McNally, 1963, ch. 3, pp. 94–141.

J. W. Getzels, 'Conflict and role behaviour in the educational setting', in W. W. Charters and N. L. Gage (eds.), *Readings in the Social Psychology of Education*, Allyn and Bacon, 1963, pp. 309–318.

R. A. C. Oliver, 'Attitudes to education', *Brit. J. educ. Studies*, vol. 2, 1953, pp. 31–41.

T. Parsons, 'The school class as a social system', *Harvard educ. Rev.*, vol. 29, 1959, pp. 297–318.

Methods of Study

E. Amidon and A. Simon, 'Teacher–pupil interaction', *Rev. Educ. Res.*, vol. 35, 1965, pp. 130–39.

J. Duthie, *Primary Schools Survey: A Study of the Teacher's Day*, HMSO, 1970.

N. A. Flanders, *Analysing Teaching Behavior*, Addison-Wesley, 1970.

D. M. Medley and H. E. Mitzel, 'Measuring classroom behaviour by systematic observation', in N. L. Gage (ed.), *Handbook of Research on Teaching*, Rand McNally, ch. 6. pp. 247–328.

B. Rosenshine, 'Research on Teacher Performance Criteria', in B. O. Smith (ed.) *Research on Teacher Education*, A symposium, Prentice-Hall, 1971, pp. 37–72.

D. G. Ryans, *Characteristics of Teachers: Their Description, Comparison and Appraisal*, American Council on Education, 1960.

K. B. Start, 'Rater–ratee personality in the assessment of teaching ability', *Brit. J. educ. Psychol.*, vol. 38, 1968, pp. 14–20.

F. W. Warburton, H. J. Butcher and G. Forrest, 'Predicting student performance in a university department', *Brit. J. educ. Psychol.*, vol. 33, 1963, pp. 68–79.

Preparation for the Classroom

D. Allen and K. Ryan, *Microteaching*, Addison-Wesley, 1969.

H. J. Butcher, 'The attitudes of student teachers to education', *Brit. J. soc. clin. Psychol.*, vol. 4, 1965, pp. 17–24.

E. Cope, 'Teacher training and school practice', *Educ. Res.*, vol. 12, 1970, pp. 87–98.

G. Dickson, *The Characteristics of Teacher Education Students in the British Isles and the United States*, Research Foundation of the University of Toledo, 1965.

A. Morrison and D. McIntyre, 'Changes in opinions about Education during the first year of teaching', *Brit. J. soc. clin. Psychol.*, vol. 6, 1967, pp. 161–3.

M. D. Shipman, 'Theory and practice in the education of teachers', *Educ. Res.*, vol. 9, 1967, pp. 208–12.

W. Taylor, *Society and the Education of Teachers*, Faber, 1969.

W. Taylor (ed.), *Towards a Policy for the Education of Teachers*, Butterworths, 1968.

R. L. Turner, 'Teaching as problem-solving behavior: A Strategy', in B. J. Biddle and W. J. Elena, *Contemporary Research on Teacher Effectiveness*, Holt Rinehart & Winston, 1964, ch. 4, pp. 102–126.

University of Exeter, 'Innovations in teaching practice', *Themes in Education No. 19*, Institute of Education, 1969.

The Teacher's Role

H. S. Becker, 'The career of the Chicago public school teacher', *Amer. J. Sociol.*, vol. 57, 1952, pp. 470–77.

H. S. Becker, 'The teacher in the authority system of the Public School', in A. Etzioni (ed.), *Complex Organizations*, Holt, Rinehart & Winston, 1965, pp. 243–51.

B. J. Biddle, H. A. Rosencrantz, E. Tomich and J. P. Twyman, 'Shared inaccuracies in the role of the teacher', in B. J. Biddle and E. J. Thomas (eds.), *Role Theory: Concepts and Research*, Wiley, 1966.

B. J. Biddle, 'Role conflicts perceived by teachers in four English speaking countries', *Comp. Educ. Rev.*, vol. 14, 1970, pp. 30–44.

J. W. Getzels, 'Conflict and role behavior in the educational setting', in W. W. Charters and N. L. Gage (eds.), *Readings in the Social Psychology of Education*, Allyn and Bacon, 1963, pp. 309–18.

N. Gross and R. E. Herriott, *Staff Leadership in Public Schools*, Wiley, 1965.

D. H. Hargreaves, *Social Relations in a Secondary School*, Routledge & Kegan Paul, 1967.

R. E. Herriott and N. H. St John, *Social Class and the Urban School*, Wiley, 1966.

R. K. Kelsall and H. M. Kelsall, *The School Teacher in England and the United States*, Pergamon Press, 1969.

F. Musgrove and P. H. Taylor, *Society and the Teacher's Role*, Routledge & Kegan Paul, 1969.

Teaching Styles and Management

K. M. Evans, *Sociometry and Education*, Routledge & Kegan Paul, 1962.

J. W. Getzels and P. W. Jackson, 'The Teacher's personality and characteristics', in N. L. Gage (ed.), *Handbook of Research on Teaching*, Rand McNally, 1963, ch. 11, pp. 506–82.

J. Glidewell, M. Kantor, L. Smith and L. Stringer, 'Socialization and social structure in the classroom', in L. W. Hoffman and M. L. Hoffman (eds.), *Rev. Child Dev. Res.*, pt. 2, pp. 221–56, Russell Sage Foundation, 1966.

L. V. Johnson and M. Bany, *Classroom Management*, Macmillan, 1970.

J. G. Kounin, *Discipline and Group Management in Classrooms*, Holt, Rinehart & Winston, 1970.

P. Sears and E. R. Hilgard, 'The teacher's role in the motivation of the learner', 63rd Yearbook, National Society for the Study of Education, pt. 1., ch. 8, 1964.

M. D. Shipman, *The Sociology of the School*, Longmans, 1968.

Communication in Classrooms

D. Barnes, *Language, The Learner and The School*, Penguin, 1969.

A. A. Bellack, *The Language of the Classroom*, Columbia University Teachers' College Press, 1966.

N. A. Flanders, *Analysing Teaching Behavior*, Addison-Wesley, 1970.

J. J. Gallagher and M. J. Aschner, 'A preliminary report on analyses of classroom interaction', *Merrill-Palmer Q. Behav. Dev.*, vol. 9, 1963, pp. 183–94.

P. W. Jackson, *Life in Classrooms*, Holt, Rinehart & Winston, 1968.

B. Rosenshine, 'Research on teacher performance criteria', 1968, in B. O. Smith (ed.), *Research on Teacher Education: A Symposium*, Prentice-Hall, 1971, ch. 2., pp. 37–72.

Teachers' Assessments

J. E. Brophy and T. L. Good, 'Teachers' communications of differential expectations for children's classroom performance', *J. Educ. Psychol.*, vol. 61, 1970, pp. 365–74.

N. L. Gage, G. S. Leavitt and C. G. Stone, 'Teachers' understanding of their pupils and pupils' ratings of their teachers', *Psychol. Monogr.*, vol. 69, 21, 1955, pp. 1–27.

H. J. Hallworth and A. Morrison, 'A comparison of peer and teacher personality ratings of pupils in a secondary modern school', *Brit. J. educ. Psychol.*, vol. 34, 1964, pp. 285–91.

P. W. Jackson, *Life in Classrooms*, Holt, Rinehart & Winston, 1968.

D. McIntyre, A. Morrison and J. Sutherland, 'Social and educational variables relating to teachers' assessments of primary school pupils', *Brit. J. educ. Psychol.*, vol. 36, 1966, pp. 272–9.

E. B. Page, 'Teachers' comments and student performance', *J. educ. Psychol.*, vol. 49, 1958, pp. 173–81.

D. A. Pidgeon, *Expectation and Pupil Performance*, National Foundation for Educational Research, 1970.

R. Rosenthal and L. Jacobson, *Pygmalion in the Classroom*, Holt, Rinehart & Winston, 1968.

R. Tagiuri and L. Petrullo, (eds.), *Person Perception and Interpersonal Behavior*, Stanford University Press, 1968.

Acknowledgements

Permission to reproduce the following readings in this volume is acknowledged to the following sources:

1 National Society for the Study of Education
2 *Harvard Educational Review*
3 Methuen & Co Ltd
4 *Journal of Experimental Education*
5 *Journal of Experimental Education*
6 *American Educational Research Journal*
7 Her Majesty's Stationery Office and Dr J. H. Duthie
8 Teachers' College, Columbia University
9 The British Psychological Society
10 Clinical Psychology Publishing Co Inc
11 Manchester University Press
12 University of Chicago Press
13 Humanities Press Inc and Routledge & Kegan Paul
14 *The British Journal of Educational Psychology*
15 Humanities Press Inc and Routledge & Kegan Paul
16 *American Educational Research Journal*
17 Clinical Psychology Publishing Co Inc
18 Society for the Experimental Analysis of Behavior Inc
19 Clinical Psychology Publishing Co Inc
20 *American Educational Research Journal*
21 University of Chicago Press
22 Holt, Rinehart & Winston Inc
23 Methuen & Co Ltd
24 W. Victor Beez, Esq
25 *The British Journal of Educational Psychology*

Author Index

Subject Index